THE GOSPEL ACCORDING TO

ST. MATTHEW

AN INTRODUCTION AND COMMENTARY

by

R. V. G. TASKER, M.A., D.D.

INTER-VARSITY PRESS

© INTER-VARSITY PRESS, LEICESTER, ENGLAND

Universities and Colleges Christian Fellowship
38 De Montfort Street, Leicester LE1 7GP

First Edition – October 1961
Reprinted 1963, 1966, 1969,
1970, 1971, 1976, 1978

HARDBACK EDITION 0 85111 611 6
PAPERBACK EDITION 0 85111 812 7

Printed in Great Britain by offset lithography by
Billing & Sons Ltd, Guildford, London and Worcester

GENERAL PREFACE

ALL who are interested in the teaching and study of the New Testament today cannot fail to be concerned with the lack of commentaries which avoid the extremes of being unduly technical or unhelpfully brief. It is the hope of the editor and publishers that this present series will do something towards the supply of this deficiency. Their aim is to place in the hands of students and serious readers of the New Testament, at a moderate cost, commentaries by a number of scholars who, while they are free to make their own individual contributions, are united in a common desire to promote a truly biblical theology.

The commentaries are primarily exegetical and only secondarily homiletic, though it is hoped that both student and preacher will find them informative and suggestive. Critical questions are fully considered in introductory sections, and also, at the author's discretion, in additional notes.

The commentaries are based on the Authorized (King James) Version, partly because this is the version which most Bible readers possess, and partly because it is easier for commentators, working on this foundation, to show why, on textual and linguistic grounds, the later versions are so often to be preferred. No one translation is regarded as infallible, and no single Greek manuscript or group of manuscripts is regarded as always right! Greek words are transliterated to help those unfamiliar with the language, and to save those who do know Greek the trouble of discovering what word is being discussed.

There are many signs today of a renewed interest in what the Bible has to say and of a more general desire to understand its meaning as fully and clearly as possible. It is the hope of all those concerned with this series that God will graciously use what they have written to further this end.

R. V. G. TASKER.

CHIEF ABBREVIATIONS

AV	English Authorized Version (King James).
RV	English Revised Version, 1881.
RSV	American Revised Standard Version, 1946.
NEB	New English Bible: New Testament, 1961.
Butler	*The Originality of St. Matthew* by B. C. Butler, 1951.
Chapman	*Matthew, Mark, and Luke* by Dom John Chapman, 1937.
Filson	*A Commentary on the Gospel according to St. Matthew* by Floyd V. Filson, 1960.
Kilpatrick	*The Origins of the Gospel according to St. Matthew* by G. D. Kilpatrick, 1946.
Knox	(For translation.) *The New Testament of our Lord and Saviour Jesus Christ newly translated from the Vulgate Latin* by R. A. Knox, 1945.
Knox	(For comments.) *The Epistles and Gospels* by R. A. Knox, 1946.
Levertoff	*St. Matthew* (Revised Version) by Paul P. Levertoff, 1940.
McNeile	*The Gospel according to St. Matthew* by A. H. McNeile, 1915.
Plummer	*An Exegetical Commentary on the Gospel according to St. Matthew* by A. Plummer, 1909.
Ropes	*The Synoptic Gospels* by J. H. Ropes, 1934.
Stonehouse	*The Witness of Matthew and Mark to Christ* by N. B. Stonehouse, 1944.
Streeter	*The Four Gospels* by B. H. Streeter, 1924.
Torrey	*The Four Gospels. A New Translation* by C. C. Torrey, 1947.
Westcott	*An Introduction to the Study of the Gospels* by Brooke Foss Westcott, 1895.
Wikenhauser	*New Testament Introduction* by A. Wikenhauser, 1958.

CONTENTS

ACKNOWLEDGEMENT

Scripture quotations from the Revised Standard Version (copyrighted 1946 and 1952 by the Division of Christian Education, National Council of Churches, U.S.A.), and from the New English Bible (copyrighted 1961 by the Cambridge University Press and the Oxford University Press) are used by permission.

When Philip ran up he heard him reading . . . and said, 'Do you understand what you are reading?' He said, 'How can I understand unless someone will give me the clue?' So he asked Philip to get in and sit beside him.

Acts viii. 30, 31, NEB

AUTHOR'S PREFACE

IN this comparatively short commentary on one of the longer Gospels I have made no attempt to deal in any detail with such matters as the Synoptic problem or Form-Criticism, but have confined my attention almost exclusively to the interpretation of the text.

One of the more unfortunate results of the general acceptance by scholars of the hypothesis that the Gospel of Mark is the earliest of the canonical Gospels has been a comparative disparagement in many quarters of the Gospel of Matthew as a reliable authority for the things that Jesus *did*, and a tendency to value it almost exclusively for the large number of His sayings which it so systematically records. I have endeavoured in this present commentary to redress the balance, and to do justice both to early Christian tradition and to what would appear to be the more reasonable conclusions of modern scholarship. The task has not been easy; and I gratefully acknowledge the help that I have received in my efforts to discharge it from many writers—not least from some of the distinguished Roman Catholic scholars, whose evaluation of the Gospel of Matthew must be more acceptable in many respects to conservative Evangelicals than that of some more liberal Protestant critics.

As this is the first volume in the present series to appear since the publication in March 1961 of the New Testament section of *The New English Bible*, I have ventured to devote a short Appendix to a consideration of some of its more salient features as exemplified in the Gospel of Matthew.

R. V. G. TASKER.

INTRODUCTION

THE Gospel of Matthew occupies the first place in all extant witnesses to the text of the four Gospels and in all early lists of the canonical books of the New Testament. This no doubt reflects not only the importance attached to it in the early Church, but also the firmly established belief, which cannot however be dated earlier than Papias, bishop of Hierapolis in the middle of the second century, that the canonical Gospel was a Greek translation of an earlier document written in Hebrew (i.e. Aramaic) by the apostle Matthew before any of the other Gospels was written. Papias, as recorded by Eusebius, stated that 'Matthew composed the oracles (*ta logia*) in the Hebrew dialect and everyone translated them as he was able'. These words were invariably understood by subsequent writers in the early Church to refer to an original work of Matthew, of which the Greek Gospel of Matthew was the accepted translation.

Irenaeus, who was consecrated bishop of Lyons towards the close of the second century, asserted that this original document was written by Matthew while Peter and Paul were at Rome preaching the gospel and founding the Church, and before the composition of the Gospel of Mark. Eusebius adds the information that 'Matthew, having first preached to the Hebrews, when he was on the point of going to other nations, committed to writing in his native tongue the gospel as he had proclaimed it, and thus supplied the want of his presence among them by his writings'. Jerome completes the tradition by asserting that the converted tax-collector Matthew (for he identifies Matthew and Levi) was the first to compose a Gospel of Christ, and that he wrote it in Judaea in Hebrew for the benefit of Jewish converts, but adds that it is not sufficiently clear who translated it later into Greek.

This traditional view that our Greek Gospel of Matthew is a translation of the original Hebrew work of Matthew the apostle, and was in fact the first of the four canonical Gospels, is still maintained by some scholars, both Roman Catholic and Protestant. The decision of the Pontifical Biblical Commission of 1911, which is binding on all Roman Catholics, leaves a loop-hole however for those who are unable on scholarly grounds to accept the priority of the Greek Gospel of Matthew but believe it to be later than the Gospel of Mark, and who regard it as a rewriting and not a direct translation of Matthew's previous work. 'According to trustworthy tradition,' the Commission states, 'the apostle Matthew was the first to write a Gospel—not merely a collection of *logia*—in the native language of Palestine; it was not written after AD 70 and the evidence of Irenaeus does not prove that it was written after Paul arrived in Rome. This Aramaic Gospel is *quoad substantiam* identical with the Greek canonical Gospel. Its historical trustworthiness and integrity must be accepted.' (Quoted by Wikenhauser, pp. 173, 174.) It is obvious that the key-words in this pronouncement are *quoad substantiam*, 'substantially'.

On the other hand, the majority of Protestant scholars have endeavoured to explain the persistent association in early tradition of the name of Matthew with the 'first' canonical Gospel, by assuming that the Aramaic work of Matthew, to which Papias refers, was *not* a Gospel but a collection of the *sayings* of Jesus, and that when these sayings were subsequently embodied in the 'first' Gospel in a Greek translation, the name of Matthew came to be associated with the larger document. The weakness of this hypothesis is that it gives to the word *logia* a far weaker and more restricted sense than later writers in the early Church accorded it. The 'oracles' of the Lord consist in fact not merely of His sayings but also of His actions. His words and deeds cannot be separated. Nor is the difficulty removed by the alternative hypothesis that by *logia* Papias meant a collection of proof-texts from the Old Testament, similar to the collections which came later to be known as *Testimonia*, and that subsequently this came to be embodied in the canonical 'first' Gospel. For the problem still remains that this was not the way in which early Christian writers understood the expression.

Most modern scholars find it very difficult to believe that our Gospel of Matthew is a translation of an Aramaic document. It bears the marks of an original Greek composition. They have also been led to the conclusion that the problem of the verbal agreements and disagreements between the three Synoptic Gospels is best explained on the supposition that the Gospel of Mark was used by both the other Synoptic writers. On this latter assumption, they tend to conclude that it is unlikely that an apostle would have made such full use of the work of a non-apostolic writer, and so conclude that Matthew did not write the Greek Gospel which has come to be described as 'according to Matthew'. As we have seen, Roman Catholic scholars disagree among themselves on both these questions. Lagrange, Chapman, and Butler uphold the view that the Greek Gospel is a direct translation of a Hebrew original and is prior to the Gospel of Mark. Wikenhauser, on the other hand, writes (p. 195), 'It may be taken as certain that an Aramaic original of the Gospel of St. Matthew can be defended only if we regard the Greek Matthew, not as a literal translation of the Aramaic, but as a thorough revision made with frequent use of the Gospel of St. Mark. This is consistent with the decision of the Biblical Commission which declares explicitly that the tradition of the early Church is preserved if we uphold the substantial identity of Greek and Aramaic Matthew. Since there are no remains of Aramaic Matthew, and no one knows what it was like, we cannot make any more accurate or more definite statement about the two forms of St. Matthew's Gospel'.

This well-balanced statement would seem to do justice both to the earliest tradition, which cannot be lightly set aside, and to what would appear to be the now more or less assured result of the intensive study of the Synoptic problem which has engaged the attention of scholars during the last one hundred and fifty years. Where modern criticism would appear to be unduly arbitrary is in the assumption that we are *never* in direct touch with the testimony of an eyewitness in the non-Marcan passages of Matthew, and in supposing that where Matthew differs from Mark in incidents and sayings which they share in common, Matthew's version is always suspect as being influenced by the author's apologetic intentions. How often is he accused of 'letting the apostles down lightly', of softening the rebukes they received from their Master, of heightening the Christology, of giving a Jewish bias to the teaching of Jesus about the validity of the Mosaic law, and of other tendentious alterations. In opposition to much of this criticism it is maintained at several points in the present commentary that the differences between Matthew and Mark may equally well be explained on the supposition that the Gospel of Matthew retains details originally handed down by the apostle of that name, and that the Gospel of Mark often draws upon Peter's reminiscences.

The indications that in the 'first' Gospel we are in touch with the apostle Matthew are, to be sure, much less evident than are the indications in the Gospel of Mark that Peter is a main source of the evangelist's information; but they are not wholly lacking. It is surely not without significance that the author not only gives the name of Matthew to the tax-collector who was called to be a disciple (ix. 9), whereas both Mark and Luke call him by what was probably his other name, Levi, but that in the list of apostles he alone of the evangelists describes Matthew as 'the tax-collector' (x. 3). Furthermore, the ambiguous reference to 'the house' where Jesus sat at table with many tax-collectors and sinners (ix. 10) may also be an indication that it was at Matthew's house that they met. Similarly, the vague references to 'the house' at xiii. 1 and xvii. 25 may also be indications that Matthew's house was often visited by Jesus. Nor can it be denied that of all the apostles whose previous occupations are known to us, Matthew would appear to be the most qualified to undertake the composition of the kind of narratives that we find embedded in the 'first' Gospel. At least he could keep accounts; and the striking references to money in this Gospel may also be small but significant clues betraying the hand of the taker of toll. 'Two parables in which the moral turns on money transactions are peculiar to the First Gospel—the parable of the Unmerciful Servant who owed 10,000 talents and that of the labourers hired for a penny a day. And it is "Matthew" who alone records that a good sum of money was paid to the watch at the sepulchre by the chief priests to ensure their silence as to the resurrection, and who also alone relates that Judas repented himself, flung back the thirty pieces of silver into the Temple, and went away to hang himself. The taker of toll gives the lesson of the bane of money.'[1]

It is conceivable that Matthew, who was in all probability bilingual, himself translated his original work or republished it in an enlarged Greek edition. But, although he may well have composed the *logia* before leaving Palestine in the early sixties, as Irenaeus indicates, the Greek revision that we possess would seem to have been made considerably later. Not only does it presuppose the circulation of the Gospel of Mark, but the remarkable insertion found in the parable of the wedding feast would appear to be a reference to the destruction of Jerusalem which was by now a *fait accompli* (xxii. 7). Moreover, the two references to 'unto this day' in xxvii. 8 and xxviii. 15 would seem to indicate, as Wikenhauser agrees, that a comparatively long period of time has elapsed since the days of Jesus. On the other hand, Chapman (p. 255), somewhat unconvincingly, supposes that a short time is implied by this expression. More effective is Chapman's remark that the reference to the 'field of blood' must have been made before the fall of Jerusalem 'for after the siege there would be no question of the field, or of the burial of strangers, or of a nickname for the place'.

It is often assumed by critics that the incidents found only in Matthew's Gospel are the latest and least reliable sections of the Synoptic Gospels, being in the nature of legendary amplifications of earlier material. Thus Streeter, assigning such material to the hypothetical source which he designated M, wrote (p. 502) 'leaving out of account the Infancy, the only

[1] W. E. Barnes, *Gospel Criticism and Form Criticism* (T. and T. Clark, 1936), pp. 23, 24.

story peculiar to Matthew which stands, so to speak, "on its own legs" is the Stater in the Fish's mouth. The rest are all, in a way, parasitic; they stand to Mark as the mistletoe to the oak.' And, speaking of the so-called 'embellishments' by Matthew of Mark's story of the passion, Streeter went on to say, 'It is noteworthy that not a single one of them looks like a genuine historical tradition; while some of them are clearly "legendary", e.g. the temporary resurrection of saints in Jerusalem at the time of the Rending of the Veil, or Pilate's washing of his hands before the multitude—an action as probable in a Roman governor as in a British civil servant in India.' In reply to this damaging subjective criticism we may well ask two questions. Can it in fact be so arbitrarily assumed that none of this special Matthew material reflects earlier and essentially reliable tradition? And is it not equally reasonable to conclude that the difficulty of knowing for certain what parts of our 'first' Gospel are incorporated from the earlier work of Matthew, and what parts came into it when the Greek Gospel was published, makes it impossible for us to speak with assurance either about the antiquity of its several parts, or about the date of its final composition?

The fixing of the date of the material found in the 'first' Gospel has been further complicated by the assumption of some scholars that the more strongly marked Jewish Christian elements in the Gospel cannot be adduced as evidence that this Gospel carries us back farthest to the Jewish environment in which Jesus lived and taught, but are in fact products of a much later Jewish *reaction* within the Christian Church. Thus Streeter (p. 512) dogmatically asserts: 'It cannot be too emphatically insisted that this element in Matthew reflects, not primitive Jewish Christianity, but a later Judaistic reaction against the Petro-Pauline liberalism in the matter of the Gentile Mission and the observance of the Law.' How different is such a conclusion from the simpler and, as some may well feel, more natural statement of Chapman (p. 256): 'Everything in Matthew (roughly speaking) is more primitive than in the other Gospels, because wholly Jewish.'

At the most we can say that a date later than AD 70 is the

probable date of the 'first' Gospel, but how much later we have no means of knowing. If those scholars who would abandon the critical hypothesis of Q, the hypothesis which assumes that the non-Marcan material common to Matthew and Luke was derived by these evangelists from a common written source, and who would substitute for it the hypothesis that Luke made use of Matthew as well as Mark, are able to establish their case,[1] one result may well be that the 'first' Gospel may be dated earlier than has hitherto been fashionable in critical circles—in the early seventies rather than in the middle eighties of the first century.

Our own tentative conclusion is that the Gospel of Matthew is not in fact the first of the four canonical Gospels, though it contains material which was originally recorded in Aramaic by the apostle Matthew before any of the other Gospels was written. As to who actually composed the Greek Gospel of Matthew we are as ignorant as was Jerome.

THE 'ROYAL' GOSPEL

It would seem reasonable to suppose that the 'first' Gospel was not given the primary place in the New Testament solely because it was believed to embody some of the earliest gospel material to be committed to writing. It was also, to judge from the frequency with which it was quoted by Christian writers in the second century, their favourite Gospel. Indeed, as Wikenhauser has pointed out, 'in the time of Irenaeus the Church and Christian literature were more deeply influenced by the Gospel of Matthew than by any other New Testament book' (p. 158). It became known as the 'ecclesiastical' Gospel, because it provided the Church with an indispensable tool in its threefold task of defending its beliefs against attacks from Jewish opponents, of instructing converts from paganism in the

---

[1] The Q hypothesis has been challenged not only, in great detail, by Catholic scholars such as Chapman and Butler, but also by other writers, particularly those who are approaching the Gospels from the standpoint of form-criticism rather than source-criticism. See e.g. Ropes (p. 93), and the essay *On Dispensing with Q* by A. M. Farrer in *Studies in the Gospels* edited by D. E. Nineham (Basil Blackwell, 1955). Some of the difficulties of the hypothesis are pointed out in the course of the present commentary.

ethical implications of their newly-accepted religion, and of helping its own members to live a disciplined life of fellowship based on the record of the deeds and words of their Lord and Master, which they heard read week by week in the orderly and systematic form provided by this evangelist. In short, the Gospel of Matthew served as an apology, a handbook of instruction, and a lectionary for use in Christian worship. In the words of Filson (p. 4): 'Its strength lay not in narrative power, literary appeal, or mystical depth, but in its proved and persistent capacity to shape Christian thought and church life.' And the same writer goes on to say (p. 5): 'Its author was a Christian teacher who has proved the teacher of centuries of Christian leaders and worshippers. The Church honoured and cherished his work because he had given it a powerful and useful tool for its common life and mission. He was great precisely because he made it his concern to serve Christ and to further the work of Christ through the Church.'

The apologetic aim of the evangelist can be summed up in the sentence 'Jesus is the Messiah, and in Him Jewish prophecy is fulfilled'. The religion, therefore, which is called 'Christian' ('Christ' being the Greek form of the word 'Messiah'), so far from being some new-fangled invention of a group of fanatics, is in fact the true consummation of the religion of Israel as embodied in the sacred records of the unique self-disclosure of God to His own people known as the Old Testament. The old law of Judaism, while it has not been overthrown, has been filled with new meaning and supplemented in the teaching of Jesus. The ancient Church of God has been transformed into the new fellowship of those who have accepted Jesus as Messiah. Only a few, to be sure, of the Jews are to be found within this fellowship, but the very refusal of the majority of them to join it is all in accord with ancient prophecy. In the demonstration of these truths, our evangelist is most concerned to show throughout his narrative that in the earthly history of Jesus, not only in its origin and its purpose, but in the actual manner of its unfolding, the activity of God was being displayed. In it God was fulfilling His own words spoken to the prophets. Hence the large number of quotations from the Old Testament found in his Gospel and introduced by some such formula as 'that it might be fulfilled which was spoken by the prophet'.

It is in the systematic arrangement of his material according to subject-matter rather than in strict chronological sequence (see the *Analysis* on p. 27) that the value of the work of this evangelist for instructional purposes is seen to lie. Ropes (p. 35) regards this as the primary task that the writer set himself—a task which he most successfully achieved. 'A well-educated man of distinguished literary ability, he undertook to provide for the instruction of Christians a systematic compendium or handbook of what was known about the deeds and words of the Founder of the Christian Church.' Kilpatrick, on the other hand, regards this orderly arrangement of his material by the evangelist as evidence primarily of his desire to provide a book suitable for reading out loud when Christians were assembled for worship. In support of this thesis, he cites the evangelist's fondness for repeating phrases which strike a solemn and liturgical note, such as 'the outer darkness', 'weeping and gnashing of teeth', and his habit of ending each of the five main collections of the sayings of Jesus which he has assembled with what is virtually the same formula: 'It came to pass when Jesus had finished these sayings' (see vii. 28, xi. 1, xiii. 53, xix. 1, xxvi. 1). This is in effect another way of saying 'Here endeth the first (or second, etc.) book of the oracles of Jesus the Messiah'. Kilpatrick also maintains that the smoother and more succinct character of Matthew's narrative compared with Mark's, in passages where both evangelists are recording the same incidents, is due to Matthew's desire to set forth his material in a manner best suited for reading in church.

In the light of these facts it is obviously very relevant to describe the Gospel of Matthew as 'the apologetic', 'the liturgical' and 'the ecclesiastical' Gospel. But if we are looking for a single epithet to describe its dominant characteristic perhaps the best available for our purpose is the word 'royal'; for, as McNeile well says (p. xvii), 'the special impression which Matthew embodies is that of royalty. Jesus is the

Messiah.' Levertoff also goes to the heart of the matter when he writes (pp. xxv, xxvi): 'These great concepts, "the Messiah" and "the kingdom", are the heart of the Gospel. The *teaching* of Jesus cannot be classified and evaluated separately from a consideration of *His Person and claims*, because He was not primarily a great religious teacher—His greatest lesson was Himself.' It may therefore be instructive if we consider the portrait of this royal Person as it has been painted by our evangelist; and in so doing we shall be in fact following a clue given by no less a person than Augustine, who wrote *Cum Matthaeus circa regis personam gereret intentionem, humanitatem Christi maxime commendavit.*

The early Fathers of the Church frequently used the symbolism of Ezekiel's vision of the four-faced cherubim (Ezk. i. 10) to distinguish, without dividing, the four Gospels. They varied, however, in the precise application they gave to the details. Usually, in the west, 'the man' was assigned to Matthew, 'the lion' to Mark, 'the ox' to Luke, and 'the eagle' to John. Augustine, with rather more insight, reversed the order of the first two symbols, so that 'the lion' designated the Gospel of Matthew. Such a fanciful exercise of the imagination does not make much appeal to the modern student of the Gospels, but he would probably admit that the animal regarded as 'the king of the forest' is from one point of view no unfitting symbol to draw attention to a striking feature of the Gospel of Matthew. Jesus is here presented first and foremost as the messianic King, the Son of the royal house of David, the Lion of the tribe of Judah. A brief review of some of the relevant details peculiar to this Gospel may help to throw this aspect of the author's portrait of Jesus into clear relief. For, as Westcott remarked (p. 328), 'The peculiarities of St. Matthew's narrative are numerous and uniform in character. With more or less distinctness they all tend to show how the Messiahship of Jesus was attested during the course of events . . . and the same feeling which directed the selection of the points of the narrative influenced the manner of their treatment.'

The opening verse of the distinctive genealogy indicates that the significance of Jesus is that He is not only Messiah, but 'the son of David' designated in verse 6 'David the king'. At the time of His birth His mother was betrothed to Joseph who was himself a direct descendant of David (i. 16) and is addressed as 'son of David' (i. 20). Jesus 'who is called Christ' is therefore legally a scion of the ancient royal house, a 'Man born to be King'. This note of Davidic sonship is sounded at other points in this Gospel. Whereas in the Gospel of Mark the title 'Son of David' is only once given to Jesus, viz. by blind Bartimaeus, in Matthew not only blind men on two different occasions (ix. 27, xx. 30), but the woman of Canaan (xv. 22), the crowds as Jesus entered Jerusalem (xxi. 9), and the children in the Temple (xxi. 15) all address Him as such; and after the healing of the blind and dumb demoniac the crowds exclaim 'Can this be the Son of David?' (xii. 23, NEB).

That Jesus was born into this royal inheritance is further emphasized by the request of the astrologers, on their arrival from the East, for information about the whereabouts of the child who was born to be 'King of the Jews' (ii. 2). The nature of His Kingship (and at this point the symbolism of the lion ceases to be relevant) is underlined by the evangelist's striking modification of the prophecy of Micah about the ruler who was to emerge from the royal town of Bethlehem (see commentary on ii. 6). It is as a *Shepherd* that this King will exercise His Kingship, caring for all the members of the flock, leading them rather than lording it over them, and taking pity on them when they are harassed and helpless (see ix. 36). In this respect His Kingship stands out in striking contrast to the worldly kingship typified by the wayward and irascible Herod the Great, and by the weak and despicable Herod Antipas, tetrarch of Galilee. The vast difference between the methods used by Jesus for the establishment of His kingdom and the methods employed by those who would build for themselves an earthly kingdom, is made clear by our evangelist when, by a reversal of their order, he makes the climax of Jesus' temptations in the wilderness the temptation to win the kingdoms of the world by paying homage to Satan. The devil's weapons of violence, cruelty and oppression have no place in the armoury of the divine 'Imperialist'. This point is further stressed when Matthew summarizes the character of Jesus at the beginning of the Galilaean ministry in words taken from Isaiah's description of the ideal Servant of God:

> 'He will not strive, he will not shout,
> Nor will his voice be heard in the streets.
> He will not snap off the broken reed,
> Nor snuff out the smouldering wick,
> Until he leads justice on to victory.'
>
> (xii. 19, 20, NEB)

And that this is a theme dear to the heart of our evangelist is further evident from the fact that he alone of the Gospel writers records that Jesus on two occasions when in controversy with the Pharisees quoted the words of Hosea, 'I desire mercy and not sacrifice' (ix. 13, xii. 7).

In the character of King Jesus there is in fact a remarkable combination of strength and condescension, a unique blending of humility, loving-kindness, gentleness, magnanimity, tenderness and compassion, as is made abundantly clear in many passages in the Gospel of Matthew where there are no parallels in the other Gospels. Though born in royal Bethlehem, by His early and long residence at Nazareth He became a despised Galilaean provincial (ii. 23), known as 'the carpenter's son' (xiii. 55). When He began His ministry it was, significantly, to the hard-worked and the heavily-burdened, as Matthew alone records, that He offered relief, bidding men come and learn from Him precisely because He was gentle and humble-hearted (see xi. 28, 29 in NEB). And when, as His ministry was drawing to a close, He deliberately chose an ass on which to make His royal entrance into Jerusalem, it is our evangelist who draws attention to His humility and gentleness, by pointing out that here was a literal fulfilment of the prophetic words addressed to the daughter of Sion: 'Here is your king, who comes to you in gentleness, riding on an ass, riding on the foal of a beast of burden' (xxi. 5, NEB). This King's compassion is emphasized by Matthew when he alone records that Jesus was deeply moved after the blind men, replying to His question 'What do you want me to do?', asked that they might be given back their sight (xx. 32–34). And His magnanimity was never more apparent than when He uttered no word of reproof to Judas, who by kissing Him had made His arrest a *fait accompli*; but, as we read only in this Gospel, said 'Friend, do what you are here to do' (xxvi. 50, NEB). Here indeed is a Messiah 'touched with the feeling of our infirmities', a King of love who ever follows love's way— to rise He stoops. And all who would experience the benefits of His reign must catch the infection of His Spirit, and value the qualities that He valued. The charter of their citizenship is delineated in Matthew's version of the Beatitudes, where the humble, the gentle, the sympathetic, the merciful and those whose hearts are set on the triumph of justice, are accounted specially blest (see v. 1–10 in NEB).

On the other hand, what Jesus condemns most strongly is the proud, uncharitable, unforgiving, jealous spirit. This is made lucidly clear in the parable of the unmerciful servant, peculiar to this Gospel (xviii. 23–35). It comes to the surface in the Matthaean version of the Lord's Prayer, where according to the probable text Jesus teaches His disciples to ask the heavenly Father to forgive them the wrong they have done because they have *already* forgiven those who have wronged them (see vi. 12 in NEB). The same truth forms the moral of the parable of the labourers in the vineyard with its climax 'Why be jealous because I am kind?' (xx. 15, NEB); it is also the highlight of the picture of the great assize, presided over by the Son of man seated in glory and designated 'the King'— the unique section with which the teaching of Jesus recorded in this Gospel ends (xxv. 31–46). We may further note that in Matthew's version of the parable of the great supper the king's anger is roused precisely because the invited guests so ungraciously make light of his generous invitation (xviii. 7). And what Jesus condemns in the Pharisees is not only their lack of justice and good faith, but also, as Matthew alone notices, their lack of mercy (xxiii. 23).

This Gospel, in common with the others, shows that Jesus

revealed His sovereignty most frequently in showing mercy and pity. His divine power was the expression of His divine compassion. His miracles are signs of the kind of Person He was. But all the Gospels are equally agreed that the death of Jesus was the supreme means by which Jesus established His rule over men's hearts by overcoming the forces of evil. He crowned His ministry of service for others by giving His life a ransom for many. On the cross 'the strong-man armed', i.e. the devil, whose strongholds Jesus had often attacked in His supernatural exorcisms, was finally overcome. We are not therefore surprised to find that some of the distinctive features of Matthew's story of the passion should especially underline the royalty that surrounded Jesus even at the time of His greatest humiliation and most bitter suffering.

In our evangelist's description of the betrayal and trials of Jesus, there is what Westcott described as 'the same open and unreserved declaration of the Saviour's majesty' (p. 328). Finding Himself in what, humanly speaking, seems a hopeless situation, His words and actions nevertheless reveal a consciousness of regal power. When His disciples want to draw the sword in His defence as His assailants approach to arrest Him, He reminds them that, should He so desire, He could even now appeal to His Father and at once more than twelve legions of angels would be sent to His relief. But not only is there no need for this intervention, for His kingdom can neither be defended nor defeated by human force, but the arrival of such reinforcements would make it impossible for Him to complete His vocation. As the Inaugurator of the kingdom of God He has to suffer many things before exercising to the full His sovereignty (xxvi. 52–54). A little later, when the high priest charges Him by the living God (a detail peculiar to Matthew) to tell him whether He is 'the Messiah, the Son of God', Jesus breaks the silence He has hitherto observed, and replies, not indeed with an emphatic 'Yes', but somewhat obliquely with the assertion 'The words are yours' (NEB). To both of these great titles He can and does lay claim; and, as He at once goes on to say, from that moment (another detail peculiar to this Gospel) His royal power will show itself,

24

and reach its climax when He returns in glory to pass final
judgment upon mankind (xxvi. 64).

After such a royal pronouncement as this the reader is not
surprised to read, in details recorded only by Matthew, that
Pilate's question to the crowd took the form 'Which would
you like me to release to you—Jesus Bar-Abbas, or Jesus
called *Messiah*?' (xxvii. 17, NEB); that it was as *Messiah* that
Jesus was mocked (xxvi. 68); and that when eventually Pilate
passed sentence of death, all the people, ready to take full
responsibility for the execution of One whom they regarded as
a *false Messiah*, exclaimed 'His blood be on us, and on our
children' (xxvii. 25). The dispenser of Roman justice had
clearly been influenced by the message from his wife urging
him to have nothing to do with this innocent man, for she had
been much disturbed in her dreams about Him during the
previous night; and seeing that his efforts to secure the release
of Jesus were unavailing and that a riot was starting,
Pilate washed his hands in full view of the people, a symbolic
expression of his own conviction that Jesus was innocent
(xxvii. 19, 24). As Westcott pertinently remarked (p. 329),
'The dream of Pilate's wife, and the symbolic purification of
the governor himself, express the influence which the righteousness of the Saviour exercised upon their imagination and
judgment.' Moreover, in some of his special additions throughout the passion narrative, Matthew emphasizes the further
truth that in all that was happening prophecy was being
fulfilled—both directly, as in the use made by the Sanhedrin
of the blood-money returned by Judas before his suicide
(xxvii. 9, 10), and indirectly, as in the addition of the words
with gall in the reference to the drugged wine in xxvii. 34, and
in the expansion of the mocking words addressed by the chief
priests, scribes and elders to Jesus as He hung on the cross
'Did he trust in God? Let God rescue him, if he wants him—
for he said he was God's Son' (xxvii. 43, NEB; cf. Ps. xxi. 9).
And it may well be that Matthew's reference to the earthquake,
the splitting of the rocks, and the emergence of many of God's
people from their graves at the moment of Jesus' death, is
meant to convey to the reader the assurance that in the hour

of His apparent defeat the regal power of the Messiah was being felt in the world of nature and in the realm of the departed—a confirmation indeed of His words 'I am God's Son' (xxvii. 51–53). It was insight into this truth that led the author of a familiar Easter hymn to write:

> For Judah's Lion bursts His chains,
>   Crushing the serpent's head;
> And cries aloud through death's domains
>   To wake the imprison'd dead.

Similarly, the peculiar traits of Matthew's resurrection narrative draw attention to the outward splendour of the mighty event by which Jesus the Messiah entered into His full sovereignty. The great earthquake frustrated all the efforts of the Roman soldiers and chief priests to bar the way to the emergence of Jesus from the tomb; and the Gospel ends with a picture of the disciples bowed in adoration before Him on a mountain in Galilee ('appointed' perhaps because it was there that He had first taught them) and hearing from His lips the solemn announcement of His universal sovereignty and the commission to go and proclaim it to all nations (xxviii. 16–20). He who had claimed authority on earth to forgive sins, and had astounded the Galilaean peasants by the note of authority that sounded through His teaching, now claims by virtue of His triumph over sin and death 'all authority in heaven and earth'. From henceforth all angelic powers are subject to Him; and His authority over all created persons and things, visible and invisible, is now an accomplished fact. In spite of all appearances to the contrary, the kingdoms of the world are destined to become the kingdoms of our Lord and His Christ. It is on that high note of majesty that the 'royal' Gospel of Matthew ends.

ANALYSIS

I. THE ORIGIN AND INFANCY OF JESUS THE
MESSIAH (i. 1–ii. 23).

  a. The Messiah's genealogy (i. 1–17).
  b. The Messiah's birth (i. 18–25).
  c. The visit of the magi (ii. 1–12).
  d. The flight into Egypt (ii. 13–15).
  e. The massacre of the infants; and the return to Nazareth
    (ii. 16–23).

II. THE BEGINNING OF THE MINISTRY OF JESUS
THE MESSIAH (iii. 1–iv. 25).

  a. The preaching of John the Baptist and the baptism of
    Jesus (iii. 1–17).
  b. The temptations in the wilderness (iv. 1–11).
  c. The beginning of the Galilaean ministry (iv. 12–25).

III. THE ETHICS OF THE KINGDOM OF GOD
(v. 1–vii. 29).

  a. Introduction.
  b. The characteristics of Christian discipleship (v. 1–16).
  c. Jesus and the Mosaic law (v.17–48).
  d. The piety of the sons of the kingdom (vi. 1–18).
  e. Single-mindedness (vi. 19–34).
  f. Judging and discriminating (vii. 1–6).
  g. Perseverance in prayer (vii. 7–11).
  h. The golden rule; the two ways; false prophets; and the
    two builders (vii. 12–29).

IV. JESUS THE DOER OF MIGHTY WORKS
(viii. 1–ix. 34).

  a. Introduction.
  b. The Healer of leprosy, paralysis and fever (viii. 1–17).
  c. Two aspirants to discipleship (viii. 18–22).
  d. The Controller of nature; the Conqueror of demons; and
    the Forgiver of sins (viii. 23–ix. 8).

e. The Friend of publicans and sinners; and the question of fasting (ix. 9–17).

f. The Restorer of life, sight and speech (ix. 18–34).

V. JESUS AND HIS MISSION PREACHERS (ix. 35–x. 42).

VI. THE CLAIMS OF JESUS THE MESSIAH (xi. 1–xii. 50).

a. The unity of this section.

b. Jesus and John the Baptist (xi. 1–19).

c. The Messiah's dirge over the unrepentant cities (xi. 20–24).

d. Jesus' thanksgiving and gracious invitation (xi. 25–30).

e. Plucking corn on the sabbath (xii. 1–9).

f. The man with the withered hand; Jesus' avoidance of publicity (xii. 10–21).

g. The Beelzebub controversy (xii. 22–37).

h. The request for a sign; the return of the unclean spirit (xii. 38–45).

i. The new family of Jesus (xii. 46–50).

VII. SEVEN PARABLES OF THE KINGDOM OF HEAVEN (xiii. 1–52).

VIII. THE REJECTION OF JESUS AT NAZARETH AND THE MARTYRDOM OF JOHN THE BAPTIST (xiii. 53–xiv. 12).

IX. WITHDRAWAL OF JESUS FROM HEROD'S DOMINION (xiv. 13–xvii. 27).

a. The feeding of the five thousand and the walking on the lake (xiv. 13–36).

b. Controversy about 'cleanliness'; the healing of the Canaanite woman's daughter (xv. 1–28).

c. Return to the lake; the feeding of the four thousand; a further request for a sign (xv. 29–xvi. 12).

d. Peter's confession and the first prediction of the passion (xvi. 13–28).

e. The transfiguration; and the cure of the epileptic boy (xvii. 1–21).

f. The second prediction of the passion; and the temple tax (xvii. 22–27).

COMMENTARY

I. THE ORIGIN AND INFANCY OF JESUS THE MESSIAH (i. 1–ii. 23)

a. The Messiah's genealogy (i. 1–17)

In the opening verse of his Gospel Matthew strikes the note which is to sound through all his narrative. He is concerned, first and foremost, to show that Jesus was the Messiah directly descended from the royal house of David, and of the seed of the patriarch Abraham, to whom the divine promises were first given and with whom 'sacred history' may be said to have begun. The primary aim of *the book of the generation*, an expression (influenced by Genesis v. 1) meaning 'the table of descent', which forms the preface to this Gospel, is to show that Jesus, as Stonehouse has well expressed it (p. 124), 'is no isolated figure, no mere innovator, but one who can be adequately measured only in terms of what has gone before'.

The tidy mind of our evangelist, a Jewish Christian familiar with rabbinical ways of thinking, leads him to find symmetry in the use of numbers. He has, accordingly, divided the generations from Abraham to Jesus into three groups—from Abraham to the establishment of the kingdom under David (verses 2–6); from David to the end of the monarchy at the deportation to Babylon (verses 6–11); and from the period of the Babylonian Exile to the birth of Jesus (verses 12–16). Each group, as he states with great preciseness in verse 17, contains *fourteen generations*. In fact, however, the third group contains only thirteen names; and in the second group three generations have been omitted according to the evidence of 1 Chronicles i–iii, which the evangelist appears to be using as his source.

It has been suggested, with considerable probability, that the significance he found in the number *fourteen* is that the numerical values of the Hebrew consonants in the word *David* add up to that number. Other scholars have seen more hidden implications in the numerical reckoning of the evangelist. 'Jewish sacred arithmetic', wrote J. H. Ropes, 'had found it necessary to calculate the future by the aid of Jeremiah's prophecy of God's salvation after seventy years; and in Daniel we find this interpreted as seventy weeks of years, or 490 years. Here in Matthew the methods of the rabbis are used, and the period from the initial promise to Abraham, by which the Jewish religion was really founded, to the birth of the Messiah is figured at three times seventy weeks of years, or three times fourteen generations which is the same thing. Thus at the exact fit time of prophecy and moreover of the lineage of David—in very truth the son of David—*Jesus who is called Christ* is born' (pp. 46, 47).

A curious feature of the genealogy is the mention in verses 2-5 of three women: Tamar the mother of Perez and Zerah (RV); Rahab the mother of Boaz; and Ruth the mother of Obed. As women's names did not normally appear in Jewish genealogies, it may be, as McNeile has stated, that the evangelist wished to disarm Jewish criticism about the birth of Jesus by showing that irregular unions were divinely countenanced in the Messiah's legal ancestry. Ruth was a Moabitess, Rahab a harlot, and Tamar an adulteress. The evangelist's argument is that Jesus, though born of a virgin mother, was none the less in the true lineage of David because Joseph was in fact legally married to His mother Mary. As he clearly asserts in verse 16 *Jacob begat Joseph the husband of Mary, of whom was born Jesus, who is called Christ* (i.e. the Messiah). *Begat* (*egennēsen*) throughout this passage indicates primarily *legal* descent. Accordingly, the variant reading in the Sinaitic Syriac MS, which created such a stir when it was discovered in 1892, 'Joseph, to whom was betrothed Mary the virgin, was the father of Jesus called the Messiah' is no evidence that Jesus was born by the natural process of generation, but is an indication that the Syriac translator misunderstood the significance of *egennēsen*. The other interesting variant in this passage, found in an important group of Greek MSS and reflected in some MSS of the Old Latin versions, 'Jacob begat Joseph to whom Mary the virgin having been betrothed gave birth to Jesus who is called Christ' represents an attempt to bring out still more clearly than the ordinary text the virginity of Mary at the time Jesus was born.

b. The Messiah's birth (i. 18–25)

In this section Matthew is not concerned to satisfy the curiosity of historians by telling the story of Jesus' birth in detail, but to draw attention to certain features of it, in which the revelation of the Old Testament was fulfilled, and some of which were wilfully misrepresented by the Jews who were not expecting the Messiah to be virgin-born. One of the slanders which the early Christians had to answer was that Jesus was born out of wedlock; for, it was asked, why did not Joseph report the matter at once to the authorities, when he discovered that Mary was pregnant during the period of their betrothal? Matthew records the answer. It is not denied that Mary became pregnant before Joseph had consummated the marriage; but it is urged that, although as a law-abiding man he was well aware that he ought to make the matter public, he nevertheless refrained from doing so from a desire to shield his betrothed from shameful exposure, and had begun to envisage the possibility of divorcing her secretly. But, before he had time to take action, he was divinely instructed in a dream not to hesitate to take Mary into his house as his wife, for it was by the power of the Holy Spirit that her child had been conceived. Joseph, though not physically the child's father, would nevertheless by virtue of his marriage to Mary give Him His true legal status. It is significant that the angel addresses him as *Joseph, thou son of David*, for it was providentially ordered that the child should be of the lineage of David. Further indication of the uniqueness of Mary's Son and of the nature of the work He would be born to perform is given in the angel's instruction to Joseph to call the child *Jesus* (Saviour), for He would rescue God's people from the guilt and power of their sins.

In this defence of Joseph the evangelist has been compelled to throw into relief the supernatural conception of Mary's child; and as he does so, he is led to see in it a fulfilment of the words spoken by God through His prophet and recorded in Isaiah vii. 14. The substitution, which he found in the LXX, of *parthenos* (virgin) for *almah* (a girl of marriageable age, or a young married woman) in the Hebrew text is to him an indication that this prophecy was in fact more far-reaching than the prophet himself was aware. Its fulfilment was not limited to the birth of Hezekiah, the good and noble son of King Ahaz. Matthew also sees great significance in the occurrence in the prophecy of the word *Emmanuel, God with us*. Because of the righteousness of King Hezekiah in observing the Mosaic law, in removing the high places and destroying the Asherah and the brazen serpent, and in giving undivided allegiance to the Lord the God of Israel, there was in his day a real tabernacling of God among His people (see 2 Kings xviii. 4-6). But when Jesus was born of Mary nothing less than the Shekinah, the revealed presence of God, was manifested (albeit in human flesh) in the midst of His people; and with His people it would continue to dwell even after the earthly life of Jesus was over, for the Gospel of Matthew ends with the great promise 'Lo, I am with you alway, even unto the end of the world'.

Joseph acted at once on the angel's instruction, and instead of trying to obtain a secret divorce took Mary home as his wife, but refrained from intercourse with her until her child was born whom he dutifully called *JESUS*.

Additional Notes

i. 18. *Jesus* should probably be omitted in this verse on the authority of the Latin and Syriac Versions and of Irenaeus, who states 'Matthew could have said "The birth of *Jesus* was thus", but the Holy Spirit foreseeing detractors and anticipating their deceitfulness says through Matthew "The birth of *Messiah* was thus".'

Was espoused (RV 'had been betrothed'). A Jewish betrothal differed radically from a modern 'engagement'. The betrothed couple could not be legally separated except by divorce, and the death of one of them rendered the other a widow or a widower (see further the commentary on xxv. 1–12).

19. *And not willing* means 'and *yet* not willing'. Joseph was torn between his desire to do what was legally correct and a natural anxiety to protect his betrothed from publicity.

To make her a publick example translates *paradeigmatisai* found in the later MSS. The more ancient reading *deigmatisai* means simply 'to expose' or 'to publish'.

20. *While he thought.* The force of the aorist participle in the original is well brought out by Knox 'But hardly had the thought come into his mind when . . .'

The angel of the Lord appeared unto him in a dream. The occurrence of these words here and the use of similar expressions in ii. 12, 13, 19, 22 do not indicate that the narratives are legendary. The evangelist is recording decisions of special significance in the manner a Jew would record them when he wished to emphasize that they were not merely the result of human deliberation but divinely prompted. As Plummer wrote (p. 16): 'We may, if we like, regard the dreams as the evangelist's own interpretation of what took place. He knew that all that was done came to pass under divine guidance; and this guidance could be most easily understood as operating through dreams. The divine ordering of events is all that is essential; the manner in which God's will took effect is of small moment.'

To take unto thee translates *paralabein*, which means 'to take to your side', so 'to take into your home'.

21. There is a play on the words *iēshua* (Jesus) and *iōshūa* (he will save). This can be brought out in translation only by inserting 'Saviour' after the word Jesus.

The word *laos*, *people*, is often used in Matthew to designate the people of God. It is the word from which 'laity' is derived.

22. This is the first occurrence of the evangelist's formula, used by him to introduce passages from the Old Testament which act as a commentary on his narrative (cf. ii. 15, 17, 23, iv. 14, viii. 17, xii. 17, xiii. 35, xxi. 4, xxvii. 9).

23. The Hebrew original has '*she* shall call', i.e. the woman who is to be the mother of the child; the LXX has '*thou* shalt call', i.e. the child's father. Matthew's '*they* shall call', the subject being unexpressed, is a common Semitic way of saying 'he shall be called'.

25. The *prima facie* meaning of this verse would seem to be that after Mary's *firstborn son* was born Joseph had normal sexual intercourse with her; and, as McNeile points out, the Greek construction used here 'always implies in the New Testament that the negatived action did, or will, take place after the point of time indicated by the particle'. On the other hand, those who assume that Mary was ever-virgin point out that *firstborn* does not necessarily imply the birth of other children, and maintain that the sentence conveys no further meaning than that given to it in Knox's translation 'he had not known her when she bore a son, her firstborn'. There is, however, strong ancient evidence for omitting *firstborn* (so RV and RSV), and it may well have been inserted here from Luke ii. 7. Some scholars would also omit the words *and knew her not till* on the evidence of an old Latin MS and the Sinaitic Syriac, arguing that the presence of the words is unnecessary, and that they were added to prevent misapprehension about the virgin birth.

c. The visit of the magi (ii. 1–12)

It would appear that the aim of the evangelist in recording the story of the magi was to show that the child, who was born of the lineage of David to fulfil the ideal of kingship associated with the name of Israel's greatest king, was acknowledged even in His infancy, and by representatives of the non-Jewish world, to be, *par excellence*, the *King of the Jews*. This story is often regarded as unhistorical; but among those who dismiss it as legendary there is no agreement as to how or why it came into being; and in fact, the features in the story which might be regarded as 'legendary' in character are very few. The conventional picture of the star leading the magi all the way from distant eastern lands is based on what is certainly a wrong translation in verses 2 and 9. What the magi say on their arrival in Judaea is 'We saw his star (i.e. what we conjectured to be a sign that he was either born or soon to be born) at its rising (*en tē anatolē*, as distinct from *en tais anatolais*, which would be rightly translated "in the east"), and are come to pay Him homage'. These trained astrologers with the insatiable curiosity characteristic of scientists had seen a remarkable astrological phenomenon, the exact nature of which is not disclosed; and, being familiar with the current widespread belief that the time was ripe for the appearance of a king to be born in Judaea who would claim universal homage and usher in a reign of peace, they set out for that country to test the truth of their conjecture.

It is not surprising that news of the enquiry made by these astrologers on their arrival should have speedily reached the ears of King Herod, and that he should have been greatly perturbed in consequence, for the last thing in the world that that ill-tempered tyrant could contemplate with composure was the presence of a rival king in Jewry; and even if the inhabitants of Jerusalem did not share his fear of the new-born child, they would certainly be alarmed at the prospect of a fresh exhibition of Herod's anger. The serious view taken by him of this possible source of trouble is reflected in the methods he adopted to get rid of it. He called the entire Sanhedrin together and made careful enquiries about what could be learned from Scripture about the birth-place of the Messiah. When told that Bethlehem would be the scene of the nativity he at once despatched the magi to that city with instructions to bring him back any information about the child they might be able to discover; but he did not allow them to leave his presence, before he had first ascertained from them the exact time when they first saw the star. It would seem that he had already decided that if he could not locate the child in question he would embark on the campaign of 'liquidation' which is recorded in verses 16–18. The reappearance of the star which they had seen at its rising was a cause of great joy to the astrologers, for it made them very sure that their conjecture would be proved true. The text states that the star *went before them, till it came and stood over where the young child was.* Plummer (p. 12) notes that this is 'the only element in the story which resembles legend', and then goes on to suggest that 'this statement of great poetic beauty may be intended to mean no more than that what they had seen in the heavens *led* to their finding the new-born Messiah'. Several weeks had elapsed since the birth of Jesus, and His mother had been able to remove *the young child* (*to paidion* as distinct from *to brephos*, 'the babe' of Lk. ii. 16) from the manger of the inn to *the house* itself (11). Here the magi paid Him their homage, and offered Him their gifts. They then returned home directly, having been providentially warned not to revisit Herod

The story has all the marks of verisimilitude. The view that it is an imaginative creation suggested by Old Testament passages, in the nature of Jewish *midrash*, though it has often been put forward, would seem to be very difficult to maintain. It is true that in Numbers xxiv. 17 Balaam foretold, in what came to be regarded as a messianic prophecy, 'there shall come a Star out of Jacob'; but, as McNeile rightly says, 'the star which pointed out the Messiah's birth-place could hardly have been derived from a star which would be the Messiah Himself. If it had been, Matthew would doubtless have quoted the passage'. It is also true that there are certain Old Testament passages that may have suggested themselves to the evangelist as he recorded this story, as they have suggested themselves to his readers; but the fact remains that he nowhere asserts that any particular prophecy was fulfilled in it, except that Bethlehem was the predestined birth-place of the Messiah.

The words *they . . . worshipped him: and when they had opened their treasures, they presented unto him gifts; gold, and frankincense* might well suggest to those familiar with the Old Testament the Psalmist's words 'Seba shall offer gifts . . . all kings shall fall down before him . . . to him shall be given of the gold of Sheba' (Ps. lxxii. 10, 11, 15), and the prophecy of Isaiah lx. 6 'they from Sheba shall come: they shall bring gold and incense'. But it is not stated that the visitors to the child Christ were *kings*, though Christians later came to think of them as such, and gave them the names, Melchior, Caspar, and Balthasar. The word 'magi', of Persian origin, almost certainly means, in the present context, 'astrologers'. To be sure, kingship is a dominant theme in this story, but it is the contrast between the kingship of Jesus and the kingship of worldly princes such as Herod that is stressed, and not least in the interesting quotation in verse 6, which may be read either as a continuation of the chief priests' reply to Herod's question, or, more probably, as an annotation by the evangelist himself.

Matthew has been accused of manipulating this prophecy of Micah v. 2 so as to favour his interpretation of the event he is recording. Certainly he does not quote the verse in the form in which it is found either in the Hebrew or the LXX. Micah actually wrote, according to the Hebrew, 'But thou, Bethlehem Ephrathah, which art little to be among the thousands of Judah, out of thee shall one come forth unto me that is to be ruler in Israel' (RV). The LXX differs comparatively little from this. In Matthew's version, the 'ruler' of the original is in effect given the title of 'shepherd' (as in the LXX); 'thousands' is changed into *princes*; *Bethlehem* is not only given geographical precision by being equated with *the land of Juda*, but, what is more important, is stated to be 'in no wise least among the princes of Judah' (RV); and the word *for* is inserted before the last clause, giving the reason for this fresh evaluation of the city. Matthew, it would seem, felt justified in making these changes, because, in the light of the actual fulfilment, Micah's prophecy is seen to be more pregnant with meaning than was apparent in its original form. Micah drew attention to the insignificance of Bethlehem among the families of Judah, but foretold that from this city of David a ruler of Israel would emerge. Matthew is influenced by the knowledge that, when Jesus the Messiah was born at Bethlehem, the Judaean princes such as Herod regarded Him as a serious rival; Bethlehem had therefore been shown to be a place of considerable importance, 'in no wise least among (or 'in the eyes of') the princes of Judah'. Moreover, the rival king that was born in

Bethlehem, Jesus, the Son of David, was destined to exercise His Kingship in accordance with the ideal of kingship which had been set before David by God Himself. This was the 'shepherd' ideal of kingship (see 2 Sa. v. 2 and Ezk. xxxiv. 23). Hence the evangelist, not unnaturally, changes 'that is to be a ruler in Israel' into 'which shall be shepherd of my people Israel' (RV), in accordance with the LXX of Micah v. 2, which stated that the ruler would 'stand and feed his flock in the strength of the Lord'.

Nor is it expressly stated by Matthew that the astrologers came from any particular part of the east, such as 'Sheba' mentioned in Psalm lxxii. Verse 1 should be read 'astrologers from the east (i.e. eastern astrologers) came to Jerusalem'; the gifts they brought could have been found in several eastern countries; and *their own country*, to which they returned, is unnamed.

Few stories have been found to enshrine so many spiritual truths as this story of the magi. Some of these have been admirably summarized by McNeile, who remarks, 'The narrative is rich in spiritual significance. It affords a type of the early history of Christianity. The Son of God was revealed "to the Jew first, and also to the Gentile"—to the mother and Joseph first, and also to the foreign astrologers. He was revealed to the humble and ignorant first, and then to the honourable and learned; to the poor first, and then to the rich; to the West first, and then to the East. It also has other lessons. He was revealed to the astrologers by a method suited to their habits and understanding; and their object in coming to Jesus was not personal advantage, but solely to give Him homage.'

Additional Notes

ii. 1. *Wise men* translates *magoi* which was used both in a good sense of learned astrologers, and in a bad sense of those who practised magical arts. It is curious that some of the early Fathers understood it here in the latter sense, and regarded the story as symbolic of the triumph of Christianity over magic and sorcery. Ignatius wrote 'A star shone forth in the heavens

above all the stars; its light was unutterable, and its strangeness caused amazement; and all the rest of the stars, together
with the sun and moon, formed themselves into a chorus
about the star, but the star itself far outshone them all. From
that time forward every sorcery and every spell was dissolved'.
But, although there is some evidence from contemporary
magical papyri that frankincense and myrrh were used to
accompany the incantations of magicians, so that magicians
might conceivably have been pictured by a Christian writer
as laying down the gold of their ill-gotten gains, and their
stock-in-trade, at the feet of the child Christ, such thoughts
seem foreign to the context of the story and to the manner in
which it is described.

In the days of Herod the king. This is the only evidence we
have in this Gospel for dating the birth of Jesus. This Herod,
later known as 'Herod the Great', was an Idumaean who
through his friendship with Marcus Antonius was given the
title of 'king of the Jews' in BC 40, though remaining subject to
Rome. He died in BC 4 when his son Archelaus (22), who
inherited the cruel nature of his father, succeeded him. It
would appear that Jesus was born in the closing months of
Herod the Great's reign and that He returned from Egypt
soon after his death. It is, however, impossible to be more
specific.

6. The absence of marks of quotations from Greek MSS
makes it difficult to decide whether the evangelist is presenting
the quotation from Micah as part of the answer of the priests
or as an addition of his own. The latter is probably correct,
for it is reasonable to suppose that the priests would have
quoted the words in a form more consonant with the Hebrew
text.

11. The mention of *three* gifts gave rise to the view that
there were *three* magi; and the tradition that these were kings
dates back to Tertullian. As time went on, their gifts were
naturally thought of as symbols of Christian truth. Thus
Epiphanius speaks of 'gold for his humanity, myrrh for his
death, and incense for his divinity; or else, gold because he is

a king, incense because he is God, and myrrh because he is mortal'.

d. The flight into Egypt (ii. 13-15)

The magi searched for the child Jesus to do Him homage and offer Him their gifts. Herod was soon to search for Him to do away with Him. But the devices of man can never thwart the ultimate purposes of God; and as Pharaoh was prevented from destroying the Israelites by divine intervention on their behalf, so Joseph is divinely warned to escape with Mary and Jesus into Egypt. The land which had once been a land of oppression is now a haven, to which the holy family can escape from danger. The word translated *departed* in verses 12, 13 and 14 (*anachōreō*) is used elsewhere in the Gospel to convey the same idea of withdrawal from danger. When Jesus hears that John is imprisoned, it is no longer safe for Him to remain in Judaea and he 'withdraws' to Galilee (iv. 12); and when the Pharisees take action with a view to killing Him after the cure of the man with a withered hand, He 'withdraws' from the district where the miracle had been performed (xii. 15). The order in which the words *the young child and his mother* are found in verses 13 and 14 indicates that from the moment of His birth this unique child took precedence over all other human beings, including the mother who had given birth to Him.

The descriptive quotation in verse 15 from Hosea xi. 1 'Out of Egypt have I called my son' is meant, it would seem, to suggest to the reader that the Messiah, Himself the personification of the true Israel, repeated in His own life story the experience of the old Israel; and also that He was a second and a greater Moses. His supreme work of salvation had as its prototype the mighty act of salvation wrought by God through Moses on behalf of His chosen people. And, as Moses was called to go to Egypt and rescue Israel, God's son, His first-born (see Ex. iv. 22) from physical bondage, so Jesus was *called* out of Egypt in His infancy, through the divine message given to Joseph, to save mankind from the bondage of sin.

e. The massacre of the infants; and the return to Nazareth (ii. 16-23)

When the astrologers failed to return to Herod with information which would enable him to take direct action against the child who might prove to be a menace to the Herodian dynasty, he felt that he had been tricked by these 'wise-acres' from the East and fell into one of his more extreme fits of passion. But though enraged he was not non plussed, for he had already conceived an effective plan for getting rid of this so-called 'King of the Jews'. He would put to death all the male children in Bethlehem and the surrounding country who had been born since the time the astrologers had first seen the star—a vital piece of information which he had been far-sighted enough to discover before they left him.

The massacre of these infants, martyrs in *deed* if not in intent, was, on the surface, one of those meaningless tragedies that lead observers to ask with understandable bitterness 'To what purpose is this waste?' But our evangelist, as he looked back upon this untoward event, was led to see in it yet another example of the biblical truth that death is the gateway to life. This becomes evident when we view the quotation from Jeremiah xxxi. 15, which he says was *fulfilled* in this terrible incident, in the light of the context in which it is originally found. It is often necessary to do this in studying the quotations from the Old Testament that we find in the New Testament; for, as C. H. Dodd has reminded us, 'sections of the Old Testament Scriptures were understood by the Christian evangelists as *wholes*, and particular verses or sentences were sometimes quoted from them rather as pointers to the whole context than as constituting testimonials in and for themselves'.[1]

When the flower of the population of Jerusalem were deported by the Babylonians it must have seemed as if God had deserted His people, and Jeremiah in this poignant passage pictured Rachel bewailing the fate of these exiles as they tramped past her tomb in Ramah on their way to a strange land. But as soon as Jeremiah voiced this lament

[1] C. H. Dodd, *According to the Scriptures* (Nisbet, 1952), p. 126.

quoted by Matthew, the Lord said to him 'Refrain thy voice from weeping, and thine eyes from tears: for thy work shall be rewarded' (Je. xxxi. 16). Rachel, who has been called the *mater dolorosa* of the Old Testament, had died in giving birth to Benjamin but she had not suffered in vain, for the sufferings of her exiled descendants would not prove to be without purpose. 'They shall come again', the Lord went on to say to Jeremiah, 'from the land of the enemy. And there is hope in thine end, that thy children shall come again to their own border.' So indeed it happened. In the sorrow of the Babylonian Exile a new life became possible for a disciplined and revivified Israel. Similarly, the sorrow of the bereaved mothers of the infants murdered by Herod was destined in the divine providence to result in great reward. Their children were the first casualties in the warfare that had inevitably to be waged between the kingdoms of the world and the kingdom of God and His Christ; and their own sorrow was akin to that of Mary, whose heart was destined to be pierced as she saw her Son tread the way that must lead Him directly to the cross—but also through death to resurrection.

The child Christ had the power of an endless life: the tyrant Herod was mortal. His death, which must have occurred very soon after he had executed his nefarious design, made possible a second, smaller, but even more momentous 'exodus' from Egypt. When Joseph was divinely bidden to return with *the young child and his mother* to the land of Israel, he assumed very naturally, and, as it turned out, correctly, that Herod *Archelaus* who had succeeded his father would show himself to be 'a chip of the old block'; and fearing his wrath he hesitated to return to his dominions. But, as he was further instructed, Galilee, not Judaea, was to be the district where the Messiah would live till the time came for Him to be publicly manifested to Israel. So it happened that the Christ, who was born in David's city of Bethlehem, was brought up in Nazareth, a small town never mentioned in the Old Testament and in a district associated with the heathen rather than with the people of God. In this was foreshadowed the universal influence that He would exercise as the Saviour of the world.

The quotation *He shall be called a Nazarene*, which is stated by the evangelist in verse 23 to have been *fulfilled* in the residence of Jesus in Nazareth, has long been an enigma, for no such words are to be found in the Old Testament. But the fact that the evangelist introduces the statement as having been *spoken by the prophets* may be an indication that he was not intending to make an exact verbal quotation, but to point out in general terms that it was entirely in accordance with what the prophets had foretold, that Jesus should come to be known as 'Jesus of *Nazareth*'. That designation of Him was at first a term of scorn and derision (see Jn. i. 46), and Isaiah had prophesied that the Servant of the Lord would be despised by men. Part of the 'fulfilment' therefore of this and other similar passages from the Old Testament lay in the contempt for Jesus shown by the religious authorities of Israel because of His association with what they regarded as a provincial backwater. This was the explanation of the passage given by Jerome and it is probably correct. Some scholars have assumed that the evangelist is playing on the verbal similarity between the word *Nazōraios*, translated *Nazarene*, and the Hebrew word *nēzer*, meaning a 'branch', and that passages such as Isaiah xi. 1 and Jeremiah xxiii. 5 were in his mind; but such a thought would seem to be somewhat irrelevant in the present context. Others have assumed a similar verbal association between *Nazōraios* and *Naziraios* (Nazirite). This would seem even more improbable, as Jesus was not a Nazirite.

II. THE BEGINNING OF THE MINISTRY OF JESUS THE MESSIAH (iii. 1-iv. 25)

a. The preaching of John the Baptist and the baptism of Jesus (iii. 1-17)

The opening words of chapter iii, *In those days*, show that the first two chapters are not a later addition but an integral part of the original Gospel. The expression is deliberately vague, as a long time has elapsed since the return of the infant

Jesus from Egypt and the settlement of the holy family at Nazareth. All that the evangelist is saying is that it was while Jesus was still living at Nazareth that John appeared in the wilderness of Judaea. Christian tradition was almost wholly silent about what have been called 'the hidden years' at Nazareth during which Jesus 'grew in wisdom and stature'. The earliest preachers of the gospel were primarily concerned with the events in the life of Jesus which began with His baptism by John; and the written Gospels seem to have followed in general outline such a summary of the primitive preaching as is contained in Acts x. 37–41: 'That word, I say, ye know, which was published throughout all Judaea, and began from Galilee, after the baptism which John preached; how God anointed Jesus of Nazareth with the Holy Ghost and with power: who went about doing good, and healing all that were oppressed of the devil; for God was with him. And we are witnesses of all things which he did both in the land of the Jews, and in Jerusalem; whom they slew and hanged on a tree: him God raised up the third day, and shewed him openly; not to all the people, but unto witnesses chosen before of God.' When we read the Gospels against this background, we are able to see them in their true light, and to understand both their contents and what might otherwise appear to be their unaccountable omissions.

Matthew assumes that his readers are familiar with John, who had long been known as *the Baptist*. Nothing therefore is said of his previous history, and it is anybody's guess whether he belonged originally to one of the Essene communities or to the Qumran sect known to us through the recently discovered Dead Sea Scrolls. What is important to the evangelist is that his appearance in the wilderness of Judaea as a preacher at this critical moment was in accordance with the prophecy of Isaiah xl. 3, which Matthew quotes in verse 3. John was divinely called to cry aloud to his fellow men, 'Prepare a way for the Lord, clear a path for Him' (see verse 3). These words originally formed part of the consoling message given to the Babylonian exiles. They were soon to return to their own land under the guidance and protection of their God and in that divinely ordered change in Israel's fortunes God would be seen to be reigning. The way back to Jerusalem was the king's highway. John, the last of the prophets of Israel, was now commissioned to utter a similar and even more wonderful 'gospel' message. The reign of God was immediately to be made manifest in Israel in all its fullness in the Person and the work of none other than the Messiah Himself. For that great coming men must prepare a way in their hearts.

John could very properly be thought of as the prophet sent, as Malachi had predicted, 'before the coming of the great and dreadful day of the Lord'—Elijah *redivivus* (Mal. iv. 5). Matthew seems to suggest this when he describes John as wearing a rough coat of camel's hair and having a leather belt about his waist (cf. 2 Ki. i. 8). And it was in the spirit of Elijah, who on Mount Carmel had called upon Israel to make a vital decision (1 Ki. xviii. 21), that John bade the people return to the Lord, and so be ready to receive the coming reign of God. The outward sign of their desire to make such a return lay in their readiness to receive John's baptism, which he describes in verse 11 as a baptism *with water unto repentance*. It was a baptism of cleansing, and those who submitted to it first made a confession of their sins (6); yet it was not an end in itself, but a preparation for the greater baptism *with the Holy Ghost, and with fire* which the *mightier* than John, whose menial slave John says he is unworthy to be, alone could bestow (11). The contrast between the symbolism of water and that of spirit and fire is well brought out by Levertoff. 'Water', he says, 'only touches the surface, and, though purifying, has no permanent result. In contrast to this is the Spirit which, wherever it works, reaches the heart, and there produces life; and fire, which, taking hold of its object, either melts or entirely destroys it.'

The Messiah's baptism would indeed endow those who submitted to His influence with sanctifying power. But it would also (and here lay the urgency of the situation) effect a separation in Israel between the true metal and the dross, between the wheat and the chaff, so that it would soon become apparent, in Paul's words, that 'he is not a Jew, which is one outwardly;

neither is that circumcision, which is outward in the flesh:
but he is a Jew, which is one inwardly; and circumcision is
that of the heart, in the spirit, and not in the letter' (Rom.
ii. 28, 29). An essential part of John's ministry therefore was
to give a severe warning to the many *Pharisees and Sadducees*
who, much to his surprise, came to his baptism. It was indeed
strange that those who were so very sure that they possessed in
their legalism and in their ritualism all things necessary for
salvation, should have felt the need to try to find some other
way of escape from the coming judgment. They were like
snakes, the title by which John tauntingly addressed them,
fleeing from a field when the scythes were mowing down the
crops, or escaping from a desert fire (7). No doubt they were
actuated by no higher motive than fear that John's popularity
with the people might lead to a movement which would
jeopardize their own position, for all regarded him as a
prophet (see xxi. 26). But John holds out hope even for the
Pharisees and the Sadducees, if their repentance proved to be
genuine. They must not, however, suppose that his baptism
was a magic prophylactic against *the wrath to come*, or that
judgment was meant only for the heathen and not also for
themselves. They must understand also that mere verbal
repentance which did not result in conduct that befitted it
would be wholly unavailing. To rely, moreover, on the merits
of their fathers, or to imagine that because God had called
Abraham to be the ancestor of His people He was committed
to bestow His blessings solely upon Abraham's physical
descendants, would be utter presumption. The great Creator
could, if He so desired, people the Judaean desert with a new
race of men and women possessing no physical ancestry, but
more fitted to be the recipients of His grace than the unworthy
sons of Abraham (8, 9). The need for repentance was vital, for
the coming judgment was so inevitable and so immediate,
that the prophet in his imagination could see a forest where the
woodman was already at work laying his axe against the root
of the trees doomed to be felled and burned because they had
failed to produce good fruit.

Because *all* Israel was confronted with the call to return to the Lord that was being sounded by John, Jesus could not remain aloof from it. We may surmise that, though unconscious of personal sin, His knowledge that a unique relationship existed between Himself and His heavenly Father, and that Jewish prophecy would be supremely fulfilled in what He would be led to say and do, made Him certain that this prophetic ministry of John had a profound significance for Himself. So He presented Himself to John for baptism. Matthew alone records that the prophet at first hesitated to accept Him. As he 'interviewed' Jesus, he seems to have felt instinctively that He was wholly different from everyone else who had come to be baptized. It is true, as we learn from John i. 31, that before Jesus was actually baptized John did not know that it was He who would 'baptize with the Holy Ghost, and with fire'. Many critics have therefore refused to accept the historicity of Matthew's statement that John tried to prevent Jesus from coming to his baptism, on the ground that it presupposes that John already possessed the knowledge that Jesus was the Messiah, when in fact that information came to him only when Jesus emerged from the water and the Spirit of God descended on Him like a dove. This conclusion is based, however, on the assumption that John's words in verse 14 mean 'I have need of Thy baptism with Spirit and fire, and comest Thou to my water-baptism?' But John's hesitation need not indicate so much as this. He may well have felt that Jesus was wholly different from the sinners who flocked to him, without yet knowing that He was the One for whose coming he was preparing. The reply of Jesus in verse 15 shows His awareness that both John and Himself had unique parts to play in the divine plan for man's redemption, and that the present moment was decisive in its execution. The significance of Jesus' action is well brought out by Levertoff: 'In undergoing baptism Jesus is accepting His destiny. As one with His people and with humanity, He takes upon Himself their sins, and in baptism thrusts them from Him with a holy hatred, dedicating Himself at the same time to His holy vocation.'

The exact form that His vocation was to take was made

clear to Jesus in His baptismal experience. It was then, as the summaries of the early Christian preaching put it, that He was 'anointed with the Holy Spirit and with power'. He did not *become* Son of God at His baptism, as certain heretical teachers in the early Church maintained; but it was then that He was appointed to a work which He alone could perform, because of His unique relationship with His Father. This is brought out in the heavenly message heard as He came up from the water. The message takes the form of a composite quotation from Psalm ii. 7 and Isaiah xlii. 1, upon both of which passages Jesus must often have meditated. In the verse from the psalm the Lord of Israel is pictured as crowning a son of David as Messiah with the words 'Thou art my Son; this day have I begotten thee'. The heavenly voice, in Matthew's account of Jesus' baptism, changes 'Thou art' to 'This is', and substitutes for the last half of the verse words from the passage in Isaiah, where the prophet speaks of an ideal servant of God who perfectly does His will as he treads the pathway of obedience and service. Jesus is thus designated God's beloved Son, chosen to be the One in whom this prophecy is to be fulfilled. He is the unique Son of God endowed with supernatural power, but it is His vocation to be a Servant well-pleasing to God, especially when called upon to suffer vicariously for His people.

It is a great paradox that upon the Messiah, who was to baptize *with fire*, the Spirit should have descended at His baptism *like a dove*, a symbol of gentleness and meekness. In Jesus we are in fact confronted with both 'the goodness and severity of God' (Rom. xi. 22); and this double truth runs right through the New Testament, and not least through the Gospel of Matthew (contrast, for example, xi. 29 and xxv. 41).

Additional Notes

iii. 2. *And saying.* These words introduce in summary form the general theme of John's preaching.

The kingdom of heaven. This is the first mention of an expression peculiar to Matthew, who with Jewish reticence substitutes *heaven* for 'God'. By *kingdom*, in most of the passages in which this expression occurs, is meant 'kingly rule' rather than the sphere in which that rule is exercised.

4. The word *agrion*, rendered *wild*, when used of plants implied that they were uncultivated. Here the reference is to honey which distils from certain trees.

8. *Bring forth*. The aorist tense of the original signifies that complete and immediate action must be taken.

Meet for repentance, i.e. 'as proof of your repentance'.

9. *Think not to say* means 'think not that you have the right to say', i.e. 'do not presume to say'.

There was probably a play in the original Aramaic on the words *stones* and *children* which it is not possible to reproduce in translation.

10. *Now also.* A better translation is 'even now' (RV).

Is hewn down. The present tense of the original is prophetic 'is to be cut down'.

11. Of the Greek word *bastasai* translated 'to bear' Moulton and Milligan wrote 'the firmly established vernacular use determines the meaning as "whose sandals I am not worthy to take off"'.

12. The word translated *fan* refers to the shovel used for throwing the corn into the air to clear it of the chaff.

14. *Forbad.* The force of the imperfect tense in the Greek is conative 'tried to prevent'.

15. *To fulfil all righteousness* means more than 'to do all that is right'. Jesus says *it becometh us* (i.e. either John and Himself, or Himself and His fellow men) to comply with all that God requires of them.

17. *In whom I am well pleased*. The Greek does not mean 'with whom I am delighted' but 'in whom my pleasure rests', i.e. 'on whom my plan for the salvation of mankind is centred'.

b. The temptations in the wilderness (iv. 1–11; cf. Mk. i. 12, 13 and Lk. iv. 1–13)

Although *then, tote,* does not always in Matthew convey the meaning of 'immediately after' what has previously been recorded, all the Synoptic Gospels imply that the temptations of Jesus followed at once after His baptism. Moreover, the expression *was led up of the Spirit* indicates that it was the divine will that Jesus, now fully conscious of His unique Sonship and fully aware of His vocation to be the ideal Servant of God, should be tempted to be disobedient to the implications of that vocation, and by overcoming such temptation should be able to embark upon a ministry which was to have as its climax His obedience unto the death of the cross. In other words, His temptations in the wilderness were temptations to rely upon the first part of the message spoken by the heavenly voice at His baptism to such an extent that He might be able to avoid treading the way marked out for Him in the second part. In Jesus, the wholly-obedient Son of God, was to be seen in perfection all that Israel, called by God out of Egypt to be His Son, had been intended to be but through disobedience had never been. But, as the author of the Epistle to the Hebrews states, He learned obedience through the things He suffered (see Heb. v. 8); and the temptations overcome in the wilderness played an all-important part in that schooling. The language in which Jesus described those temptations to His disciples (for it must have been from His lips that they obtained this precious piece of autobiography) reveals His awareness that He must succeed where the old Israel had failed, that whereas they had shown constant disobedience He must be consistently obedient.

The first temptation should probably be understood not as a temptation to doubt His Sonship, for the word *if* in verses 3 and 6 could convey the meaning 'since'. The devil is in fact not challenging Jesus to show some proof that He really is God's Son, but tempting Him to display an unwillingness to render to His Father the complete obedience that true Sonship demanded. According to Matthew's account, this temptation to disobedience came at the end of a long fast.

Jesus, the greater Moses, had abstained from food other than what the desert provided for the same length of time, *forty days and forty nights* (*forty nights* being found only in Matthew), as Moses had fasted when he was 'with the Lord' on Mount Sinai (Ex. xxxiv. 28). It was now very plausibly suggested to Him that it would be fitting for Him to exercise His supernatural power to create bread for Him to eat. But Jesus, whose long meditations upon Scripture during 'the hidden years' at Nazareth were now bearing fruit, was well aware that His Father had subjected Him to the discipline of this fast for precisely the same purpose that Israel had been 'suffered to hunger' in the wilderness; it was that the supreme lesson might be learned that *man shall not live by bread alone, but by every word that proceedeth out of the mouth of God* (see Dt. viii. 3). The Father, who had called Him and submitted Him to temptation, would in His own good time supply the physical necessities of His Son. The duty of Jesus was to be obedient to that call, and not to decide for Himself either the moment or the manner in which His fast should be ended.

The second temptation, in the order found in Matthew, was, it would seem, to doubt whether the Father who had called Him really would enable Him to be true to His vocation in the face of widespread opposition and the constant refusal of men to believe without witnessing spectacular signs of His divinity. Surely, so the devil suggested, it would be folly for Jesus to enter upon His ministry with the prospect of possible failure. Should He not obtain more definite proof of His Father's protection by creating a situation in which He would be forced to come to the aid of His Son? Jesus is tempted, therefore, to imagine Himself seated on a *pinnacle of the temple* with the crowds assembled in the courts beneath, perhaps at the time of the evening sacrifice, and to contemplate jumping down among them—a leap which in the case of everyone else who attempted it would be suicidal, but from which upheld by angels' hands He would escape unscathed. This temptation was made more attractive by the scriptural language in which it was framed. Divine protection from physical disaster was promised to the faithful in the quotation from Psalm xci. 11,

12 quoted by the tempter in verse 6. But when the devil quotes Scripture for his own purpose he rarely quotes it accurately. So in this instance he significantly omitted the words 'to keep thee in all thy ways' after *charge concerning thee*. The omission in fact destroys the truth of the original, which does not encourage the faithful to tempt God by taking unnecessary risks, but assures him that God will keep him safe wherever his way may lead, provided he is obedient to the divine will. Jesus counteracts the devil's suggestion by recalling another passage of Scripture. He understands that He is being tempted to do what the Israelites did at Massah, when they murmured against Moses and forced him to entreat God to provide His people with a miraculous supply of water from the rock. They were in effect tempting 'the Lord, saying, Is the Lord among us, or not?' (Ex. xvii. 7). And Jesus remembers how subsequently the Lord recalled this incident to the people in the words 'Ye shall not tempt the Lord your God, as ye tempted him in Massah' (Dt. vi. 16). The ways that Jesus was to be called to tread in discharging the obligations of His ministry included the most difficult of all ways, the way of the cross; and we may be very sure that He was sustained in His determination to follow it by the assurance contained in the psalmist's words, which the devil had failed to mention, that His Father would keep Him in all His ways, if He remained subservient to His will.

To escape the way of the cross by being disobedient to the vocation of the suffering Servant despised and rejected by men, upon whom was to be laid the iniquity of us all, was Jesus' greatest and most persistent temptation; and, according to Matthew's account, it was the climax of the wilderness temptations. Jesus was in effect tempted to subscribe to the diabolical doctrine that the end justifies the means; that, so long as He obtained universal sovereignty in the end, it mattered not how that sovereignty was reached—as though, forsooth, if the means by which an object is sought are corrupt, the object itself will not suffer corruption in the process. The devil was once again mimicking Scripture. When Moses on Mount Nebo surveyed the land that lay before him, he was told that this was the land of which God had said to the patriarchs 'To your seed I will give it'. Similarly, the devil presents to the imagination of Jesus, standing on an *exceeding high mountain*, a vision of the kingdoms of the world which were destined to become 'the kingdoms of the Lord and His Christ', and he offers them to Him without toil or tears or the loss of His own life, on the single condition that Jesus would pay homage to him.

This was the temptation to use the devil's weapons of cruelty, ruthlessness, and force in a heartless thrust for universal dominion, instead of winning men and women by self-sacrifice and suffering and so making them willing subjects of the kingdom of God. But the truth that evil can never be overcome by evil, and the reign of God never established by Satanic means, was axiomatic to one who knew the Scriptures as Jesus knew them. The Israelites, He remembers, were divinely warned that when they came to possess the land of promise, they would be tempted to be self-satisfied, to trust solely in their own powers, and to forget the Lord their God, so that the kingdom of Israel, instead of being the reign of God's people, might prove to be little different from the kingdoms of the world. This warning often went unheeded; Israel forgot the divine injunction 'Thou shalt fear the Lord thy God, and serve him, and shalt swear by his name' (see Dt. vi. 10-13). But whereas Israel forgot, the Messiah remembered; and it was with these very words that He withstood the devil's presumptuous offer and bade him depart. For the third time 'the word of God' had provided Him with 'the sword of the Spirit' with which to combat the forces of evil (see Eph. vi. 17). And His obedience was rewarded, so Matthew seems to suggest, not only by the devil's departure, but by the consciousness of renewed spiritual strength.

These three temptations re-asserted themselves on subsequent occasions in Jesus' ministry, a truth which Luke seems to imply by the addition of the words 'for a season' after *the devil leaveth him*. First, Jesus was continually tempted, we may believe, to shrink from what was involved in the words 'My meat is to do the will of him that sent me, and to finish his work' (Jn. iv. 34), for it must often have meant a temporary failure to find satisfaction for His own physical needs. Secondly, He had constantly to resist the temptation to oblige the idly curious by working some 'sign' that might gain their temporary allegiance (see xvi. 3). And thirdly, when all the ways leading *from* Jerusalem and the cross lay open before Him, He had to resist the temptation to avoid the way that led directly *to* it, even when the mouth-piece of such temptation was none other than Peter, His apostle (see xvi. 23).

c. The beginning of the Galilaean ministry (iv. 12–25; cf. Mk. i. 16–20 and Lk. vi. 14, 15, v. 1–11)

Both Matthew and Mark state that it was after John the Baptist's arrest that Jesus returned to Galilee, but Matthew alone records that *leaving Nazareth, he came and dwelt in Capernaum*, on the western shore of the Sea of Galilee in the district once known as Zebulun and Napthalim but now incorporated in the larger circular area known as Galilee. Capernaum now became, as Matthew describes it in ix. 1, 'his own city'. The evangelist is interested in the fact that the Messiah resided at Capernaum not merely because he himself lived in it, but also because he finds in this a fulfilment of Isaiah's prophecy that a great light would one day dawn upon that down-trodden region ravaged by the Assyrian invader (see Is. ix. 1–7). The expressions *by the way of the sea* (i.e. towards the Mediterranean) and *beyond Jordan* (i.e. west of Jordan) depict the district from the viewpoint of the Assyrian invaders. Levertoff brings out the significance of Matthew's reference to this particular prophecy as follows: 'The prophet, after prophesying judgment and doom, proclaimed the dawn of a new hope in the birth of a descendant of David who would establish a kingdom of peace. Yet not in Jerusalem and Judah will the light first dawn, but in the northernmost part of the land of Israel, a region which lay in darkness and death at the time Jesus came to fulfil the ancient prophecy, and which even the Baptist had not been able to reach by his call to repentance.'

The early Galilaean ministry of Jesus had two complementary features. It consisted of both preaching and healing. In verse 17 the evangelist gives a summary of the preaching. Unless the reading of the Old Syriac versions, supported by one important Old Latin MS, is followed, which omits the words *Repent* and *for*, there is an exact verbal similarity between this summary and that of the preaching of John, given in iii. 2. Both the Baptist and Jesus, the one held by the people to be 'a prophet' (xxi. 26) and the other known to them as 'the prophet of Nazareth of Galilee' (xxi. 11), call Israel to repentance in view of the coming kingdom of God. It is probable that the longer reading is original, for John's ministry did not influence more than a few Galilaeans, and Jesus was constantly pressing upon His hearers the need to repent. But while there is a verbal similarity between the summaries of the teaching of these two 'prophets', in fact with the arrival of Jesus in Galilee the kingdom of God had become a present reality. In the beneficent and merciful ministry of teaching and healing exercised by Him the powers of evil were being broken, and men and women were coming to experience the reign of God. Such a ministry was in fact a proclamation in word and deed of victorious good news—a 'gospel' (*evangelion*). Hence the activity of Jesus is summarized in verse 23 as *preaching the gospel of the kingdom, and healing all manner of sickness*.

The distinctive expression *From that time* (*apo tote*) in verse 17 is repeated in xvi. 21, where the evangelist records that 'from that time' Jesus began to teach His disciples about the necessity of His forthcoming death. It would seem, therefore, that iv. 17 is to be regarded as a summary of the public teaching of Jesus in Galilee during the first part of His ministry, and xvi. 21 as a summary of the private teaching given later to His disciples after they had through their spokesman Peter acknowledged Him as the Messiah, the Son of the living God. Consequently, it may not be entirely without significance that between the summary of Jesus' preaching in verse 17, and the general description of His Galilaean ministry in verses 23-25, the evangelist interposes the story of the call of two pairs of brothers who formed the nucleus of the apostolic band. In

Mark the narratives are reversed. Because the response of these four fishermen to follow Jesus was so immediate and so sacrificial, they would be able to learn in the company of Jesus all that they needed to know before receiving from Him the appointment to be *fishers of men*, by whose teaching and example many would be brought to experience the reign of God. Three of these men, Peter, James and John, seem to have been more intimate with Jesus than the rest of the Twelve. At any rate, it was they who were specially privileged to be alone with Jesus at the raising of Jairus' daughter (Mk. vi. 37), on the mount of transfiguration (xvii. 1), and in Gethsemane (xxvi. 37).

Jesus' ministry, though it was exercised throughout *all Galilee*, was confined almost exclusively, so this Gospel emphasizes, to the people of Israel. It was in the *synagogues* for the most part that His teaching at first was given; and it was *among the* (Jewish) *people* (*en tō laō*) that His hand was stretched out to heal (23). But news of what He was doing in *all Galilee* inevitably spread *throughout all Syria*, which lay to the north and north-east of Palestine. There was no kind of illness, the evangelist suggests, that Jesus failed to cure; and among the numerous patients that were brought to Him were those tormented by the most acute forms of physical and mental derangement—demoniacs, epileptics, and paralytics. And wherever He went, Matthew adds, great crowds followed Him, consisting not merely of Galilaeans but of those who journeyed from the free Greek cities that lay south-east of the Sea of Galilee and were known as *Decapolis*, and also of visitors from Jerusalem, Judaea, and trans-Jordania (25).

III. THE ETHICS OF THE KINGDOM OF GOD
(v. 1–vii. 29)

a. Introduction

The expression 'the Sermon on the Mount', by which this section is usually called, is somewhat misleading, as it would seem most probable that in these chapters the evangelist is not recording a single discourse delivered on one occasion, but is assembling in an orderly form small groups of the sayings of Jesus about discipleship given at various times during His ministry. The fact that many of the sayings here recorded are found in different contexts in Luke's narrative confirms this conclusion, as also does the general consideration that it would have been unlikely that any teacher would have condensed so much instruction into a single sermon. Chapman's suggestion (p. 216) that the original sermon, if not developed, might have taken an hour to deliver, but that if there were developments and explanations it might have lasted as long as three hours, is somewhat unconvincing. Moreover, the setting given by Matthew to the 'sermon'—*a mountain*, and the posture of the preacher—*when he was set* (sitting being the usual practice of the Rabbi when teaching), seems to suggest that the evangelist is deliberately portraying Jesus as the second and greater Moses, who on a 'mountain' (though in fact it was a Galilaean hill-side) gives to the new Israel a new 'law', though to be sure a very different kind of law from that promulgated by Moses from Mount Sinai. The 'law' prescribed by Jesus is no external code of rules which can be followed to the letter, but a series of principles, ideals, and motives for conduct, more akin to the 'law' which Jeremiah foretold the Lord would put in men's 'inward parts' and 'write it in their hearts' when He established a new covenant with them (see Je. xxxi. 33). The fact that Luke records a much shorter but similar collection of sayings about discipleship in what is often called 'the Sermon on the Plain' (Lk. vi. 20–49), and that both collections begin with a series of beatitudes and end with the parable of the two builders, is accounted for by critics either on the supposition that both evangelists were drawing upon a pre-existent collection of sayings, which Matthew has expanded, or, less commonly, on the assumption that Luke was abbreviating the narrative of Matthew.

In this section we find crystallized into the form of direct instructions the teaching of Jesus about the way men and women must tend to behave when they have become subject to the reign of God. Some of this teaching is found in a more poetical form in the illustrative parables delivered by Jesus on other occasions. Thus, the best commentary on the first beatitude (v. 3) is the parable of the Pharisee and the publican (Lk. xviii. 10–14); and the truth contained in the fifth beatitude (v. 7) is illustrated in an unforgettable manner in the parable of the unmerciful servant (xviii. 23–35). Similarly, the parable of the good Samaritan exemplifies how the injunction *love your enemies* (v. 44) can be practised. The recollection of these other literary forms in which the same teaching of Jesus is found should help us to resist the temptation to regard 'the Sermon on the Mount' in a legalistic spirit, and to remember that it was largely in opposition to that spirit as it found expression in the teaching of the scribes and Pharisees that Jesus was speaking. Much misunderstanding and frustration are caused if we regard the precepts contained in this section as rules which can be obeyed literally by anybody, under any circumstances, by the exercise of the human will, in the same way that the laws of an earthly state can be complied with by any of its citizens. The ethics of the 'Sermon on the Mount', as C. H. Dodd has pointed out,[1] 'are the absolute ethics of the kingdom of God. We are not to suppose that we are capable in this world of loving our enemies, or even our neighbours, to the full measure in which God has loved us; or of being as completely disinterested and single-minded, as pure of worldly desire and anxiety, and as unreserved in self-sacrifice, as the words of Jesus demand; and yet these are the standards by which all our actions are judged.' The same writer makes the same point elsewhere,[2] when he writes: 'The precepts of Christ are not statutory definitions like those of the Mosaic code, but indications of *quality* and *direction* of action which may be present at quite lowly levels of performance.'

[1] *The Bible Today*, p. 84.
[2] *The Gospel and the Law of Christ* (Longmans, 1947), p. 19.

b. The characteristics of Christian discipleship (v. 1–16; cf. Lk. vi. 20–23, xiv. 34, 35, xi. 33; Mk. ix. 50)

The beatitudes, as they are usually called, are descriptions given in an exclamatory form of the qualities, all of which must be found, and in fact are found in varying degrees, in the lives of those who have come under the influence of the kingly rule of God. They are also a declaration of the blessings which all who display those virtues experience already in part, and will enjoy more fully hereafter. The future tense used in the description of those blessings in verses 5–9 emphasizes their certainty and not merely their futurity. The mourners will *indeed* be comforted, etc. The beatitudes in Matthew would appear to be eight in number, for in verse 11 Jesus abandons the exclamatory form 'How blest are' and addresses the disciples directly in the words *Blessed are ye*. The eight qualities here set forth, when blended together (and no single one of them can in fact exist in isolation from the others) make up the character of those who alone are accepted by the divine King as His subjects (3, 10), who alone can see Him who is invisible (8), and who alone are worthy to be His sons (9). In consequence, anyone who claims to be God's son, or to know Him, or to belong to His kingdom, or to be a member of His body, the Church, in whom these qualities are conspicuous by their absence, is 'a liar and knows not the truth'. Many of these qualities had already been counted blessed by the psalmist. It is the assembly of them by Jesus, so that they form a kind of mosaic of the Christian character, that is His unique contribution.

The *poor in spirit* are not the 'poor-spirited', as this somewhat unfortunate English translation might suggest. They are those who recognize in their heart that they are 'poor' in the sense that they can do no good thing without divine assistance, and that they have no power in themselves to help them do what God requires them to do. The *kingdom of heaven* belongs to such, for from that kingdom the proudly self-sufficient are inevitably excluded.

They that mourn are those who are sorrowful both for their own sins and failings, and also for the evil that is rampant in the world and the cause of so much suffering and misery. The sympathy that arises from such sorrow brings consolation even now to those who display it, and the day will surely come when God 'will wipe away *all* tears from their eyes'.

The meek are those who humble themselves before God, because they acknowledge their utter dependence upon Him. In consequence, they are gentle in their dealings with others. Moses exhibited this quality in a remarkable degree; and the possession of it by Jesus was one of the grounds on which He invited sorrowing men and women to come to Him (see xi. 29). When God has finally destroyed all who in their arrogance resist His will, the meek will alone be left to *inherit the earth*.

Those who *hunger and thirst after righteousness* are those who, because they long to see God's final triumph over evil and His kingdom fully established, long also to do what is right and just themselves. All such have the growing satisfaction of knowing that they are furthering and not thwarting God's purposes.

The merciful are those who are conscious that they are themselves the unworthy recipients of God's mercy, and that but for the grace of God they would be not only sinners but condemned sinners. In consequence, they endeavour to reflect in their dealings with others something of the mercy God has shown to them; and the more they do so, the more God's mercy is extended to them.

The pure in heart are the single-minded, who are free from the tyranny of a divided self, and who do not try to serve God and the world at the same time. From such it is impossible that God should hide Himself. They endure as already seeing Him who is invisible, and one day they will see Him as He is (cf. Heb. xi. 27 and 1 Jn. iii. 2).

The peacemakers are those who are at peace with God 'the author of peace and lover of concord'; and who show that they are truly *children of God* by striving to use every opportunity open to them to effect reconciliation between others who are at variance.

Those who are *persecuted for righteousness' sake* suffer solely because they uphold God's standards of truth, justice and purity, and refuse to compromise with paganism or bow the knee to the idols that men tend to erect as substitutes for God. As Paul reminded his friend Timothy, 'all that will live godly in Christ Jesus shall suffer persecution' (2 Tim. iii. 12); but to such Jesus gives the assurance that they are citizens of the only kingdom that abides, *the kingdom of heaven.*

In verse 11 Jesus turns to His disciples and warns them that in their case suffering *for righteousness' sake* will mean being subjected to abuse, persecution, and every kind of calumny *for* His *sake.* When He, the Messiah, is withdrawn from them, the hatred of the world, directed against Him while He is on earth, will be turned against His followers. They must rejoice greatly in the knowledge that such suffering is an indication that they are in the true line of descent from the prophets who foretold the Messiah's coming.

Those prophets and the people to whom they spoke were a 'peculiar' people, and the disciples of Jesus must also, by the very nature of their calling, be 'distinctive'. It is this truth which is expressed in Jesus' description of them as *the salt of the earth.* The most obvious *general* characteristic of salt is that it is essentially different from the medium into which it is put. Its power lies precisely in this difference. So it is, says Jesus, with His disciples. Their power in the world lies in their difference from it. The Christian is as different from other men as the salt on a plate is different from the food into which it is placed. Moreover, another primary function of salt is to preserve, to arrest decay, to act as an antiseptic, so that the germs latent, for example, in meat may be rendered ineffective when salt is rubbed into it. The disciples, accordingly, are called to be a moral disinfectant in a world where moral standards are low, constantly changing, or non-existent. But they can discharge this function only if they themselves retain their virtue—and this calls for much self-discipline—not least in speech, for, as Paul said, a Christian's speech must be 'alway with grace, and seasoned with salt' (Col. iv. 6). As Jesus goes on to point out, if a disciple has lost his 'virtue' he is like salt which has lost its saltness and so becomes a wholly useless commodity, fit for nothing else except to be thrown out on the street and trampled on by passers-by. In the Lucan version of the saying it is implied that it would be a waste of time and energy to scatter it on the land or put in on the compost heap (Lk. xiv. 35).

But the disciples of Christ must not, through fear of being an unworthy influence, remain silent about their religion. They can, and they must, bear witness to the faith that is in them through personal example. This is the truth underlying the metaphor used by Jesus when He tells them they are *the light of the world*. They obtain their light from Him who is supremely the Light of the world, but if it is to shine in the world's dark places, it must be in a conspicuous position itself and unobscured by intervening objects. It is the city set on *an hill* that is visible to those who live on lower levels. And it would be absurd, Jesus adds, to put a *candle* (RV, rightly, 'lamp') under a meal-tub (*modios*, translated *bushel*, being a measure containing about a peck, used for measuring meal) instead of placing it on a *candlestick* (RV, rightly, 'stand'), and then to expect the occupants of a house to see by it! So the disciples must not hide themselves, but live and work in places where their influence may be felt, and the light that is in them be most fully manifested to others—not for their own glorification, but that others may see that the light of real Christian goodness, finding expression in practical acts of loving-kindness and service, is a light not of this world but coming from God, and may in consequence be led to give honour and praise to its Giver.

c. Jesus and the Mosaic law (v. 17–48; cf. Lk. xii. 57–59; Mk. ix. 43–48, x. 11, 12; Lk. xvi. 18, vi. 29, 30, 32–36)

In this section Jesus insists that in His teaching He is in no way contradicting the Mosaic law, though He is opposed to the legalistic type of religion that the scribes had built upon it. That He regards the Old Testament as possessing permanent validity as the Word of God is clear from the uncompromising sayings in verses 17–19. At the same time, it is also clear that He regards His own teaching as equally binding; and His emphasis upon this truth has sometimes given readers of this section of the Gospel of Matthew the impression that in some instances the abiding nature of the old law seems to be denied. Six times in this passage Jesus appears to be setting His own pronouncements in antithesis to what has been previously spoken, and in every instance the earlier utterance consists of, or at least includes, a quotation from the Mosaic law. If, however, there was in fact any real antithesis between what the law stated and the fuller implications of it unfolded by Jesus, the statements in verses 17–19 would be unintelligible.

In three of these apparent antitheses Jesus is clearly bringing out what is implied in the Mosaic commands in opposition to the strictly literal or legalistic interpretations of them by the scribes. In what He says in verses 21–26 about the sin of anger, in verses 27–30 about the sin of lust, and in verses 43–48 about hatred of one's enemies, He is obviously not impinging in the least degree upon the permanent validity of the sixth and seventh commandments and upon the levitical injunction to love one's neighbour. What He *is* saying is that God's demands in these matters are far more comprehensive and exacting than current interpretations of them by the scribes might seem to suggest. Murder, He insists, has its birth in anger fostered by an uncontrolled spirit of revenge, and such anger is itself an infringement of the sixth commandment. Similarly, adultery is but the final expression of lustful thoughts harboured in the imagination and fed by the illicit contemplation of the object of desire, so that the lust of the eyes and the lust of the flesh cannot be dissociated. Moreover, when Jesus says *Ye have heard that it hath been said, Thou shalt love thy neighbour, and hate thine enemy. But I say unto you, Love your enemies, and . . . pray for them which . . . persecute you* (43, 44), it is clear that the real antithesis lies not between the command of Leviticus xix. 18, 'Thou shalt love thy neighbour', and what Jesus Himself goes on to teach, but between the wrong inference drawn by the scribes from these words (and expressed in the addition they made to it, *and hate thine enemy*) and what Jesus proceeds to teach. As Stonehouse has well pointed out (p. 201), 'the expressions in chapter v "Ye have heard that it was said" or "It was said" are not intended to correspond to the expression "It is written" which Jesus often employs in appealing to the authority of Scripture.' They embrace the limited or erroneous interpretations of the law given by the scribes to the people.

In the three other antitheses in this chapter, concerning divorce (31, 32), the taking of oaths (33–37) and the *ius talionis* (38–42), Jesus appears indeed at first sight to be abrogating what stood written in the law of Moses. He seems to be setting aside the Mosaic provisions which allowed for the dismissal of a wife, for swearing and for retribution, and to be substituting for them absolute prohibitions. It is seen on investigation, however, that no such contradiction is intended. The quotation from Deuteronomy xxiv. 1 is introduced in verse 31 not to contradict it, nor to deny its validity, but because it was a passage which some of the Pharisees were accustomed to quote in order to justify a much laxer attitude to divorce than was here permitted. Stonehouse would appear to be interpreting the passage correctly when he paraphrases verse 31 'Ye have heard of the appeal of Jewish teachers to Deuteronomy xxiv. 1 in the interest of substantiating a policy which permits husbands, freely at their own pleasure, to divorce their wives simply by providing them with a duly attested document of the transaction' (p. 203). Jesus does not disallow the law which permitted divorce when the husband found 'something unseemly' in his wife, but He condemns the lax interpretation of these words that was often given. This matter is dealt with more fully by Jesus in xix. 3–9, where the commentary should be consulted.

Similarly, there is no real antithesis between Jesus' teaching about the taking of oaths and the relevant Old Testament laws. The words quoted in verse 33 as 'said to them of old time' (RV) are not a precise quotation but an accurate summary of Old Testament teaching on the subject. This teaching was represented, however, by the scribes as implying that if only swearing was not to a false proposition and did not profane the actual name of God, there was no need to regard oaths as binding. Hence oaths *by heaven*, or *by earth*, or *by Jerusalem*, or *by thy head* where the divine name was unspoken, could be disregarded (see xxiii. 16–22) even though all those things, as Jesus points out, were indissolubly connected with God. Jesus, as Stonehouse remarks, 'condemns such vain efforts to avoid a reckoning with God, by the declaration that His disciples are not to swear at all'. That His prohibition is limited to personal relationships and does not apply to the taking of an oath in a civil court of law seems clear from the fact that when put on oath Himself by the high priest He readily assented (see xxvi. 63). Finally, it would seem that what Jesus is opposing in the section dealing with the *ius talionis* is the justification of unlimited personal vengeance in the light of the circumscribed Mosaic precept *An eye for an eye, and a tooth for a tooth*, which had in fact been given to put a restraint upon the lust to avenge. Jesus insists that a disciple should be ready to suffer loss rather than to resort to personal vindictiveness.

It can be concluded therefore from this section that the moral law of the Old Testament is recognized by Jesus as possessing divine authority, but that as Messiah He claims authority to supplement it, to draw out principles that lie latent within it, and to disclaim the false deductions that had been made from it. This is what He seems to have meant when He said *I am not come to destroy, but to fulfil* (17).

Additional Notes

v. 18. *Jot* (originally spelt 'iote' in AV) renders the Greek *iōta* which probably represents *yod*, the smallest letter of the Hebrew alphabet, whose insertion often makes no difference to the sense. *Tittle* (Latin *titulus*) renders the Greek *kerea*, by which is probably meant in this connection the stroke that is sometimes placed over words in the Hebrew Old Testament. The view that *kerea* (literally 'horn') refers here to the projection which differentiated letters of the Hebrew alphabet which otherwise would be the same, is improbable, as such differences greatly alter the sense, and in the present context only minute changes are envisaged.

20. By *righteousness, dikaiosunē*, would seem to be meant here 'the conduct that God requires, which is only possible when the law is regarded as an inspiration rather than a burden as the scribes tended to make it'. Knox, while admitting that the translation 'justice' only expresses a part of what is implied in this difficult word, renders 'If your justice does not give fuller measure than the justice of the scribes'; and he paraphrases 'your justice' as 'your notion of what is due from you to your fellow men'.

21. In this verse, and in verses 27 and 33, *by them* should be 'to them'.

21, 22. The words *without a cause* are omitted by RV and RSV following some ancient MSS. Both readings are well attested; but, though the words probably give the sense Jesus intended, it is perhaps more likely that He would have expressed the antithesis without qualification.

The main difficulty of these verses is due to the fact that while there seems to be, as Knox puts it, 'clear gradation of peril, the gradation of guilt is less easy to trace'; for the Greek word *mōre*, rendered *Thou fool*, seems to be more or less equivalent to *Raca*, an Aramaic word meaning something like our 'nitwit'. To avoid this difficulty, some scholars think that in these verses there may be a double contrast between what the Rabbis say and what Jesus says. 'Rabbis tell you not to murder, I tell you not to be angry; Rabbis tell you that Raca is a dishonourable expression, I tell you not to call your brother a fool.' But, as Knox goes on to say, 'the run of the sentence is against this (not impossible) expression'. As another way out of the difficulty, it has been suggested that the *Raca* clause and the *fool* clause reflect two interpretations current in the early Church of the previous words *shall be in danger of the judgment*. Some, it is supposed, referred this to the judgment of *the Sanhedrin*; others interpreted it of the divine tribunal; hence the reference to *hell fire*.[1] It is difficult, however, not to feel that a gradation of guilt is implied as well as a gradation of punishment. Perhaps the least unsatisfactory solution of this very difficult passage is that *mōre* is not here the Greek word for 'fool', which Jesus Himself uses in addressing the Pharisees

[1] See B. T. D. Smith, *St. Matthew*, Cambridge Greek Testament, 1927.

(see xxiii. 17), but a transliteration of the Hebrew *mōreh* meaning 'persistent rebel against God' or 'apostate' which is found in Jeremiah v. 23 and Psalm lxxviii. 8. Hence *Raca* would mean 'worthless fool' and *mōre* 'outcast' (see Torrey, p. 291). On this assumption, Jesus would be saying that the man who tells his brother that he is doomed to hell is in danger of hell himself!

23, 24. These verses are complementary to the previous one. If the Christian who harbours thoughts of hatred and gives way to explosive expressions of anger is in a dangerous condition, so too is the Christian, against whom a brother has cause for complaint, if he does nothing to try and clear the matter up. Conduct is more important than formal worship. God does not want to receive offerings from Christians who are not at peace with one another; and, as verses 25 and 26 imply, the offender who does not come speedily to terms with the brother he has offended may have severe penalties imposed upon him if the case is taken to court.

29, 30. *Offend* translates the difficult word *skandalizō*, here rendered 'causeth thee to stumble' (RV) and 'causes you to sin' (RSV). Jesus is expressing in metaphorical language the all-important truth that a limited but morally healthy life is better than a wider life which is morally depraved. This is true Christian asceticism. If certain books, certain places, certain activities and certain people are causes of temptation to sin they must be eschewed whatever the cost. The *eye* is here regarded as the medium through which temptation comes, and the *hand* as the instrument by which sin is committed.

32. *Fornication* renders *porneia*, which is a general term for 'unchastity', the word by which RSV here translates it. RV follows AV. There is no MSS evidence for the omission of this exception-clause, and it must be supposed that Jesus favoured the interpretation put on Deuteronomy xxiv. 1 by the stricter school of Jewish interpreters.

33. *Forswear thyself* is rendered less archaically 'swear falsely' by RSV and 'perjure thyself' by Knox.

36. McNeile comments 'The *head* might be thought to be a man's absolute possession, but God alone can make a man look old, or preserve the dark hair of his youth'.

37. Better sense is obtained if the second *yea* and the second *nay* are construed as predicates, as in James v. 12; 'Let your word "yes" really mean yes', etc.

39. *Evil* (*tō ponērō*) is much too general a translation, and the doctrine that evil should never be resisted is a wrong deduction from this verse. If the adjective is masculine, it should be rendered 'the man who injures you', and if neuter 'injury' (so Knox and Torrey).

The following illustrations in verses 39*b*–42 are not to be taken literally; they serve to drive home the point (almost to the point of absurdity) that a Christian rather than avenging himself upon a brother who has done him a personal wrong had better go to the opposite extreme!

44. The clauses *bless them that curse you, do good to them that hate you*, and *which despitefully use you* are omitted in the most ancient MSS, and would appear to be later assimilations to the text of Luke vi. 27, 28.

48. *Perfect* is here a misleading translation of *teleios*, and is largely responsible for the erroneous doctrine of 'perfectionism'. Men can never be perfect as God is perfect; and Jesus Himself taught that at best, when men have done everything possible, they are unprofitable servants, who have only done their duty (see Lk. xvii. 10). Torrey would seem right in supposing that the underlying Aramaic word was active in sense, and that the meaning here is 'all-including (in your good will) even as your Father includes all'. '*Be therefore perfect*', he writes, 'would be mere nonsense, even if it were not wholly unprepared for in this context. Nothing here leads up to the idea of perfection—to say nothing of equalling the perfection of God Himself! In this paragraph the disciples are taught that they must show kindness *to all men*, just as the heavenly Father makes no exception.'

d. The piety of the sons of the kingdom (vi. 1–18; cf. Lk. xi. 2–4 and Mk. xi. 25, 26)

The best attested reading in vi. 1 is 'righteousness' (RV). *Alms* was a later but natural substitute for it, partly because it brought the sentence more into line with verse 2, and partly because almsgiving was so essential a part of 'righteousness' as the Jews had come to understand it, that the words had become almost synonymous. 'Doing alms', the expression used in verse 2, was a work that merited salvation. It is almost certain, however, that verse 1 was intended as an introduction to the whole of this section, and that 'righteousness' (*dikaiosunē*) is here used as a general term for 'piety' or 'religious practice'.

In the following verses examples are given to show that pious acts are vitiated when performed to 'be seen of men'. Jesus states that the three expressions of Jewish piety, almsgiving, prayer and fasting (mentioned here in the order of importance assigned to them) are also characteristics of the sons of the kingdom of God—but only when practised with an entire lack of ostentation and without any desire to win praise from men. As Levertoff well says, 'although the disciples are to be seen doing good works, they must not do good works in order to be seen'. It was a mark of the hypocritical type of Pharisee to draw attention to himself when he was about to bestow his gifts (2). It was also his practice not only to select the most public places in which to say his prayers (5) but to lengthen his rambling and often meaningless devotions, as though he was a heathen addressing a god, whose favours to his devotees depended upon the volume of their incantations (7). And when he fasted, he took a perverted delight in defacing himself by the application of cosmetics that made him 'look like death' so that others could not fail to notice the intensity of his self-mortification (16). Such elaborate efforts to 'put on a show' might well elicit from those who witnessed them the verdict 'What a religious man he is!' But this, says Jesus with great emphasis (the *verily* of 2, 5 and 16), is the *only* reward such a hypocrite will ever receive. The word translated *have* in verses 2, 5 and 16 (*apechousi*) is used in Hellenistic Greek in receipting bills, and indicates that payment has been made *in full*. All such ostentation reflects an entire disregard of the truth that God sees not as a man sees. A man can see only the outward signals that others bring to his notice; God sees the inner recesses of the heart, and needs no external display to attract His attention (4, 6, 18). In direct contrast to this 'showing off', the sons of the kingdom must be prepared to give anonymously (3), to pray in places where they can be absent from their fellows and alone with God, and to show the same cheerful demeanour when fasting as they would when keeping a festival (17). For all such, the reward is still to come, the heavenly Father's reward given to those who love Him for His own sake and desire to please Him whether they win the approval of other men or not.

In verses 9–15 Matthew inserts teaching given by Jesus, as we know, on other occasions. The Lord's prayer is also found in Luke xi. 2–4, and it may well have been taught by Jesus more than once and in more than one form. Matthew makes the four following additions to Luke's version. *Our* assumes that the prayer will be used corporately. *Which art in heaven* is a Jewish expression found twenty times in Matthew as an epithet of the Father-God. The clause *Thy will be done in earth, as it is in heaven* is probably an explanation of the preceding words *Thy kingdom come*, made, as Chapman suggests (p. 224), 'because Jews would naturally understand that clause of the coming of the external "reign of God" over the world, and not of His reign over hearts who would serve Him'. This addition is not, as Levertoff rightly points out, 'a resigned sigh, but an expression of desire for the fulfilment of the divine purpose'; and it was used by Jesus Himself in Gethsemane (see xxvi. 42). If we are right in regarding this as an explanatory addition, then the words *in earth, as it is in heaven* should be construed with it alone, and not with the two preceding clauses as well. Similarly, the words *but deliver us from evil* (RV, rightly, 'the evil one') were probably added to make clear that God is not, as the previous clause might possibly be taken to imply, the author of temptation. (See James i. 13.) Temptation is the work of the devil, a fact of which Jesus had first-hand experience (see iv. 1–11). The final doxology at the close of verse 13 is not found in the oldest witnesses to the Greek text, and is almost certainly a later liturgical addition. The only other difference between Matthew's version of the prayer and Luke's is the substitution by Matthew of *debts* in verse 12 for 'sins'. *Debts* is a Jewish way of regarding sins, and, as we do not in English use the word in this connection, Knox felt justified in using here the word 'trespasses' even though the Vulgate rendering is *debita*. It is important to notice that the last clause in verse 12 does not imply that the forgiveness of our sins is in *proportion* to our forgiveness of the sins of our fellows. The point, under-lined in the words of Jesus recorded in verses 14, 15, which are found in a different context in Mark xi. 25, 26, is that unless we ourselves show a forgiving spirit we cannot expect to be forgiven.

Additional Notes

vi. 2. *Therefore (oun)* has here the implication 'for example'.

4, 6. *Openly* should be omitted on the authority of many ancient MSS. The contrast is not between the secrecy of the Father's seeing and the openness of His rewarding, but between the wonderful reward that *the Father* gives and the comparatively miserable 'reward' of human approval.

5. *Pray standing* puts an emphasis on *standing* which is not in the original. The emphasis is upon the conspicuous places where men 'stand and pray'.

6. *Thou* indicates that it is personal prayer that is here envisaged. Contrast *ye* in verse 7 and 9.

Closet. The Greek word *tameion* was used for the store-room where treasures might be kept. So the implication may be that in the inner room where the Christian regularly prays there are treasures already awaiting him which he can draw upon and add to. As Maisie Spens has well said:[1] 'For Jesus prayer was never something which had in cold-blooded travail to be created almost for the first time at each fresh "turning to

---

[1] *Concerning Himself* (Hodder and Stoughton, 1937), p. 85.

prayer". It was rather a *continuity*, a withdrawal into already accumulated and imperishable spiritual treasure, to reach out farther from thence to God.'

7. *Vain repetitions* was an attempt to translate the otherwise unknown word *battalogēsēte*, which Tyndale had rendered 'babble overmuch'. The Vulgate rendered it *multum loqui*, translated by Knox 'use many phrases'. The old Syriac version understands by it 'do not say idle things'. It would seem probable that it is meaningless rather than repetitive speech that is primarily indicated by the word. Our Lord repeated Himself in prayer (see xxvi. 44); so if the AV translation is retained, emphasis should be placed on *vain* rather than on *repetitions*. Probably Tyndale's rendering is as good as any other.

8. Although the Father already knows the needs of His children, He wishes them to show their trust and dependence by praying to Him.

9, 10. In these verses, the verbs, placed first in the original, are in each instance emphatic. In English, emphasis is obtained by placing them last. We should therefore translate 'Thy name be hallowed. Thy kingdom come. Thy will be done'.

11. *Daily* renders the word *epiousion*, found only here and in the corresponding passage in Luke. By derivation it would seem to mean 'bread for the immediate future'. Jerome, treating the word as though it were *epousion*, rendered it in this verse, though not in Luke xi. 3, *supersubstantialem*, which has often been understood by Roman Catholics as a direct reference to the Eucharist.

13. The word *peirasmos*, translated *temptation*, also means 'outward trial'. Many commentators regard this as the primary meaning here. Christians are to pray to be spared the trials which will precede the consummation of the kingdom. The words may perhaps have a more general significance. 'Give us the necessary strength so that life's trials do not become for us occasions of spiritual temptation.'

e. Single-mindedness (**vi. 19–34; cf. Lk. xii. 33, 34 and xi. 34–36**)

It has already been suggested in verse 6 that by prayer the disciple has access to heavenly treasure which accumulates as he grows in perseverance and holiness. This spiritual treasure, Jesus now asserts, though invisible and intangible, is far more real and lasting than the material good which men and women in their undue anxiety about the future are at so much pains to amass. These possessions, even if they escape the clutches of the marauder, are only too likely to become moth-eaten and rusty. To set one's heart, therefore, upon *them* is to live in perpetual, even if unrecognized, insecurity; it is also to deprive oneself of heavenly treasure which is beyond the reach of thieves and secure from the ravages of moth and rust (20). A man's heart inevitably follows his treasure; he is in love with what he believes to be his highest good (21). Jesus bids His disciples therefore never to regard earthly possessions as *treasure*, much less as permanent treasure to be held on to at all costs. On the contrary, he implies, they should make it their aim to use their material wealth wisely and generously, for by such wisdom and generosity they may well be adding to their true and abiding spiritual riches.

Matthew has appended to Jesus' words about *treasure in heaven* His difficult saying about the eye being *the light* (RV 'lamp') *of the body*, which is found in another context in Luke xi. 34–36. The eyes were looked upon by the ancients as the windows through which light entered the body. If the eyes were therefore in good condition the whole body was lit up and receptive of the benefits that light can bestow; but if the eyes were bad the whole body was plunged in the darkness that breeds disease. Jesus, using this language metaphorically, affirms that if a man's spiritual sense is healthy and his affections directed towards heavenly treasure, his whole personality will be without blemish; but if that spiritual sense is diseased by a false sense of values, or by covetousness, or by a grudging ungenerous spirit, he will rapidly become disingenuous. AV, by rendering *haplous single* in verse 22, has given us the expression 'a single eye', indicating 'devotion to one purpose';

and this interpretation probably expresses the fundamental truth of the passage. There is about the single-minded person an essential moral healthiness and a simple unaffected goodness, which are absent from those whose motives are more mixed and who are trying to serve more masters than one. RSV keeps closer to the original metaphor by rendering *haplous* 'sound', and *ponēros* (AV *evil*) 'not sound' in verse 23. It may also be significant for the understanding of these verses that 'an evil eye' was a Jewish metaphor for 'a grudging or jealous spirit', so that the opposite expression, a *single eye*, might also be taken to indicate 'a generous spirit'. The last sentence in verse 23 seems to imply that if the only source of light to guide men along the path of moral rectitude is itself dark, i.e. if their spiritual sense is perverted by false philosophies and debased ethics, then the darkness that already exists in them through the inherent perversity of their nature becomes darkness indeed.

In verse 24, Jesus reaffirms in the language of slavery the truth that heavenly treasure and earthly possessions cannot both be 'laid up' by men at the same time. Men cannot *serve* (i.e. 'be slaves of') *God and mammon* (Knox 'money') at once, for single ownership and full-time service are of the essence of slavery. The accumulation of wealth is so absorbing an occupation that sooner or later money enslaves its victims, and leads them to despise the God to whom they may have imagined they could render a limited allegiance. The closing sentence of this verse Knox regards as 'a concealed disjunctive'. 'You must serve God or money. You cannot serve both.' As McNeile points out, 'The Lord states the principle without compromise or limitation.'

What leads men to hoard material possessions and to give to money the supreme position that ought to be given to God is not only the covetousness that is deep-seated in the human heart, but also, as Jesus teaches in verses 24-34, undue anxiety as to whether they will have the means to provide food and clothing for themselves and their dependants. Jesus is not here decrying careful provision for the future, as the misleading archaism of the AV rendering *Take no thought for* might suggest. Rather does He bid His disciples refrain from fretting unduly about what tomorrow may bring. Their heavenly Father, He reminds them, gave them their life and their bodies. He who made the greater can provide for the less; He can supply the food that sustains life, and the clothing that protects the body (25).

In verses 26–29, Jesus is in effect contrasting the fussiness, worry and distracting anxiety of faithless men and women with the birds and the flowers which are intrinsically of much less value. The birds also are largely concerned with providing for the future. They work hard building their nests and obtaining food for their young, and yet they do not fuss. They have no seed-time and harvest to worry about, but live their lives unconsciously fulfilling the purpose for which God created them. Similarly, the wild flowers in their own instinctive way are looking to the future. Their activities are all directed to producing the bloom which is their glory. And yet, so calm and tranquil is their life, that they appear to be doing nothing at all. Neverthless, God clothes them with a beauty surpassing the most resplendent raiment that can ever be manufactured even by the richest of kings. Jesus does not bid us *imitate* the birds and the flowers, for that is impossible, but He does ask us to observe God's providential care for creatures which are less valuable in His sight than men and women.

The uselessness of anxiety is stressed by Jesus in the rhetorical question in verse 27. By worrying, He insists, a man cannot add a single hour to his life, though, as we understand today, he may very well shorten it. This is the probable meaning of the words here recorded; for, though *pēchus*, translated *cubit*, is literally a measure of *space*, and *hēlikia* often means *stature* (as in Lk. xix. 3), yet the former word can also be used metaphorically of a measure of *time* and the latter often indicates 'age' (as in Jn. ix. 21). Men worry more perhaps over their length of life than over their physical height!

But Jesus condemns anxiety not only on the ground that it is useless, but also because it is a mark of faithlessness, and symptomatic of a failure to put first things first. Pursuit of food and clothing as the supreme good is a characteristic of the godless (32), who know nothing of a heavenly Father in

77

whose sight each one of His children is infinitely precious and who is fully aware of all their needs. The distinctive mark of the Christian is that he desires first and foremost that God's triumph over evil should be completed; that He should reign in the hearts of men; and that His righteousness, i.e. His standards of justice, should be universally accepted. Jesus bids His disciples therefore have faith that if this is their primary objective, then their other necessary requirements will be satisfied. In other words, if they *first* pray 'Thy kingdom come', their 'daily bread' will be provided. Origen attributes to 'the Saviour' a saying which seems to be in effect a variant of verse 33. 'Ask for the great things and the little things will be added to you, and ask for the heavenly things, and the earthly things will be given you as well.'

Verse 34 has no parallel in Luke and was probably spoken in a different context. As McNeile points out, 'though *Be not anxious* forms a link with the preceding verses, the thought is different; for the trust in God, enjoined in verses 25–33, involves a happy confidence that no day shall have its *evil*, because He will provide'. Nevertheless in the closing sentence of this verse, each day is said to have troubles enough of its own.

Additional Notes

vi. 19. The word *brōsis*, translated *rust*, means literally 'devouring', and it might be used here for 'devouring by vermin'. Some commentators prefer this interpretation on the ground the 'stores' in question would be more likely to consist of grain, etc. than of material liable to corrosion. *Corrupt* is better rendered 'consume' (RV).

24. *Mammon*, a transliteration either of a Hebrew word meaning 'what is stored up' or of another Hebrew word meaning 'what is entrusted', is here a personification of wealth.

28. The Codex Sinaiticus has the interesting variant here 'they card not, toil not, spin not'.

28, 29. If no other words of Jesus had survived except those found in these verses, we should have known at least two things about Him—first that He looked out upon nature with the eyes of a poet, and secondly that He was familiar with the story of the fabulous wealth of King Solomon. Humanly speaking, the world of nature and the traditions of the Jewish people were the sole sources of His 'culture', and it is remarkable how they are blended together in this unforgettable passage.

f. Judging and discriminating (vii. 1–6; cf. Lk. vi. 37, 38, 41, 42)

The form of the prohibition in verse 1, translated *Judge not* (*mē* followed by the present imperative), makes it clear that it is the *habit* of censorious and carping criticism that Jesus is condemning, and not the exercise of the critical faculty, by which men are able and expected on *specific occasions* to make value-judgments and to choose between different policies and plans of action. Such censoriousness depresses those against whom it is directed, and weakens rather than strengthens their moral fibre. It also increases the self-righteousness of those who display it, and invites others to retaliate by indulging in equal measure in the same type of nagging fault-finding. It is wisest, therefore, if only to avoid becoming the victim of similar censure himself, for a man to be generous in his criticism of others. Moreover, many of our own failings, about which we are not at all concerned, even if we are aware of them, are often so glaringly obvious to others, protruding from our eye, as Jesus with deliberate exaggeration expressed it, like a large piece of timber, that it ill-befits us to draw attention to the tiny speck (*mote* being an archaism for 'dust') which we may happen to notice in the eye of another. And when we sanctimoniously offer to put an offender right in some trivial defect, having made no effort to put ourselves right first in a much more serious failing, we are, Jesus tells us, *hypocrites*. As McNeile well comments, 'our unkind criticism takes the form of a kindly act'; evil is in fact parading as good.

The form of the prohibition contained in the saying of Jesus recorded only by Matthew in verse 6 (*mē* followed by the aorist subjunctive) gives it the meaning 'Never think of giving'. This injunction makes it clear that it is not every kind of judging that comes under the ban expressed in verse 1. In Levertoff's words 'We may not judge, or condemn, anyone, but on the other hand we must have "a sense of judgment" in our contacts with our fellow-men'. We must, in other words, discriminate carefully between those who possess and those who lack the sensitivity necessary to appreciate such intellectual, artistic, or spiritual benefits that we may have it in our power to bestow. A Jew, as Jesus suggests by the language used in this verse, would not invite a pagan to share his religious feasts, for that would be like throwing meat consecrated for sacrifice to an unclean pariah-dog. Nor would he risk the jibes of his Gentile neighbours, by placing before them spiritual 'food' which they could not assimilate; for that would be like trying to feed unclean pigs with pearls, the only result being that the pigs, finding the pearls inedible, trample them under foot and turn savagely upon the donors. Similarly, the truths that Christ taught, His pearls of great price, must not be broadcast *indiscriminately* to those who would ridicule and despise them, and become increasingly antagonistic. As has often been said, 'want of common sense does great harm to religion'.

g. Perseverance in prayer (vii. 7–11; cf. Lk. xi. 9–13)

The force of the present imperatives in verse 7 is iterative. The disciple is never to weary of asking, seeking and knocking. He must be persistent in bringing his requests before the throne of grace, for it is the persistent petitioner whose prayers will be answered, and who will receive the blessings which the heavenly Father is only too eager to give His children when they acknowledge their dependence upon Him (cf. the parable of the importunate widow, Lk. xviii. 1–7). But the disciple must never imagine that persistency in prayer is necessary in order to overcome some unwillingness on the Father's part to respond to His children's requests. Nor need he ever fear that the Father will 'put him off' by offering him some shabby substitute. It would be incredible conduct, says Jesus, on the part of any earthly father, however *evil* (i.e. 'unkind' or 'ungenerous') he might be, to mock his child by handing him something resembling what the child requested but in fact basically different—a stone instead of bread, or a serpent instead of a fish. How much more incredible that the *heavenly* Father should stoop to such indignities, or refrain from presenting gifts to His children, in answer to their prayers, equally as *good* (Knox 'wholesome') as those which earthly parents endeavour to bestow. In fact they are intrinsically better, for more often than not they are *spiritual* gifts—a truth which Luke brings out when he substitutes 'Holy Spirit' (some MSS read 'good spirit') for the *good things* of Matthew vii. 11 (see Lk. xi. 13).

h. The golden rule; the two ways; false prophets; and the two builders (vii. 12–29; cf. Lk. vi. 31, xiii. 23, 24, vi. 43, 44, xiii. 26, 27 and vi. 47–49)

The saying recorded in verse 12 serves as a general summary of much of the teaching in chapters v–vii. It is in effect a new version of 'the golden rule' which in its Jewish form was phrased negatively 'whatever you would *not* wish done to you, do *not* yourself to another'. The addition, found only in Matthew, of the words *for this is the law and the prophets* reiterates the truth that generally speaking Jesus 'fulfilled' the precepts enjoined under the old covenant by giving them a more positive content.

The ideal set before the disciple in this passage is a very high one; and if he is to practise it he must be prepared to travel the narrow way of personal commitment and self-renunciation so conspicuously trodden by Jesus Himself. *That* way, and that way alone, leads to the narrow gate by which entrance to eternal life is obtained. In Luke xiii. 23, in reply to the question 'Are there few that be saved?', Jesus bids His hearers 'strive to enter by the narrow door' (RSV); and there is no subsequent mention either of an alternative entrance or of two different 'ways'. It is probable therefore that it is the wide *gate* that leads to destruction, and the narrow *gate* that leads to life, though it is also possible grammatically to construe both relative clauses with *way* rather than *gate*. There is some textual evidence for omitting *gate* in each verse (the evidence for omission being stronger in verse 13 than in verse 14), but it would seem that these omissions were later attempts to simplify the somewhat difficult adjacent references to two gates and two ways. The implication of the text as we have it would seem to be that each of the two ways leads up to and passes through a gate—the one wide and the other narrow; and that once either of these gates has been entered there is no possibility of return. There is plenty of room, Jesus affirms, on the wide road leading to the wide gate, and crowds will be found journeying on it; but the road to the narrow gate is narrow and restricted and only a few are able to find it. If this is the correct exegesis, it follows that, although Jesus did not answer directly the question put to Him in the Lucan passage, He knew that 'the saved' would in fact be few. The vital truth is that there are only two ways open for men and women to tread—described in Jeremiah xxi. 8 as 'the way of life' and 'the way of death'. And if by the grace of God a man keeps to the former, he must inevitably pass through the gate that leads to life; but it is equally certain that the man who continues to tread the latter way must eventually enter the gate that leads to destruction. Paul echoes the same uncompromising truth when he differentiates sharply in 1 Corinthians i. 18 between 'those who are perishing' and 'us who are being saved' (RSV).

What makes the narrow way hard to find is the existence of numerous false teachers who have their own formulas for man's welfare, and who cry aloud (in the days of Jesus 'from the house-tops' and in the streets, and in our own time from the pages of newspapers, novels and journals) 'This is the true way, walk in it'. The people of God under the old covenant were constantly subjected to the pernicious influence of false prophets (see Dt. xiii. 1–5 and Ezk. viii. 1–15), as also are His people under the new. In verse 15, in a statement found only in Matthew, Jesus warns His disciples that the most dangerous characteristic of all these false teachers is that their teaching often appears at first sight to bear resemblance to the truth. It may well be some time before its pernicious elements are detected, and the teachers themselves shown up in their true colours. It is only on closer inspection that the apparently harmless *sheep* are seen to be in fact *wolves* who in their greed for personal gain are primarily concerned to 'sell' their false philosophies to an unsuspecting public. Paul predicted that after his departure from Ephesus 'grievous wolves' of this kind would bear down heavily upon the fold of Christian disciples (Acts xx. 29), and we know from the later books of the New Testament that his prophecy was proved true.

In the form in which it is found in the original, the pertinent question in verse 16, recorded only by Matthew, has the nuance 'Men do not gather grapes from thorns, do they?' It serves to connect the previous verses about false prophets with verses 17–20, which contain the simile about the essential relationship between the quality of a tree and the quality of its fruit. This simile is also found in Luke vi. 43, 44, where it illustrates more generally the vital connection between what a man is and what he does. 'Any sound tree will bear good fruit, while any tree that is withered will bear fruit that is worthless' (Knox). In the present context the implication of this axiom is that because belief and practice, creed and conduct, are vitally connected, then false philosophies and erroneous doctrines, however attractive at first sight they may appear to be, will *in the long run* produce a perverted morality, even if their original exponents may themselves be moral. And the logical conclusion is that, where such a result is seen to follow, the doctrines that led to it should be discarded with the ruthlessness that men do not hesitate to display when they cut down a tree which fails to bear good fruit and throw it on the fire (19).

But it is not only false teachers who make the narrow way difficult to find and still harder to tread. A man may also be grievously *self*-deceived, and fondly imagine that he is walking along the right road when he is not. He may use the believer's vocabulary, repeat the believer's formulas, recite the believer's creed, and take part in the believer's activities without being a real believer himself. Knox rightly points out that the rendering *Not every one* in verse 21 'imparts a logical precision which is not in the original'. *Not every one that saith* is in fact a Semitic way of saying 'It is not the people who say'. Jesus is here asserting with great emphasis that it is right conduct, the doing of the Father's will, and not lip-service, which is the passport through the narrow gate that leads to life and results in a verdict of acquittal *in that day* (i.e. the day of judgment). When that day comes, Jesus asserts, many will call Him *Lord, Lord,* and assert that they have *prophesied in* (His) *name* (i.e. by claiming His authority to do so), that they have *cast out devils in* (His) *name* (i.e. by using His name as the formula of exorcism), and that *in* (His) *name* (i.e. due to His power) they have been able to perform their miracles. But because they have made little or no response to His moral demands, Jesus says unequivocally that He will *profess* (i.e. 'say openly') to all such false-pretenders 'You were no friends of mine; depart from me, you that traffic in wrong-doing' (Knox's translation of verse 23).

Matthew brings the present collection of the sayings of Jesus to a conclusion by recording the parable of the two builders, which is an outstanding example of the poetical form in which our Lord presented much of His teaching. The parable underlines the truth that, in the spiritual realm above all others, hearing is valueless if it does not result in action. The Christian way of life can never be practised unless it is based on a solid foundation, and the only sure foundation is Christ Himself (see 1 Cor. iii. 11). The man whose faith in Christ is whole-hearted, can and will build on that faith an edifice of Christian character, which will weather the storms of misunderstanding and disappointment, of cynicism and doubt, of suffering and persecution, when they threaten to overwhelm him. He will, in the words of 2 Peter i. 5–7, 'make every effort to supplement (his) faith with virtue, and virtue with knowledge, and knowledge with self-control, and self-control with steadfastness, and steadfastness with godliness, and godliness with brotherly affection, and brotherly affection with love' (RSV). On the other hand, the man who pays but lip-service to Christ, and whose heart is far from Him, has no solid foundation on which to build, and though the edifice of his character may for a time look as safe and sound as that of the man of faith, nevertheless when the day of trial and adversity comes it will fall with a resounding crash.

In verse 28 Matthew marks the conclusion of this collection of the sayings of Jesus by using for the first time the formula which occurs in four other places in his Gospel at the close of similar collections (see xi. 1, xiii. 53, xix. 1, and xxvi. 1).

IV. JESUS THE DOER OF MIGHTY WORKS
(viii. 1–ix. 34)

a. Introduction

In this section Matthew records nine mighty works of Jesus in three groups, each group containing stories of three miracles. The first group (viii. 1–17) is separated from the second (viii. 23–ix. 8) by an account of two would-be followers of Jesus (viii. 18–22). This insertion is skilfully made. The two aspirants speak to Jesus *after* He has given orders to cross the sea (18), but *before* the actual embarkation (23). The result is that a 'bridge' is formed between the first and second groups of miracle-stories by a narrative which has all the appearances of being strictly chronological. In Chapman's summary (p. 23) 'The dating is clear: After the cure of Peter's wife's mother come the evening healings of the sick; then, seeing the crowds, Jesus gives the order to cross to the other side, and on His way to the lake is accosted first by a scribe who wishes to accompany Him, and then by a disciple who wishes not to do so. He then enters the boat, followed by His disciples'. But as Luke records the story of these two men in a totally different setting, we cannot be certain about the chronology; and most scholars regard both Matthew's and Luke's arrangement as editorial. Chapman, on the other hand, strongly supports the priority and chronological accuracy of Matthew as against Luke.

Between the second group of miracles (viii. 23–ix. 8) and the third (ix. 18–34) our evangelist, giving the same sequence of events as Mark and Luke, interposes the record of his own call to discipleship and the subsequent feast in his house attended by publicans and sinners, followed by a story of conflict between Jesus and the Pharisees arising out of a question about fasting and issuing in two sayings of Jesus showing the incompatibility between Pharisaism and His own teaching about the kingdom of God (ix. 9–17).

b. The Healer of leprosy, paralysis and fever (viii. 1-17; cf. Mk. i. 40-45; Lk. v. 12-16, vii. 1-10; Mk. i. 19-34; Lk. iv. 38-41)

It is clear from His reply to the message of John the Baptist (xi. 5) that Jesus regarded the cleansing of lepers as one of the signs that He was the long-expected Messiah, although this was not specifically stated in the messianic prophecies of Isaiah which He seems to have been most conscious that He was fulfilling (viz. Is. xxix. 18, 19, xxxv. 5, 6, lxi. 1). The Levitical law contained detailed regulations about leprosy, and it was the duty of the priests to see that they were obeyed. Lepers were regarded as unclean, both physically and ceremonially, and outcasts (see Lv. xiii); and when they were cured, thanksgiving for their cleansing had to be accompanied by sacrificial offerings (see Lv. xiv). The leper in the present passage (viii. 1-4) came near enough to Jesus to be seen prostrating himself before Him and for his request to be audible. He had learned, we may suppose, that Jesus was displaying remarkable powers of healing; his only doubt was whether He would be willing to use those powers to cure one who solicited His favours as he was doing. There is pathos in the words 'Sir (*Lord* is too strong a rendering in this context), if you are willing you can cleanse me'. Mark alone tells us that Jesus was 'moved with compassion' at the sight of this afflicted man; but all the Synoptic Gospels state that Jesus, in defiance of the regulations, *put forth his hand, and touched him*, and that, after expressing His willingness, He uttered the word of power which effected the cure. Jesus allowed the constraint of divine love to take precedence over the injunction against touching a leper; but He insisted that the healed man should report to the priest and make the offering required by the Mosaic legislation. The primary meaning of the difficult words *for a testimony unto them* would seem to be 'that the priests may be able after the necessary examination to certify your cure without necessarily knowing how it has come about'. Some commentators, on the other hand, understand them to imply 'that the priests may know that I possess supernatural power'. It would seem improbable, however, that Jesus would follow the injunction to the leper to keep silent about his cure with what would be virtually a command to make known to the priests the miraculous power by which it had been effected. Nevertheless, later readers of the Gospels, not unnaturally, feel that the words contain this implication for *them*, because they are aware that the story was recorded as an example of the might of Jesus the Messiah. Knox's translation is intentionally ambiguous 'to make the truth known to them'.

The hypothesis first put forward by Wrede in 1901, that the various commands to keep silence after Jesus has performed mighty works are due to a literary device on the part of Mark (followed by the other evangelists), in order to explain why Jesus was not more generally recognized as Messiah in His life-time, was described by Sanday as 'wrong-headed'. It is the more regrettable, therefore, that it has been resuscitated by some recent scholars, notably in England by R. H. Lightfoot. The injunction to silence in the case of the leper can be adequately explained on other grounds, as e.g. in the words of Stonehouse (p. 62), 'Except for restraint on his own part and on the part of others, the situation might easily have got out of hand and his public ministry brought to an untimely end.'

It is clear from the Gospel of Matthew that Jesus' ministry was confined almost exclusively to *Israel* (see e.g. x. 5, 6, xv. 24), and that it was *Israel's* belief in Him as Messiah that

He hoped to obtain. The centurion who met Him as He entered Capernaum (5) was a Gentile stationed in Jewish territory; but, as his faith exceeded any that Jesus had found so far even in Israel (10), Jesus did not hesitate to heal his paralysed *servant* (possibly 'boy' as the Greek *pais* is ambiguous) who was 'in terrible distress' (6, RSV). The faith of the centurion is reflected in his response to the challenge put to him by Jesus in the words of verse 7, which should probably be construed as a question, 'Am I (emphatic, '*I*, a *Jew*') to come and heal him?' The centurion answers this by acknowledging his unworthiness to receive Jesus under his roof; but he also expresses his conviction that Jesus has only to say the word and his servant will be healed. If verse 7 is construed as a statement, as in AV, then *answered* in verse 8 indicates the centurion's reaction to the expressed intention of Jesus. As a non-commissioned officer in the great Roman military machine, he knows what it is to obtain the instant obedience of subordinates, though he himself has to submit to superior authority. How much more easily, therefore, could Jesus, who is subject to no man, give orders affecting the welfare of human beings which would be instantly obeyed, whether He was in their presence or not.

The RV translation of *kai gar ego* in verse 9 'for I also am' is inferior to AV *for I am*. The force of *kai* is to emphasize *ego*, so that the implication is 'I know that you can do this, for even I . . .'. There is also no emphasis on *man*, which was probably unrepresented in the original Aramaic. The Arians, translating 'I *too* am a *man*', wrongly supposed the meaning to be 'I am only a man like yourself'. The real emphasis is on the centurion's understanding of authority. 'I myself', he says in effect, 'know what it is both to be under authority and to exercise it'. It was at *this* that Jesus marvelled.

In the parallel story in Luke vii. 1–10, the centurion does not visit Jesus in person, but sends a deputation of Jewish elders, who report that as a lover of the Jewish race who has contributed to the building of their synagogue he is a man deserving of help; and, at a later stage, when Jesus is on the way to his house, the centurion despatches friends to express his feeling of unworthiness and his desire that Jesus should not enter his home but merely speak the word of healing power. The differences between Matthew's and Luke's accounts confront the student of the Synoptic problem with serious difficulties. On the one hand, they provide a strong argument for those who discountenance the Q hypothesis, which supposes that Matthew and Luke used the *same* written source for the non-Marcan material they have in common. On the other hand, those who argue that Luke used Matthew as his second primary source can do so only on the supposition that Luke retold the present story in the light of another version of it. Augustine attempted to harmonize the narratives on the principle that 'he who does something through another does it also through himself'. Knox, who quotes this, makes the further suggestion that the noticeable omission of Matthew's almost invariable rubric 'came and fell down before him' may be an indication that the man did not come himself.

Before he notices, in verse 13, that the centurion's faith resulted in the granting of his request, and that it was at the moment when Jesus gave him that assurance that his servant was healed, our evangelist inserts, in verses 11 and 12, some words of Jesus which indicate that the centurion's faith could be regarded as a first instalment of the faith in Jesus destined to be exhibited by Gentiles in all parts of the world. The faith of these Gentiles would win for them the places at the Messiah's banquet, when His kingdom was finally established, which would be forfeited by the *children of the kingdom*, who thought they had a natural right to its privileges but who would be left outside in the dark. Similar words of Jesus are found in Luke xiii. 28–30 appended to sayings, recorded also in Matthew vii. 13 and 21, about the many who would be refused entrance into the kingdom in spite of their verbal acknowledgment of Jesus as Lord.

The narrative of the healing of Peter's mother-in-law (14, 15) is interesting because of the evidence it affords that Peter had a house at Capernaum. Mark's statement that it was 'the house of Simon *and Andrew*' reflects Peter's unselfish reference to it. This narrative also shows once again the power of Jesus' touch; and the words *she arose, and ministered unto them,* as well as affording undeniable evidence of the cure, are a reminder to all readers of the Gospel that those who receive blessings from Jesus show their gratitude to Him by trying to serve Him.

The summary record in verse 16 of the numerous exorcisms and healings by Jesus on the evening of the day when Peter's mother-in-law was cured, affords the evangelist the opportunity of introducing, by means of his usual formula, a quotation from Isaiah liii. 4 to show that all this benevolent activity of Jesus was evidence that He was filling the role of the ideal Servant of God. Matthew seems to be following the Hebrew 'he bore our griefs and carried our sorrows' (so AV) rather than the LXX 'he bears our sins and is grieved for us', but he understands by 'griefs' physical maladies rather than moral infirmities. Both the Greek words in Matthew's version, *elaben* and *ebastasen,* translated *took* and *bare,* could mean either 'carried' in the sense of 'bore the burden of', or 'carried away', i.e. 'removed'. The latter gives the better sense in the present context, for though Jesus bore the burden of men's *sins,* there is no evidence that He endured physical maladies on their behalf.

c. Two aspirants to discipleship (viii. 18-22; cf. Lk. ix. 57-62)

If *another of his disciples* in verse 21 is interpreted strictly, it would be necessary to suppose that the *certain scribe* of verse 19 was either already a disciple when he made his rash assertion, or became one later. On the former assumption, it would seem that Jesus felt it necessary to impart to this inexperienced and over-confident follower some idea of the physical privation and discomfort that would be the experience of all who threw in their lot with Himself. It is possible that the present tense of the verb translated *thou goest* conveys the sense 'wherever you are going *now*', but it is more probable that this enthusiast in his exuberance was offering to accompany Jesus on *all* His journeys. On the other hand, the possibility must be allowed for that this man was *not* yet a disciple; for, although we need not follow Levertoff in concluding that because he addressed Jesus as *Master* (i.e. Rabbi) rather than 'Lord' this scribe was offering to follow Jesus *as a scribe*, nevertheless we are bound to remember that in Luke's narrative he is introduced simply as 'a certain man' who accosted Jesus on the road. But whether a disciple or not, Jesus' response to his offer is to point out that He, the Son of man, has no settled home—not even a temporary place of refuge such as holes in the earth afford the foxes, or 'roosting-places' provide for the birds.

The second man, described as a disciple, though he had already been called to follow Jesus appears to be anxious to postpone committing himself to the full implications of his vocation till after the funeral of his father, who may be dead already or expected to die soon. By the apparently harsh words with which He counters the man's request, Jesus, as Levertoff rightly points out, 'is not trying to turn him away from his family ties: it is simply a case of the good news of the kingdom being more urgent than an obligation which could just as easily be fulfilled by someone not yet spiritually "alive" '. In Luke's version the words 'go thou and preach the kingdom of God' take the place of *Follow me*.

Additional Notes

viii. 20. As it is *temporary* resting-places that are here in question, *nests* is an inaccurate translation, for birds construct *nests* for one purpose only—rearing their young.

The Son of man. This is the first of many occasions on which this expression is found in the Gospel. It is used only by Jesus, and always, it would seem, with reference to Himself. We may believe that He singled out this 'title' for constant use because it expressed better than any other the two sides of His nature. On the one hand, it drew attention to the limitations and sufferings to which He was of necessity subjected during His earthly existence; as a real man (the Hebrew 'son of man' being equivalent to 'man') He was lower than the angels (see Heb. ii. 6, 7). On the other hand, it also suggested His transcendence which would be seen in all its glory when men beheld the Son of man coming in judgment on the clouds of heaven and claiming all kingdoms as His own (see Dn. vii. 13, 14).

d. The Controller of nature; the Conqueror of demons; and the Forgiver of sins (viii. 23–ix. 8; cf. Mk. iv. 35–v. 20, ii. 1–12; and Lk. xiii. 22–35, v. 18–26)

The psalmist regarded the quieting of the troubled sea as a supreme manifestation of the saving power of Almighty God. 'O Lord God of hosts,' he cried, 'who is a strong Lord like unto thee? . . . Thou rulest the raging of the sea: when the waves thereof arise, thou stillest them' (Ps. lxxxix. 8, 9). In the incident recorded in viii. 23–27 Jesus is shown to possess the same power over nature; and, in consequence, the disciples, amazed at what they have witnessed, come to understand that He is One whom *even the winds and sea obey*. When the great storm arose 'so that the boat was being swamped by the waves' (RSV), Jesus was found to be still asleep. In Mark's account, based no doubt upon what Peter remembered of the incident, the disciples awoke Jesus as He lay on a cushion in the stern, and asked whether He was not concerned at their peril. Whereupon Jesus rebuked the wind; and addressing the sea, as though it were a person, said 'Peace, be still'. Then, when all became quiet, He asked the disciples why they were afraid and had no faith. In Matthew's account, Jesus is roused with the cry *Lord, save us: we perish* (Knox 'we are sinking'), a cry obviously spoken by those who believed that Jesus *had* power to save them. Nevertheless, the terror displayed even by those who uttered this prayer was evidence to Jesus that their faith did not in fact go very deep. Consequently before *he arose, and rebuked the winds and the sea*, He chided His disciples with the words *Why are ye fearful, O ye of little faith?*

It is true, as Knox points out, 'that this short and simple passage is a headache for the solver of the Synoptic problem'.

We may add that it is particularly so, when it is assumed to be a case of accepting either Mark's *or* Matthew's account as primary. May it not be that, while both narratives are fragmentary, each retains truthful echoes of what was said and done by Jesus and His disciples in a crisis that was as dangerous as it was bewildering? Though some showed more faith than others, as is indicated by the different versions of their cries, none was exempt from their Master's censure for not understanding that if He was in the boat with them, all must be well; and He may have spoken reproving words both before and after He bade the sea 'Be still'.

The two demoniacs who accosted Jesus when He landed on the south-eastern shore of the lake lived a solitary life, for, as Matthew alone tells us, they were regarded as so dangerous that no other human beings dared to come near the burial-place which they haunted (28). But when they saw Jesus, they knew instinctively that they were confronting no ordinary person, but the *Son of God*—who had the power to destroy them. In consequence, they who struck terror into the hearts of others were now the victims of fear themselves; as James had occasion to remark, 'the devils also believe, and tremble' (Jas. ii. 19). What astonished these particular demons was that the time for their defeat appeared to have come so soon; and in their bewilderment they cried out 'Why dost thou meddle with us, Jesus, Son of God? Hast thou come here to torment us before the appointed time?' (Knox). But if the time for them to be exorcized had in fact arrived, they requested that they might not remain disembodied but be reincarnated in the herd of swine which was grazing some distance away. The favour was granted, but it proved to be the demons' undoing, for the swine stampeded and rushing down the cliff were drowned in the sea. This was incontrovertible evidence to the swineherds that something supernatural in origin had occurred. It was also evidence to all who subsequently heard the story, that Jesus was ready to sacrifice the less important of God's creatures in the interests of the highest. He came to save men and women, and only men and women; though, as Paul foretold, the day will eventually come when the *entire* creation, groaning and travailing in pain at present, will be free to enjoy the liberty of the sons of God (see Rom. viii. 18–22). Jesus, in this and similar actions, was sounding the death-knell of the forces of evil, but their complete defeat was not yet.

When the inhabitants of the neighbouring town heard from the swineherds what had happened, they were more concerned with the further loss of property that might be entailed if Jesus remained among them, than with the wonderful news that two of their fellow men had been rescued from the miseries of mental derangement, and they put pressure on Jesus to leave the district. Levertoff describes verse 34 as 'a terrible phrase', and comments 'All down the ages the world has been refusing Jesus because it prefers the pigs!'

A clear distinction would seem to be drawn in the Gospels between Jesus' works of healing and His exorcisms. The stories of the casting-out of evil spirits reveal Him, as we have seen, as the Messiah in victorious combat with the forces of evil, but they do not reveal Him as the Saviour of sinners. It was misfortune, rather than sin, which caused the demons to make their abode in some particular human victim. In contrast to the story of the Gerasene demoniacs, the story of the healing of the paralytic in Jesus' *own city* (i.e. Capernaum), with which Matthew follows it in ix. 2–8, makes it very clear that, before this particular man could be healed physically, his sins had to be forgiven; for his disease was the result of his sin. The heart-warming pronouncement by Jesus of forgiveness, made in response to the faith of the man's friends who, as Mark records, had taken great trouble to bring him to Jesus (Mk. ii. 2–4), is in itself an expression of His divinity. As the scribes were rightly thinking, it is blasphemy for a mere man to claim the authority to forgive, for no human being can with absolute justice assess the motives, and therefore the guilt, of another. But Jesus, who could read their thoughts, was aware that these scribes were also harbouring a malicious grudge against Himself (4). They were envious of One, who convinced them by His manner that, as Knox puts it, 'He was not merely announcing the divine pardon, but bestowing it as by His own right'. Jesus therefore attests the validity of His credentials by bestowing upon the sufferer the power to get up and return home carrying his bed.

Additional Notes

viii. 24. *He was asleep.* The imperfect tense in the original indicates that Jesus 'continued to sleep'.

26. *He arose.* The Greek *egertheis* could mean 'when He was roused from sleep', but it would seem to be the posture of authority adopted by the Lord when He rebuked the wind that the writer wishes to indicate.

27. *The men* is best taken as a reference to the disciples in the boat. McNeile however finds in the expression a more general reference to the people who came subsequently to hear the story.

28. *Gergesenes.* The best attested reading in Matthew is 'Gadarenes' (so RV and RSV)—Gadara being a town some six miles from the lake. Mark and Luke have 'Gerasenes'—Gerasa being a town some thirty miles south-east of the lake. The reading *Gergesenes*, which became established in the later Greek MSS, seems to have been due to Origen, who, as McNeile notes, asserted that neither Gadara nor Gerasa satisfied the requirements of the narrative.

Two. Mark mentions only one man, whose name is 'Legion'. It is, however, pressing the implications of the hypothesis of the priority of Mark too far, when critics suggest that Matthew deliberately doubled the number, because he was conscious of having left out the story of exorcism recorded in Mark i. 23–26. It is more probable that there were two men, but that Mark confines his attention to one of them, about whom he has more details to give. Matthew's account is concerned almost exclusively with the transference of the demons into the swine (see the comment on viii. 30).

29. The Greek rendered *What have we to do with thee?* is literally 'What to us and you?'. It represents a Hebrew idiom, found also in Mark i. 24 and John ii. 4, which suggests that the two parties in question have no common concern. The meeting of the Son of God with demons can result only in the latter's discomfiture.

Jesus, not found in the most ancient witnesses to the text, is due to assimilation to the narratives of Mark and Luke.

31. *If thou cast us out.* The present indicative in the Greek implies that it is almost certain that Jesus intends to do so. Hence Knox's translation 'If thou hast a mind to cast us out'.

ix. 2. Matthew alone has *tharsei* rendered by AV *be of good cheer*. RSV 'take heart' and Knox 'take courage' come nearer to the meaning of the word.

5, 6. The point of these verses, which it is almost impossible to bring out clearly in translation, is well indicated by Knox who comments 'The bystanders could detect a bogus claim to healing powers, but not a bogus claim to spiritual authority; therefore it is "easier" to say "Be forgiven"; and one who effects a cure when he says "Be cured" must, *a fortiori*, be given credit when he says, "Be forgiven".' It is a question, he adds, 'which formula can be used with least fear of detection'.

Power translates *exousia*, which is 'delegated power', i.e. 'authority'—in this case, divine authority exercised by the Son of man.

8. *Marvelled* is the reading of the later MSS, and is due to assimilation to Mark ii. 12 and Luke v. 26. The older MSS have 'were afraid' (RV), i.e. 'were awe-struck'.

All three accounts add that those who witnessed the cure *glorified God*, but Matthew alone adds *which had given such power unto men*. This is an indication that some of the crowd understood the expression *Son of man* (6) as a synonym for 'man', as in Psalm viii. 4 and in the book of Ezekiel *passim*. Mark and Luke record the reaction of others in the crowd, expressed in the words 'We never saw it on this fashion' (Mk. ii. 12) and 'We have seen strange things today' (Lk. v. 26).

e. The Friend of publicans and sinners; and the question of fasting (ix. 9–17; cf. Mk. ii. 14–22 and Lk. v. 27–39)

It is evident from xi. 19 that Jesus was aware that He was known by the 'religious' people of His day by what they regarded as the uncomplimentary title 'friend of publicans and sinners'. It was true that He had come to offer the kingdom, or reign, of God to all who were conscious of their need of it, and who were humble and penitent enough to receive it. Among these were some of the *publicans*, despised because they took on a job which probably only Jews who were unable to find other employment were prepared to do—the collecting of taxes for a hated foreign power in return for such profit as they were able to extort from their victims. *Sinners* in this context is almost a technical term for those who either *could* not because of their ignorance, or *would* not because of the intolerable burden involved, observe the intricacies of the Jewish law as elaborated by the traditions of the scribes. The sympathetic approach of Jesus to these outcasts in Israel finds expression in the semi-satirical saying with which He replies to the criticism of the Pharisees, spoken to His disciples, when those superior persons found Him sitting at table with some of these bad characters in the house of Matthew, who had but recently left his customs-house on the shore of the lake to follow Jesus. 'Those who are well', He told them, 'have no need of a physician, but those who are sick. . . . I came not to call the righteous, but sinners' (12, 13, RSV). These words imply that in fact all men are sinners, that 'there is none righteous, no, not one' (Rom. iii. 10), and that the recognition of this is a prime condition for receiving the salvation that Jesus came to bring. Accordingly, Jesus bids these doctrinaires, in a passage found only in this Gospel, to read their Bible again, and to discover from Hosea vi. 6 how completely in accordance with the will of a merciful God it was that He should make contact with these 'sinners' instead of avoiding them in the interests of ritual correctness. It was mercy that found favour with God, not sacrifices offered by those who felt themselves to be morally superior. The failure of the Pharisees to understand the truth revealed in this text from Hosea is underlined by Jesus again at xii. 7.

In His controversy with John's disciples over fasting, recorded in verses 14 and 15, Jesus condemns it except as an expression of real sorrow. The point is that John's disciples and the Pharisees were continuing to observe their fasts mechanically, oblivious of the fact that with Jesus the age of the Messiah had arrived, an age which was often regarded in Jewish thought as a joyful marriage-feast. It would therefore be wholly incongruous for the disciples of the Messiah, *the children of the bridechamber* ('the wedding guests', RSV), to go into mourning while the wedding festivities were still going on. Nevertheless, the growing opposition of the Jewish authorities to Jesus, the Bridegroom, would soon bring those festivities to an end. His disciples would then experience, for a time, intense sorrow, till their tribulation was turned into joy by the resurrection. This is the first reference in the Gospel to Jesus' consciousness that sooner or later He would suffer a violent death, and that for a period, later described by Him as 'a little while' (see Jn. xvi. 16–21), His disciples would be plunged into grief which would inevitably cause them to abstain from food.

The two illustrations with which this passage ends indicate Jesus' awareness that it was becoming more and more certain that there was a fundamental incompatibility between the old Israel, paralysed by self-righteousness and overloaded with petty regulations, and the new Israel humbled by the consciousness of sin, and turning in faith to Jesus the Messiah for forgiveness. The old garment could not contain the new cloth. The new wine of messianic forgiveness could not be preserved in the parched wine-skins of Jewish legalism.

Additional Notes

ix. 9. From early days the tax-collector Matthew was identified with Matthew the apostle mentioned in x. 3 and regarded as the author of the Gospel. In the parallel passages in Mark and Luke the publican is named Levi. The difference has been explained on the ground that Mark and Luke wished to disguise the fact that Matthew was a publican, for they omit this description of him in their lists of apostles (see Mk. iii. 18 and Lk. vi. 15). It may be that Levi was his original name and that he became known as Matthew after his conversion.

10. In place of *in the house* Mark and Luke have 'in his house', leaving it ambiguous whether 'his' refers to Jesus or Matthew. The latter is more probable; and it is possible, as is suggested in *The New Bible Commentary*, that Matthew's expression is an indication that he is telling the story himself, and saying in effect 'when Jesus was sitting at table at home' (i.e. 'in my house').

13. *I will have* is more explicitly rendered 'I desire' in RV and RSV.

To repentance is the certain reading in Luke v. 32, but is omitted in many ancient witnesses for the text of Matthew. Its later insertion was due to harmonization.

14. There is a good deal of external evidence for omitting *oft*. Internal evidence is against it, as the question at issue is not the frequency of fasting but the practice of it at all.

16. The Greek *agnaphou* translated *new* is better rendered 'unshrunken' by Torrey (RSV 'unshrunk').

f. The Restorer of life, sight and speech (ix. 18–34; cf. Mk. v. 21–43; Lk. viii. 40–56 and xi. 14, 15)

The narrative of the raising of a *ruler*'s daughter, which contains within it an account of the cure of a woman suffering from prolonged haemorrhage, portrays Jesus as 'the Lord and giver of life', who exercises His restorative power in response to faith—either, as in the case of the woman, the faith of the sufferer, or, as in the case of the ruler, the faith of near relatives or friends. Faith did not play a psychological part in the actual working of these miracles, as happens today in what is called 'faith-healing'. The power to heal proceeded from Jesus and from Him alone, as is indicated in Mark's reference to the consciousness of Jesus that power went out from Him at the moment when the afflicted woman was healed (Mk. v. 30). Nevertheless, belief in Jesus played a vital part in the release of His divine activity. The narrative does not necessarily imply that the girl, whom Mark describes as the twelve-year-old daughter of Jairus, a ruler of the synagogue, was raised from *death*. The words *the maid is not dead, but sleepeth* (24) could be understood literally, as there is no other instance in the New Testament of the verb *katheudō*, here used for 'sleep', being used metaphorically of the sleep of death. The girl may have been in a deep coma which her relatives not unnaturally mistook for death. Moreover, the fact that our evangelist has grouped this narrative with stories of the cure of blindness and dumbness may indicate that it is not entire loss of life, but the temporary failure of vital powers, that Jesus was concerned to remedy in the case of these particular sufferers. On the other hand, Jesus reported to John the Baptist that the raising of the dead by Himself was an indication that He was none other than the Messiah (xi. 5); and it is unlikely that the raising of Lazarus, reported in John xi, was the sole occasion on which Jesus displayed His supernatural power in this way. Moreover, His instructions to His mission-preachers included the injunction 'Raise the dead' (x. 8).

The narrative of ix. 18-26 with its parallels in Mark and Luke raises the problem of the mutual relationship of the Synoptic Gospels in an acute form. While it is possible that all three evangelists obtained their information from different sources, the fact that they give the same general outline, and agree that Jesus was delayed on His journey to the ruler's house by the intervention of the woman, would seem to render the hypothesis of literary interdependence almost certain. It is usually acknowledged that Luke is here making direct use of Mark; but the relationship between Matthew's brief and concise narrative and Mark's long and detailed story is much more difficult. Those who assume the priority of Mark conclude that Matthew made a précis of what lay before him. If so, he has done his work with remarkable skill, for he has succeeded in producing an account so clear and consistent, that no reader would suspect how many details he has in fact omitted. On the other hand, those who believe that Matthew's narrative is primary regard it as a more reasonable hypothesis that Mark has supplemented Matthew's outline with a large number of life-like details recalled by Peter from memory.

A distinctive feature of Matthew's narrative is that the father reports the *death* of the child immediately he meets Jesus, whereas in the other accounts he states that she is *in extremis*, and news of the actual decease does not reach Jesus till a later point in the story. It would seem either that Matthew is indicating, as Augustine suggested, what was in the father's mind but not what he actually said; or, more probably, as Knox points out in a footnote to his translation, 'Matthew has here combined two separate appeals made by the ruler of the synagogue.'

Verses 27-31 are peculiar to Matthew. The narrative stresses once again the vital part played by faith in the miracles of Jesus. The two blind men address Jesus by the messianic title *Son of David*; but Jesus, before acceding to their request, tests their sincerity by asking the direct question *Believe ye that I am able to do this?*, and not until He is satisfied that their faith is genuine does He restore their sight, accompanying the act of healing with the words 'Your faith shall not be disappointed' (Knox's translation of verse 29). In spite of the strict injunction of Jesus that they should keep quiet about the manner of their cure, these men in their exuberance could not refrain from spreading the news.

The story of the healing of the dumb-demoniac by exorcism, recorded in verses 32-34, is also peculiar to this Gospel. The words *as they went out*, similar to *when Jesus departed thence* in verse 27, may be a literary device of the evangelist to link up stories originally disconnected. If they are strictly chronological, then it would seem that *they* in verse 32 includes the blind men who had just got back their sight. In that case the first person on whom they set eyes, other than Jesus, after they could see again, was a fellow-sufferer, a dumb man destined to experience the same divine power as themselves.

The mention of *the multitudes* in verse 33 is an indication that this miracle took place out-of-doors in a frequented district. Verse 34, though omitted by a strong combination of witnesses to the text (the bilingual Codex Bezae, the old Latin Codex Bobbiensis and the Sinaitic Syriac) is probably original. It is unlikely to have been inserted from xii. 24 as there is no mention in it of 'Beelzebub'. The way Jesus countered this constant criticism of the Pharisees can be seen in xii. 25–30.

Additional Notes

ix. 18. *Is even now dead* is more lucidly rendered by RSV 'has just died'.

20. *An issue of blood*, i.e. in modern medical terminology *menorrhagia*.

The hem. Matthew and Luke agree against Mark in stating the woman touched *the hem* of Jesus' cloak. The agreement may be only a coincidence, or Luke may be here copying Matthew. If the reference is not merely to 'the edge' of the garment, but to 'the fringe' or 'tassel' attached to it to remind the wearer of the sacred law (see Nu. xv. 38; Dt. xxii. 12), it is more likely that a Jewish writer such as Matthew, rather than a Gentile such as Luke, would have drawn attention to its significance.

23. The mention of *the minstrels* (RSV 'the flute players'), found only in Matthew, is an indication that he is writing for readers familiar with Jewish mourning-customs. These 'musicians' were hired to play their dirges in the house where a death had occurred.

V. JESUS AND HIS MISSION PREACHERS (ix. 35–x. 42)

This section contains the second large collection of the sayings of Jesus to be found in this Gospel. It might not unreasonably be supposed, from the way the evangelist arranged these sayings, that all of them were spoken by Jesus when He sent out the twelve men, whose names are recorded in x. 2–4, on a mission through Palestine, even though some of the instructions (e.g. in verse 18) would not appear to be relevant to the conditions prevalent during His lifetime. Nevertheless, on the assumption that He was preparing His apostles for future missions in Gentile lands at the same time as He was sending them forth on this more restricted venture, it is not impossible to read the section as the record of a single discourse. The difficulties that prevent many from doing this will be mentioned later.

During a long tour of preaching and healing in the towns and villages of Galilee, Jesus has become deeply moved by the spiritual condition of the people. They are confused and helpless with no-one to look to as their leader. But the very extremity of their need, He seems to imply, may render them more receptive of the good news of the kingdom of God, if only there are enough messengers to proclaim it (35–38). So He decides to enlist for this purpose the services of twelve disciples who have been closely associated with Him. He sends them out in pairs, as *apostles* or missionaries, with strict instructions to avoid entering Gentile territory or any Samaritan town. They are to confine their attention to Israelites, for the good news is for the Jew first. Moreover there would not be time for them to visit all the towns in Palestine during the earthly life of the Son of man, even if He wished them to do so and had no other claims to make upon their time. Only after His death, when He would come back to them in the triumphant power of His resurrection, would they receive from Him the commission to evangelize the *Gentile* world (5, 6, 23; and see xxviii. 18–20). At the moment, they are to proclaim the advent of the kingdom within the confines of *Jewry*, and to perform such works as all who have eyes to see will recognize as signs that the messianic age has come (7, 8). They have been given special power for this life-giving ministry as a free gift, and they must exercise it with an equally lavish generosity (8).

Such a mission calls for a rare combination of innocence and wariness in the missioners, for they will meet with cruel opposition (16). Not every house will welcome them; and the King's business calls for such haste that they must not linger at any house which will not receive them (11–13). They are ambassadors on an urgent errand and must be seen to be such. Accordingly, they are to take with them only the bare necessities, and to trust that those who are led to respond to the message will also supply the physical needs of the messengers (9, 10). When persecuted, they are not to be anxious about what they are to say, but to rest assured that the divine Spirit will put the necessary words in their mouth (19, 20). Persecution they must expect, for they are disciples and envoys of a Master who is Himself despised and abused, and whose teaching will always cause divisions among men, not least among members of the same household (18, 21, 22, 35, 36). But no amount of persecution will be able to prevent these apostles of the Messiah from proclaiming in public what they have learned from Him in secret (26, 27). Nor need they fear those who may kill their bodies but will be unable to destroy their souls (28). Eternal salvation awaits all who are under the protection and loving care of the heavenly Father (29–31), as surely as destruction awaits the towns which will reject their message (15). Moreover, the Master who has commissioned them will never disown them, so long as their loyalty to Himself takes precedence over every other loyalty (32, 33, 37). On the contrary, He will acknowledge before His Father all who acknowledge Him before the world (32). As they go on their way fearing God, but otherwise fearless (26, 28), ready to sacrifice their lives for the Master's sake (38, 39), and determined to hold out to the end (22), they will find that they have gained a higher life (39). Their reward will be great, precisely because they have looked for no reward. Similarly, all who welcome them into their homes will not go unrequited, for in welcoming them, whether they know it or not, they will be welcoming Jesus who sent them, and in welcoming Jesus, they will be welcoming the Father who sent Him into the world to be His Apostle (40). The smallest act of service to the most insignificant of Christ's disciples will be rewarded as though it had been rendered to Christ Himself (41, 42).

If all this teaching had been recorded only in the form in which it is found in this Gospel, there would be less difficulty about regarding this section as a single discourse. But the presence of most of it in different places in Mark and Luke gives the critic considerable ground for hesitation. When the Gospels are studied in a synopsis, it is seen that verses 5–8 of chapter x are peculiar to Matthew; verses 9–16 have parallels in Mark vi in the account of the sending out of the Twelve, and also in two different contexts in Luke, viz. in chapter ix where the Twelve are being commissioned, and in chapter x when the Seventy are being despatched; verses 17–25 have parallels in the eschatological discourses in Mark xiii and Luke xxi; verses 26–30 have no parallels in Mark, but are found in four different places in Luke, viz. xii. 2–9, 51–53, xiv. 26, 27, and xvii. 33; and finally verses 40–42 are peculiar to Matthew.

The most widely accepted critical 'solution' of these literary phenomena is that Matthew is here combining with great dexterity material drawn from his two main sources—the Gospel of Mark and the hypothetical collection of the sayings of Jesus, spoken of as Q, used very differently by Luke and himself. On the other hand, those who reject the Q hypothesis on other grounds, and who accept the ancient tradition of the priority of Matthew, find additional support for their thesis in the consideration that the verses in this chapter, which are peculiar to Matthew, are so deeply embedded in the present context, that it is improbable that they have been merged into an artificial collection of sayings drawn from extraneous sources. Rather would they appear to be parts of an original unity (see Chapman, pp. 236–242 and Butler, pp. 102–106). The problem is complicated, and the debate continues. Meanwhile, all who are engaged in witnessing to the gospel of Christ can turn to this chapter for inspiration, encouragement and advice in their difficult task, confident that they are listening to the words of the Master Himself, even if the occasions on which some of them were spoken must remain uncertain.

Additional Notes

ix. 35. *Among the people* is absent from many ancient witnesses to the text, and is probably a later addition taken from the very similar summary of the Galilaean ministry of Jesus in iv. 23.

36. The metaphor of *sheep having no shepherd* is found in Numbers xxvii. 17 where Moses prays God to set a man over the congregation that they be not 'as sheep which have no shepherd'; cf. also 1 Kings xxii. 17.

The words rendered *fainted* and *scattered abroad, eskulmenoi* and *erimmenoi*, are better translated 'were harassed and helpless' (RSV). The crowds are like sheep worried by dogs and left lying on the ground unable to exert themselves.

37, 38. These verses are also found in Luke x. 2 at the beginning of Jesus' instructions to the Seventy.

x. 2–4. Matthew, unlike Mark, lists the apostles in pairs, corresponding perhaps to the groups into which they formed when Jesus sent them out 'by two and two' (Mk. vi. 7).

2. There is little doubt that *The first (prōtos)* means 'first and foremost'. It is not surprising that this designation of Peter is not found in Mark, for the leading apostle was humble enough not to harp upon the position assigned him by Jesus.

Who is called Peter, i.e. who is known by that name at the time the evangelist is writing. Mark's words 'Simon he surnamed Peter' may reflect Peter's constant reference to his failure to live up to the great name, chosen for him by his Master (cf. Jn. i. 42).

3. *Matthew the publican*. Of the Synoptic writers Matthew alone refers in the list of apostles to Matthew's previous profession. This may well be an indication that we are here listening to Matthew himself. Others might like to forget that an apostle was once engaged in this despised work, but Matthew himself never ceased to wonder that a social outcast such as himself should have been selected by Jesus for this high office.

Lebbaeus, whose surname was Thaddaeus translates the reading that became established in the late Greek MSS. The original reading in Matthew is *Thaddaeus*, as in Mark. Luke substitutes for this 'Judas . . . of James', both in Luke vi. 16 and Acts i. 13. It may be that Judas was his original name, but later owing to the stigma attaching to the name Judas Iscariot, Thaddaeus (meaning perhaps 'warm-hearted') was substituted for it.

4. *The Canaanite* is virtually a transliteration of the Greek *kananaios*, which probably represented an Aramaic word meaning 'zealous'. Luke who calls him Simon 'the zealot' has almost certainly given the sense. Simon was not a native of Canaan, nor an inhabitant of Cana of Galilee, as Jerome supposed, but probably a member of the Zealot party which advocated revolutionary tactics to overthrow the power of Rome. It was as remarkable that Jesus should have chosen a Zealot to be an apostle, as that He should have chosen a tax-collector, and both facts have been handed down in the gospel tradition.

5. *Go not into the way of the Gentiles*, i.e. 'do not take any road which will lead you into Gentile territory'.

7. *Is at hand*. The original *ēngiken* means 'has drawn near' and so 'is upon you'.

10. *Scrip* (RV 'wallet', RSV 'bag') translates *pēran*, probably a pack for carrying provisions.
Nor yet staves. The oldest MSS have 'staff'. Mark says that the Lord bade them take 'nothing except a staff'. This is a variation difficult to harmonize. We should not resort to allegory, as Augustine, who supposed that the reference in Matthew is to a 'walking-stick', and in Mark to the right of the apostles to live at the expense of those to whom they ministered! It is best to suppose that Jesus bade the apostles take nothing with them that was not necessary. This might sometimes involve carrying a stick and sometimes not (see Chapman, p. 240).

11–14. The second person plural in these verses refers to the particular pairs of apostles who were to work and lodge together.

11. *Till ye go thence*, i.e. 'until you leave the town for good'. They are not to change their lodgings.

13. *Your peace*. This shows that the salutation mentioned in verse 12 was the Semitic greeting 'Peace be unto you'. The benediction is to be withdrawn from the house that has shown itself unworthy of it.

14. To 'shake the dust from the feet' is an indication that they had been treading on what was virtually heathen soil, which must not be carried back to 'holy' land.

18. By *governors* is meant Roman provincial governors, and by *kings* the Herodian princes who were sometimes given the courtesy-title 'kings'.

Against them; better 'to them' (RV) or 'before them' (RSV).

22. *For my name's sake*, i.e. 'because you are loyal to Me'.

23. This very difficult verse, found only in Matthew, is best understood with reference to the coming of the Son of man in triumph immediately after His resurrection, when He appeared to the apostles and commissioned them to make disciples of all nations (xxviii. 18–20). If it is taken as a reference to the final coming of the Son of man 'in the clouds of heaven' (see xxiv. 30), we are forced into one or other of two very unsatisfactory conclusions. Either, the words were a genuine prophecy of Jesus which proved to be mistaken; or, they have been attributed to Him erroneously, and reflect the fervent belief in the immediate *parousia* of Jesus held by many in the early Church.

27. The *house-top* is mentioned because it was a favourite spot for gossip and discussion.

34, 35. *I am come to send*. Consequences are often expressed in the Bible as though they were intentions. So here the divisive result of Jesus' coming, particularly in the sphere of family relationships, is described as though He had deliberately come to bring it about.

The language in which this result is described in verse 35

was used by Micah to indicate the degenerate conditions of his age (Mi. vii. 6).

37. The Lucan form of this saying (Lk. xiv. 26) is apparently much more harsh. It is, however, the same saying presented in Semitic fashion. What is in fact a comparison is stated as though it was a contrast. 'If a man come to me and hate not his father . . . he cannot be my disciple.' Matthew's version clearly gives the sense.

38. *Taketh not his cross*, i.e. be willing to suffer a martyr's death, like a condemned criminal forced to carry the cross-beam to the place of execution.

39. *Findeth his life*, i.e., in Knox's words, 'secures his life by denying his faith under persecution, or otherwise making terms with the world at the expense of his own conscience'.

40–42. Levertoff's understanding of these verses would seem most probable. 'The passage', he writes, 'seems to imply that as of old kindness shown to a prophet because he represented God (e.g. Elisha and the widow), and to a righteous man because he was righteous, was rewarded by God according to the measure of the merit of the prophet or the righteous man; so now even the simplest kindness shown to the most insignificant disciple of Christ, because he is a disciple of His, will be rewarded according to the merit of Christ Himself.' It is unlikely that there is any reference to a class of Christian prophets or any group of Christians known as 'righteous men.' Verse 41 is peculiar to Matthew.

VI. THE CLAIMS OF JESUS THE MESSIAH
(xi. 1–xii. 50)

a. The unity of this section

In this part of his Gospel the evangelist has assembled a variety of narratives which all reveal directly or indirectly the reality and the nature of Jesus' Messiahship. It is this which gives unity to what might at first sight appear to be little more than an assembly of heterogeneous and disconnected passages. The reply of Jesus to John's messengers expresses His consciousness that His works of healing and exorcisms are indications of His Messiahship (xi. 2–6). His subsequent teaching to the people about John draws attention to the place occupied by the Baptist in the divine dispensation: as the immediate forerunner of the Messiah John is greater than the prophet, who foretold Messiah's coming, but he is not himself a subject of the kingdom which the Messiah had come to inaugurate (xi. 7–15). In the following parable of the children's games Jesus criticizes His contemporaries for their failure to see that the age in which they are living is in fact the critical age of divine revelation, the age of fulfilment, in which God in His wisdom is justifying His ways to men through the ministry of two very different people, John the greatest of men yet born of women, and Jesus the unique Son of man (xi. 16–20).

Similarly, the tragedy of the rejection of Jesus by the cities where He had laboured most arose from their failure to repent when confronted with deeds, which were not the work of some magician, but the actions of the Messiah Himself (xi. 20–24). On the other hand, Jesus could and did give thanks to His Father that such a rejection of Himself by those privileged to witness those actions had in no way thwarted the divine purpose, for the Father had enabled the less sophisticated and more receptive of His people to understand the unique relationship that existed between Jesus and Himself and, in consequence, the unique character of the knowledge of the divine will which Jesus possessed (xi. 25–27). Our evangelist would further seem to suggest, by inserting at this point the sayings of Jesus found in the last three verses of chapter eleven, that the invitation to *all* whose work is hard and whose burdens are oppressive, to come to Him and find relief for their souls, would have been presumptuous, and indeed almost repellent, on the lips of anyone but God's Messiah (xi. 28–30).

The story of the conflict of Jesus with the Pharisees about plucking ears of corn on the sabbath, in the form that Matthew records it, brings to the surface the truth that something greater is now taking place than ever happened in the days when rigid sabbath observance and meticulous temple ritual played such a significant part in the religion of Israel. That 'something' is the presence among men of Him who fulfils the Law and the Prophets, the divine Son of man, who is greater than David, and is Himself the Lord of the sabbath (xii. 1–8, verses 5–7 being found only in Matthew). Moreover, the insertion by Matthew into the following account of the healing of the man with the withered hand on the sabbath, of the illustration of the rescue of a sheep fallen into a ditch, brings into relief both the fact and the nature of Jesus' Messiahship. The argument is that if it is accepted that the saving of a stricken animal is a suitable occupation for the sabbath, then, *a fortiori*, the saving of a stricken human being is an even more suitable occupation, and especially so for Him who is Lord of the sabbath, and who displays His power supremely by showing mercy and doing good (xii. 9–14, verses 11 and 12 being found only in Matthew).

It was pre-eminently the gentleness of Jesus together with His unobtrusiveness which was the most distinctive characteristic of His Messiahship. The evangelist accordingly goes on to notice that this was why, for the most part, Jesus gave strict injunctions to those whom He cured not to make Him known. His works were indeed messianic, but He Himself was no conventional Messiah, for He combined in a unique manner the office of Messiah and the role of the divine Servant delineated by Isaiah. He would never therefore deliberately advertise Himself, or seek out occasions for a noisy assertion of His claims. Moreover, His sympathy for the weak and the afflicted, the sinful and the oppressed, would, as the prophet had predicted, render the knowledge that one day He would discharge His messianic function as the victorious Judge, a message not of terror but of hope for mankind (xii. 15–21, verses 17–21 being found in Matthew only). That final triumph over sin and evil, in which the kingdom of God would be completely manifested and its King fully vindicated, was foreshadowed, as the evangelist now proceeds to show, by such an incident as the healing by Jesus in the power of the divine Spirit of a man whose blindness and dumbness were evidence that he was demon-possessed. In a very real sense, a battle was here and now being fought which would prove decisive. Satan was already being rendered impotent and his panoply destroyed by Him who was armed with the ultimately irresistible power of God. The death-knell of the prince of evil was sounding as the reign of God in the ministry of Jesus the Messiah was becoming a reality among men. Consequently, the wilful refusal to accept this evidence, or the attribution of what was essentially divine work to Satanic influence, were not only nonsensical, but supreme blasphemy, the outpouring of an evil heart, which condemned without any possibility of reprieve him who uttered it. This gentle Son of man will forgive when He is personally insulted or abused, but when God's redemptive work is regarded as evil, He is the prophet of the inevitability of the divine wrath (xii. 32–37).

The unbelieving Pharisees were not only unwilling to accept Jesus' exorcisms as evidence of His Messiahship; they also, as Matthew makes clear by the next incident he records, attempted to discredit Him still further by challenging Him to do a 'sign' which would show unmistakably that He was the Messiah in the sense in which they understood that term. To be an exorcist was in itself, they argued, no qualification for that high office. There were many successful Jewish exorcists, as Jesus admitted, but they did not claim to be Messiahs. But because Jesus' conception of His Messiahship is so radically different from that of the Pharisees, He asserts categorically that no 'sign' will be performed such as would compel all and sundry to believe. Any belief in Him as Messiah that was unaccompanied by repentance would in fact be unbelief. Moreover, what He had already said and done should have been sufficient to cause men to repent. As it was, their failure to repent would render them subject to condemnation on the day of judgment by the Ninevites, who repented at the preaching of Jonah; and Jonah, prophet though he was, was far inferior to Him in whom all prophecy was fulfilled. The messianic nature of Jesus' words and actions would indeed be divinely acclaimed, when He was raised from the dead, after having accomplished in His death the supreme work He had come on earth to do. His miraculous emergence from the grave after a brief space of time among the dead would be the prelude to a mission of repentance and hope among the Gentiles; and a type of that mission could be seen in the mission to the Ninevites of Jonah, who had himself been miraculously preserved for the purpose. Similarly, no special 'sign' in the sky could vindicate Jesus' claims to Messiahship more than the wisdom that was inherent in what He taught. And the refusal to recognize that wisdom would render the men of Jesus' generation subject to condemnation on the day of judgment by the queen of the south; she traversed the earth to sit at the feet of King Solomon, and Solomon's wisdom, though it exceeded that of any of his contemporaries, was essentially 'earthly' wisdom, and was therefore far inferior to 'the wisdom that is from above' which was embodied in Jesus the Messiah (xii. 38–42).

But not all who witnessed the deeds of Jesus failed to repent. There were some penitents, however, whose repentance did not go very deep; and if it was not followed by a more whole-hearted surrender to Jesus and a more complete acknowledgment of His claims, it might lead them into a state worse than before. This would seem to be the point of the story of the exorcized spirit which could find no other residence and so returned to its original home only to make it a greater den of iniquity than before (xii. 43–45). In contrast to these unbelievers or half-believers there was the small company of people, who by their acceptance of Jesus as Messiah and by their determination to do His Father's will, were bound to Him by spiritual ties as close as the physical ties which weld together the members of a human family. The evangelist accordingly closes the section with the words of Jesus, *Whosoever shall do the will of my Father which is in heaven, the same is my brother, and sister, and mother* (xii. 46–50).

b. Jesus and John the Baptist (xi. 1–19; cf. Lk. vii. 19–25)

John, though a unique figure in biblical history, was no

superman. He was subject, as are all human beings, to depression and disappointment. It is not therefore surprising that when he was confined to prison in the fortress of Machaerus by the Dead Sea, after his arrest by Herod the tetrarch of Galilee, denied access to reliable information, and forced to form his judgment upon what was happening in the world outside from such fragments of garbled information as might reach him, he was becoming impatient and beginning to wonder why Jesus was not asserting His messianic claims more forcibly and more openly. He was perhaps also expecting that if Jesus was the Messiah, He would secure his release from prison, where he was the victim of the evil machinations of Herod Antipas and Herodias, who may well have seemed reincarnations of Ahab and Jezebel. Ought not Messiah 'with the breath of his mouth to slay the wicked'?

It is true that Luke's account of the present incident would seem to imply that some of John's disciples had recently brought him news about what the people of Nain, who had witnessed the raising by Jesus of a widow's son, were saying about Him. Their verdict was 'A great prophet is risen up among us' and 'God has visited His people'. So far, John may have thought, so good. But *other* great prophets had appeared in Israel; and God had *often* visited His people. Such acclamation of Jesus by the villagers of Nain did not amount to an acknowledgment that He was Messiah. Yet John had been led to believe that He *was* the Messiah, and that He would administer a twofold baptism with spirit and with fire. But there was no evidence that men were being subjected to a messianic fire of judgment, nor any sign that the mighty were being put down from their seats, or the proud scattered in the imagination of their hearts! And so, to set his troubled mind at rest, John put to Jesus through the medium of his disciples the pertinent question, 'Is it thy coming that was foretold, or are we to wait for someone else?' (Knox). Jesus at once perceives that the cause of John's distress is lack of reliable evidence. So He supplies him with the information he needs. He bids the envoys carry back to their disappointed master the reassuring news that Jesus is in fact doing precisely what

Isaiah had prophesied that He would (see Is. xxxv. 5 and lxi. 1). It is true that He is not yet displaying His divine sovereignty in all its fullness. Nor is He now passing final judgment upon mankind. But He is attacking the citadel of evil by restoring health and sanity to human beings suffering from the ravages of sin and disease. John could not, indeed *would* not, take offence at Jesus, or lose confidence in Him, for what might appear an undue limitation of the Messiah's activities and an irksome delay in the exercise of His prerogatives.

As John's messengers were leaving, Jesus pointed out to the assembled company the precise significance of John. It was no ordinary sight, such as a reed-bed swaying in the wind, that they had gone out into the wilderness to see. Nor had they gone to such an unpromising spot to gaze upon some courtier, dressed in finery, in attendance upon an earthly monarch. They had gone to see a prophet, and indeed more than a prophet, for other prophets of Israel had foretold in connection with the Messiah what they would never live to see, but John was a contemporary of the Messiah and privileged to bear Him personal testimony. There was a sense therefore in which it was true to say that with John prophecy had come to an end. John was in fact the divine herald, sent to usher in the messianic age and the advent of the kingdom of God, the 'Elijah' mentioned in Malachi iv. 5, as those who had the necessary spiritual insight would readily understand. But, because John could never enjoy the benefits of that kingdom, for he was destined to die a martyr before the greatest of those benefits had been secured, he must be pronounced less blessed than the humblest of that eager throng, who in their desperate need were violently striving to be the recipients of what Jesus had to bestow.

There were, however, very many others who were blind to the significance of both John and Jesus, and who refused to accept either of them as a messenger of God. It was with these unbelievers in mind that Jesus spoke at this juncture the parable of the children's game. The wording of the parable does not enable us to reconstruct in every detail the game which the children are playing. From Matthew's account, in which the children are said to be *calling unto their fellows*, it might seem as if one group of children is blaming another group for refusing to join in *either* of the games which the *first* group has suggested, whether it be a game of weddings in which some played festive tunes on pipes while the others danced, or a game of funerals in which some imitated the wailings of the hired professional mourners, while the others smote their breasts in mock sympathy or shed tears of affected grief. On the other hand, from Luke's account, in which the children are said to be 'calling to one another', it might be reasonable to suppose that there are *two* groups of children, *neither* of which will join in the game proposed by the other. When one complains *We have piped unto you, and ye have not danced*, the other replies 'Yes, and *we have mourned unto you, and ye have not lamented.*' The understanding of the parable does not depend, however, on the exact details of the game. It is the general characteristics of children at play to which Jesus directs attention. They think they know what they want, when in fact they do not. They tire so easily and so quickly at the game they are playing, and are constantly wanting to start something fresh. They are by nature restless and perpetually striving to obtain some further and more satisfying pleasure. And only too often because of their peevishness, their way-wardness and their discontent, the game ends in a quarrel; and it makes no difference then whether the game has been one of weddings or funerals!

In John the men of Jesus' generation were confronted with one who was solemn in demeanour and ascetic in his manner of life; and they heard from his lips a severe, though hopeful, message. But he proved unacceptable to them; and when they had ceased to be awed by him, they rejected him as a madman who had a devil. This hermit, living apart from the haunts of men, with little experience of the world as it is, with his unconventional dress, his extremes of self-denial, and his unsociable habits—who was he to point the way to others whose duties made it imperative for them to mingle with the world? In Jesus, on the other hand, the men of His generation were face to face with One who, although He was the divine Son of man, was outwardly like any other son of man; but they were no more satisfied with Him than they were with John. Who was He, they were no doubt saying, to call others to deny themselves and take up the cross, when He was seen feasting with fraudulent tax-collectors and outcasts; or to claim to be different from others when He behaved like every one else; or to say He was fulfilling the law when He was associating with those who were deliberately breaking it? So they dismissed Him with the insinuation that He was little better than the company He kept, 'a glutton and a drunkard, a friend of tax collectors and sinners' (RSV). And yet, as Jesus implies in the concluding verse of this section, both John and Himself, however different they might be in personality and in the kind of work they were called to perform, were children of the divine wisdom, with essential parts to play in the working out of God's plan of redemption. Moreover, God's actions are vindicated in no uncertain manner by the changed lives of all who have responded to their influence; who have learned the truth that John so clearly proclaimed, that without repentance there can be no salvation, no coming of the reign of God to the human heart, no avoidance of the divine wrath; and who have come to see that it was precisely because Jesus came to seek and save that which was lost, that He must move in circles where the lost were especially to be found. Men may reject John as a mad fanatic, and they may dismiss Jesus as a pretentious upstart or a disappointed idealist, but as long as the miracle of the new birth is taking place *wisdom is justified of her children.*

Additional Notes

xi. 2. By using the word *Christ* absolutely, 'Matthew expresses', as McNeile points out, 'his own knowledge of what the Baptist only suspected and hoped' viz. that Jesus was the Messiah.

For *two of his disciples* RV and RSV, following the more ancient reading *dia*, have 'by his disciples'. As *two* (Gk. *duo*) is the undisputed reading in the parallel passage in Luke, its presence here in the later MSS of Matthew is probably due to an attempt to harmonize the two accounts.

3. *He that should come* translates the Greek present participle *ho erchomenos*. RV construes 'he that cometh' and RSV 'he who is to come'. The expression 'the Coming One' was virtually, though not technically, a title for the Messiah owing to the frequent references in the Old Testament to His coming.

4. There is nothing in the Greek to justify the translation *again*, and it should be omitted.

5. *The poor* is used in the same sense as in v. 3 of those who feel their spiritual need.

7. The word *began* is often used loosely in the Gospels. The meaning here is well brought out by Knox 'took occasion'.

10. The quotation in this verse from Malachi iii. 1 is regarded by McNeile as an editorial insertion by the evangelist, but as the verse is found in precisely the same place in the Lucan account, this conclusion seems improbable. Jesus substitutes *thy* and *thee* for 'my' and 'me' in the original, so that the passage becomes an announcement made by God to the Messiah.

11. The adjective translated *least* is a comparative, and is taken in that sense by RV 'but little'. But, as the comparative more often than not has a superlative force in New Testament Greek, *least* is almost certainly the right translation.

12. The word translated *suffereth violence* can be construed as middle as well as passive. So RSV margin 'has been coming violently', i.e. in the exorcisms and other mighty works of Jesus. This makes good sense and avoids having to make the second clause tautological. It also finds some support from the fact that Luke's version of what would appear to be the same saying, though it is found in a different context, is 'the good news of the kingdom of God is preached' (Lk. xvi. 16, RSV). The passive rendering is necessary if the kingdom is thought of here as wholly future. Either rendering is possible on the more probable assumption that it is the *present* aspect of the kingdom that is prominent in the passage. In the above commentary the passive translation has been adopted. For a full discussion of this difficult verse and other explanations see McNeile *ad locum* and Stonehouse, pp. 246-248.

19. For *children* a few of the most ancient MSS have 'works', the reading followed by RV. As all witnesses to the text except the Codex Sinaiticus have 'children' in the corresponding passage in Luke, it is very possible that the reading 'children' here in Matthew is due to harmonization. *Works* may be explained as the evangelist's adaptation of the saying. It would imply that God is proved to be right in the events of history, especially in the unique intervention into human life made through the incarnation of His Son. The two versions are virtually complementary, but *children* seems to fit the context better, and to have the greater stamp of originality.

c. The Messiah's dirge over the unrepentant cities (xi. 20-24)

As we have already noticed, Jesus the Messiah did not (perhaps to the disappointment of John) *execute* judgment upon those who attempted to thwart the divine will. But as these verses make clear, He did foretell the doom that awaited the unrepentant cities, where His messianic works had been performed, at the final judgment, though He did so in a mood of sorrow and pity and not in a spirit of vengeance. The wealthy and wicked cities of Tyre and Sidon are often denounced in the Old Testament. But Jesus asserts that if they had been privileged to witness such a work of the Messiah as the miraculous feeding of the crowd, which probably took place in the open country near Bethsaida, their pride would have melted, and their genuine repentance would have shown itself in the outward signs of mourning and fasting. Accordingly, their lot will be more fortunate than that of Chorazin and Bethsaida when the judgment comes.

The important town of Capernaum on the shore of the

Sea of Galilee, through which the great road ran from Damascus to the Mediterranean, was secure and prosperous, satisfied and self-sufficient. It was tempted therefore to say, so Jesus implies by the form of the question He now addresses to it (23, RV), what Isaiah pictured Babylon as saying, 'I will ascend into heaven, I will exalt my throne above the stars of God . . . I will ascend above the heights of the clouds; I will be like the most High'. And a doom awaits it for its arrogance similar to that foretold in the words addressed by the prophet to Babylon 'thou shalt be brought down to hell' (Is. xiv. 13–15). It is a doom greater than that which will come to Sodom on the day of judgment; for, says Jesus, grievous though the sins of Sodom were, it would have been spared the visitation of the divine wrath which reduced it to ashes, and would have still been standing, if the Messiah had performed in its streets the deeds that He had wrought in Capernaum. It would have recognized in them, as Capernaum did not, the hand of God outstretched to heal and to save.

Additional Notes

xi. 20. *Then* has no strict temporal significance. This section, which is found in a wholly different context in Luke (see Lk. x. 13–15), is placed here because it deals with the messianic claims of Jesus.

For the significance of *began* see the note on xi. 7.

21. *Woe unto you* should not be understood as a curse, but as an expression of grief. It would be better rendered 'Alas for you'.

The mention of *Chorazin* is a reminder that many deeds of Jesus are unrecorded in the Gospels, and that the latter were never intended to be complete biographies.

23. For *which art exalted unto heaven* RV and RSV, following the oldest and best attested and more vigorous reading, have 'shalt thou be exalted unto heaven?'

For *hell* RV and RSV, transliterating the original, have 'Hades', which is equivalent in this context to 'the depths'.

d. Jesus' thanksgiving and gracious invitation (xi. 25–30; cf. Lk. x. 21, 22)

The prosperous and self-sufficient inhabitants of the Galilaean towns might be blind to the true nature of Jesus and the significance of His actions. But Jesus Himself, so far from feeling personal resentment, thanked God that there were some, for the most part the less sophisticated and the less important, who turned instinctively to Him to satisfy their deepest needs; for they understood who He really was.

It is often in a person's prayers that his truest thoughts about himself come to the surface. For this reason the thanksgiving of Jesus here recorded is one of the most precious pieces of spiritual autobiography to be found in the Synoptic Gospels. It shows that the dominant characteristic of His incarnate life was obedience to His Father's will. A wonderful self-effacement and self-surrender underlies the words *for so it seemed good in thy sight*. They bear eloquent testimony to the truth that *whatever* the Father's gracious will might be, it was accepted without question by His Son, even if humanly speaking acceptance might involve Him in much disappointment and distress.

All things in verse 27 is obviously a more inclusive term than *these things* in verse 25. As the rest of the passage shows, it comprises first the entire truth about the nature of Jesus, which has been made known to Him by His Father, for the Father alone has full knowledge of Him; and secondly, the entire truth about the Father's redeeming love, of which the Son alone is fully cognizant, for He alone has an intimate understanding of the Father's will, and to Him and to none other the Father has entrusted the task of passing on this knowledge to whom He will.

The gracious invitation which brings chapter xi to a close is recorded only by Matthew. It is addressed in the first instance to those upon whose backs the Pharisees were laying heavy burdens by demanding meticulous obedience not only to the law itself but to their own intricate elaborations of it. Every law-abiding person is of necessity under a yoke, and the expression 'the yoke of the law' was a commonplace in

Judaism (cf. Acts xv. 10). Jesus the Messiah also calls His disciples to accept a 'yoke', but how different is *His* yoke! In the first place it is not really obedience to any external law at all, for it is first and foremost loyalty to a Person, which enables the disciple to do gladly, and therefore easily, and without feeling that he is struggling under a heavy burden, what that Person would have him do. If men loved Him, Jesus said, they would inevitably keep His commandments (see Jn. xiv. 15, RSV). Where such a relationship exists between the disciple and Himself (His) *yoke is easy, and* (His) *burden is light*. Moreover, the way of life that He desires His disciples to follow is His own life. In consequence, the Christian's guide to conduct is no law-book full of baffling perplexities but the *exemplum Christi*. *Learn of me* is His instruction. And to be a pupil of Jesus is to have a very gentle and humble-minded Teacher, who is never impatient with those who are slow to learn and never intolerant with those who stumble. It would of course be boastful for any merely human teacher to claim gentleness and humility as his primary qualifications. But Jesus the Christ does not hesitate to do so. 'Learn from me,' He says, 'for I am gentle and lowly in heart' (RSV). It is precisely this feature of the divine invitation which renders it, in the description of it in the Book of Common Prayer, a 'comfortable' word; for we all know from experience that it has been the teachers who have possessed something of these lovely qualities who have most influenced us for the better. It is surely very significant that these are the characteristics of Jesus that Paul singles out as the qualities he himself would most desire to show in his dealings with his converts (see 2 Cor. x. 1).

Rest in verses 28 and 29 (*anapausis* not *katapausis*) would perhaps be more accurately, and less misleadingly, translated 'relief'. Certainly Jesus does not promise His disciples a life of inactivity or repose, nor freedom from sorrow and struggle, but He does assure them that, if they keep close to Him, they will find relief from such crushing burdens as crippling anxiety, the sense of frustration and futility, and the misery of a sin-laden conscience.

Additional Notes

xi. 25. *At that time.* By this expression the evangelist conveys the impression that the Messiah uttered this great thanksgiving when the early days of 'popularity' had passed and He was faced with much opposition. Luke, introducing the prayer with the words 'In that hour', associates it with the return of the Seventy after their successful mission which he has just recorded (see Lk. x. 21).

Answered. This word, as so often in the Gospels, does not indicate an answer to a specific question, but draws attention to the speaker's reaction to a particular situation. It is not found in the parallel passage in Luke; and its insertion here by Matthew suggests that he understands the thanksgiving as Jesus' reaction to the different ways in which His messianic claims were being received. Knox translates 'said openly', which implies, probably rightly, that Jesus was anxious that it should be known that gratitude based on an unflinching loyalty to the divine will was His own reaction to the situation.

Because thou hast hid . . . and hast revealed. As McNeile rightly points out, 'Jesus was thankful not that the wise were ignorant, but that the babes knew'. This can be brought out in translation by inserting 'though' before *thou hast hid* and by substituting 'yet' for *and*. The English versions render literally what is in fact a Semitic idiom; cf. Romans vi. 17, where Paul does not mean, as AV might at first sight suggest, 'God be thanked that ye were the servants of sin', but, as RV rightly renders 'thanks be to God, that *whereas* ye were servants of sin', etc.

The wise and prudent are those who imagine that the mind of God can be known by human reason unaided by revelation, and they are contrasted with *babes* who are the receptive and the open-minded, whatever their age may be. The former are often so preoccupied with the natural that they are unable to recognize the supernatural; to the latter, on the other hand, the supernatural is as real as the natural.

These things in the present context means the truth about Jesus' Messiahship to which the Galilaean towns had for the most part been blind.

26. *Even so* (Gk. *nai*) could also be construed as picking up the opening words of the thanksgiving, 'Yes indeed I thank thee'. AV regards it as a confirmation and approval of what has just been stated.

In thy sight is a Hebraism for 'to thee'.

27. For a further discussion about the significance of the Father-Son relationship see the present writer's *Tyndale Commentary on St. John's Gospel*, p. 87.

e. Plucking corn on the sabbath (xii. 1–9; cf. Mk. ii. 23–28 and Lk. vi. 1–5)

By inserting *were an hungred* Matthew emphasizes that it was a real need and not just a desire to be provocative that led the disciples technically to violate the law by 'harvesting' on the sabbath (1). It was a similar necessity, Jesus reminds the Pharisees when they draw His attention to this 'law-breaking', that drove *David* to break not indeed the *sabbath*-law but the law that forbade any but the priests to eat the hallowed bread. This incident related in 1 Samuel xxi. 1–6 was doubtless familiar to the Pharisees, but, as Jesus suggests by the words *Have ye not read*, they had not grasped the spiritual principle set forth in it, that human necessity must take precedence over legal technicalities (3). They were similarly blind, He implies, to the great truth enshrined in Hosea vi. 6, quoted also by Him in ix. 13, *I will have mercy and not sacrifice* (7). God Himself is merciful, and He expects His people to show mercy to others and not to be censorious of those who are merciful. The absence of such mercy cannot be made good by the offering of sacrifices however numerous.

It is not however only the general truth that 'the sabbath was made for man, and not man for the sabbath' (Mk. ii. 27), that Matthew sees displayed in this story. In fact he omits these words, and by so doing concentrates the reader's attention on their sequel *For the Son of man is Lord . . . of the sabbath day* (8). If David had the right to 'violate' the law, so *a fortiori* had great David's greater Son—the Messiah Himself.

Similarly, by recording what the other evangelists omit, viz. the reference by Jesus to the duty of the temple priests to violate with impunity the letter of the law about sabbath observance, followed by His great assertion *But I say unto you, That in this place is one greater than the temple* (6), Matthew makes it clear not only that the disciples of Jesus are *guiltless* in this incident, but that with His coming the Temple and all that it stood for is in fact superseded. The Temple was believed to enshrine the divine presence, but in Jesus, the Messiah, the divine presence is incarnate.

Additional Notes

xii. 1. *Were an hungred* translates *epeinasan*, which is an inceptive aorist and should be rendered 'became hungry'. It is omitted in Mark and Luke.

4. The *shewbread* is more lucidly translated 'the bread of the Presence' by RSV and 'the loaves set forth before God' by Knox.

5. The priests 'profaned' the sabbath by burning incense, changing the shewbread (Lv. xxiv. 8), and offering a double burnt-offering (Nu. xxviii. 8f.).

6. *One greater* translates the masculine *meizōn* found in the later Greek MSS and in the Vulgate. The neuter *meizon* is the reading of the most ancient MSS and is followed by RSV 'something greater', the reference being to the kingdom of God now being inaugurated by the Messiah.

8. *Even* translates *kai* found here, in Matthew, only in the late MSS. It should be omitted as an insertion from Mark ii. 28 where it is translated 'also' in AV.

f. The man with the withered hand; Jesus' avoidance of publicity (xii. 10–21; cf. Mk. iii. 1–6 and Lk. vi. 6–11)

Luke makes it even clearer than Matthew that the presence of the incapacitated man in the synagogue on the sabbath was the occasion for the scribes and the Pharisees to put a test question to Jesus with the hope of proving Him a law-breaker (see Lk. vi. 7). As everyone knew, it was lawful to heal a man on the sabbath if his life was in immediate danger. In the present instance, the man's life was not in danger, and presumably Jesus could have waited till the sabbath was over before healing him. But what angered Jesus (see Mk. iii. 5) was the wrong scale of values of which His would-be accusers were guilty. As He makes clear in the illustration found, in this context, only in Matthew's version of the story (11, 12), they would not hesitate to rescue a sheep fallen into a ditch on the sabbath, but they would stop and argue whether a man was sufficiently ill or maimed to justify them coming to his aid on the sabbath. In God's scale of values a man is worth more than a sheep; and God's Messiah does not hesitate to use His messianic power on this occasion to render a lifeless hand as sound as the other.

The strict injunction of Jesus to the large number of sick folk whom He healed not to make Him known (16) affords our evangelist the opportunity of introducing a descriptive passage of the ideal Servant from Isaiah xlii. 1-4. As has already been noticed, it is one of the more perverse features of a certain type of modern Gospel criticism that it regards these injunctions of Jesus to keep silent about Himself as a literary device of Mark, followed by Matthew and Luke, to explain why Jesus was not more widely recognized as Messiah in His lifetime. As Matthew here makes very clear, it was the fact that Jesus was the ideal Servant as well as the Messiah, and that therefore His whole conception of what Messiahship involved was radically different from the conventional Jewish one, that led Him when He performed cures and exorcisms on Jewish territory to issue the command for silence.

Additional Notes

xii. 10. In the apocryphal *Gospel of the Hebrews*, according to Jerome, the man said to Jesus 'I was a mason earning a living with my hands. I pray you Jesus to heal me that I may not have shamelessly to beg for bread', an interesting illustration of how biographical details tended to be added to the canonical stories as time went on.

11. *One* does not imply that the man in question possessed only one sheep, and that he would therefore be particularly anxious to rescue it. The Greek *hen* is often used in New Testament Greek as if it were an indefinite pronoun, and the implication here is that, even if one out of a large flock of sheep had fallen into a ditch, its owner would pull it out.

14, 15. Mark adds that the Pharisees took council at this point with the Herodians. In other words, the religious and secular authorities were now united in their desire to form a plot to bring about the destruction of Jesus. Jesus left the place where He was, because He had no desire deliberately to provoke the Pharisees to a conflict. This was in strict accord with His character as delineated in the quotation which follows.

g. The Beelzebub controversy (xii. 22-37; cf. Mk. iii. 23-30; Lk. xi. 17-23, xii. 10, vi. 43-45)

In this section passages common to all three Synoptic Gospels, passages common to Matthew and Luke, and passages peculiar to Matthew are so interwoven that it is impossible to be certain whether the three evangelists are dependent on each other, or following three more or less independent traditions.

The cure of a blind and dumb demoniac astounds all who witness it, and leads them to entertain, though very tentatively, the hope that Jesus may be *the son of David*, or Messiah. The Pharisees however take steps at once to shatter that hope by suggesting that the supernatural power being displayed by Jesus is in fact evil. Jesus with unassailable logic points out how vulnerable is this thesis of the Pharisees. For all their learning their criticism of Him is astonishingly naïve (25, 26), and it can be turned directly against themselves (27). Civil war, says Jesus, always has disastrous results, and that is as true in the spiritual as in the physical realm. Satan is not engaged in committing suicide! The real truth is that in the exorcisms being performed by Jesus, God Himself is at work exercising His dominion over the realm of evil and its prince. In consequence, the long-expected reign of God has now arrived, though not yet in its fullness. Satan is already bound though not so as to be rendered completely impotent (28, 29). Nevertheless, the campaign between God and Satan has begun in earnest, and in that campaign neutrality is impossible. Not to be allied with Jesus and the kingdom of God is to be allied with Satan and the kingdom of evil; and to try to prevent men and women from accepting Jesus as their King, as the Pharisees were trying to do (see 23, 24), is to disintegrate and *scatter* those who would otherwise be 'the sons of the kingdom' enjoying its reign in their hearts, and that is the devil's main objective (30).

To call good evil, and light darkness, as the Pharisees were in effect doing, had a curse pronounced upon it by the ancient prophet (see Is. v. 20), and it is now denounced by Jesus as *blasphemy against the Holy Ghost*. All who persist in it must, He asserts, remain for ever unforgiven. Every other sin that men may commit, even speaking against the Son of man, could be forgiven, but *not* the sin of him who wilfully rejects the truth when once he has seen it, or who denounces as evil what he knows to be good (31, 32). Peter could be said to have spoken *a word against the Son of man*, when he tried to stand in the way of Jesus when He was taking a course of action which would lead to His death (see xvi. 23), or when he three times disowned Him at the time of His trial. But in all this Peter was merely being unstable and inconsistent. He was not deliberately speaking *against the Holy Ghost*; he was temporarily, but not fundamentally, divided against himself. At heart he was loyal, and he remained a disciple. Judas, on the other hand, always acted consistently with his nature; he was permanently in the service of himself and Satan, even while professing to be an apostle. He could be said therefore to be speaking *against the Holy Ghost*, and so he readily became the tool of Satan, and betrayed Him who was bringing in the kingdom of God in the power of the Holy Spirit. The root of his nature was bad, and therefore the fruit of his character was also bad. Jesus, on the other hand, was radically good, and it was no more possible for Him to be allied with Satan than it was possible for a sound tree to produce bad fruit (33).

The Pharisees for all their religious pretensions were fundamentally evil, a *generation of vipers*, as Jesus now calls them, following the example of John the Baptist (see iii. 7). Their words were evil, because they overflowed from an evil heart (34). What the mouth utters is often what has been occupying the thoughts for so long that it must now find vocal expression. It was while he was musing, the psalmist said, that the fire kindled, and at last he spake with his tongue (see Ps. xxxix. 3). If therefore the affections and thoughts of men are evil, their utterances must also be evil (35). And if speech is such an unfailing indication of character, it is very natural that it is by men's words, no less than by their deeds, that they will be either acquitted or condemned on the day of judgment (36, 37).

Additional Notes

xii. 22. *Then* (*tote*) does not indicate 'at that moment' or 'directly after that' but is a literary device of the evangelist for linking together stories which are fundamentally similar.

23. The question is introduced in the Greek by *mēti*, which expects the answer 'No' but allows for the faint possibility that it may be 'Yes'. So rsv and Knox 'Can this be?'

This (*houtos*) is somewhat contemptuous as in verse 24, where it is rightly rendered *this fellow*. Apart from His miracles, Jesus did not seem to the people much like what they supposed that *the son of David* would be. It was popularly believed that the Messiah would be of the lineage of David; and in Matthew's Gospel this expression is virtually a messianic title.

24. *By* means 'with the aid of'.

All English versions follow the Latin and Syriac versions in giving the prince of the devils the name *Beelzebub*. The Greek mss have Beelzebul. Both words would seem by derivation to be terms of abuse denoting worthlessness.

26. Jesus clearly regards *Satan* and *Beelzebub* as the same person. Various names are found in Jewish literature for 'the prince of devils'.

27. *Your children*, i.e. 'your fellow-Jews'.

28. The word translated *is come* (*ephthasen*) denotes in modern Greek 'is just coming'. Here it implies that the kingdom has in a real sense arrived, but not yet in its fullness. Jesus was indeed performing works of the kingdom, but the supreme work of the kingdom, His death and resurrection, still lay in the future.

31. AV rightly translates *pasa hamartia*, *all manner of sin*, for the sense is clearly 'every other kind of sin'. *Blasphemy against the Holy Ghost* is not therefore included in this expression. RV by rendering the Greek literally as 'every sin' tends to obscure the sense.

32. *This world . . . the world to come* are better translated as in RSV *this age . . . the age to come*. The Jews contrasted the present evil age with the blessed age to come.

33. The imperatival clauses in this verse are virtually conditional. 'If you make the tree good, then the fruit will also be good.'

34. *Abundance* (*perisseuma*) is better translated by Knox 'overflow'.

36, 37. These verses, found only in Matthew, introduce a somewhat different thought; for in verse 34 it is not *idle* speech that is under consideration, but speech that is the overflow of deliberate thought. The word *idle* (Gk. *argon*, translated 'careless' by RSV and 'thoughtless' by Knox) means by derivation 'ineffective' or 'useless'. The Vulgate translates it *otiosum*.

h. The request for a sign; the return of the unclean spirit (xii. 38–45; cf. Lk. xi. 29–32, 24–26)

It is clear that the *sign* demanded by the Pharisees as a *sine qua non* for accepting Jesus as Messiah was something different from the exorcisms and other beneficent works He was performing. It was a sign which Jesus Himself would not originate, so that there would be no mistaking it for the work of one who could be regarded as an ordinary man endowed with magical power. The sign they were asking for is called, in the similar incident recorded in xvi. 1, 'a sign *from heaven*'. But Jesus was always insistent that the divine activity displayed in His works should be sufficient to lead men to repentance and a life of faith. He therefore states emphatically that no sign of the kind the Pharisees were demanding will be given except when His Father raises Him from the dead. Of this supreme sign, which would be the Father's unmistakable vindication of His Son, the emergence of Jonah from what was a temporary living death was in some sense a foreshadowing. It is true that the resurrection of Jesus was such a unique event that only indirect prognostications of it could be found in the Old Testament. The *sign of . . . Jonas* is in fact similar to what might be called 'the sign of Isaac'. As the Epistle to the Hebrews states, Abraham was ready to offer up his son, considering that God was able to raise men even from the dead; and from the dead, the author goes on to say, he did, figuratively speaking, receive him back (see Heb. xi. 17-19, RSV). Similarly, Jesus here implies, Jonah was, figuratively speaking, 'raised from the dead' to discharge the work to which God had called him.

Many critical scholars have regarded the reference in verse 40, found only in Matthew, to the sign of Jonah as unauthentic, but, it would seem, on inadequate grounds. 'The verse', says McNeile, 'cannot be genuine. It differs from Luke; the title "the Son of Man" as applied by Jesus to Himself occurs too early; and as a prediction it is inaccurate, for the Lord was in the heart of the earth not three but two nights.' It will be argued however in this commentary that the unspecified reference to the sign of Jonah in xvi. 4 with its parallel in Luke xi. 29 has the same significance as in the present passage. Nor can we say dogmatically when Jesus first applied the title Son of man to Himself. And, as any part of the twenty-four hours constituting a day and night could in contemporary Jewish idiom be referred to as though it were a complete day and night, the last objection seems somewhat pedantic.

Repentance can be regarded as a kind of exorcism, for it involves an expulsion of the demon of self-centredness. But if turning to God away from the sinful ego, which constitutes repentance, is to be something more than a temporary phenomenon, the 'exorcized' man must be 'possessed', and at once, by a new spirit, otherwise the demon will return reinforced to occupy his old home. The Spirit of God must take possession of the penitent if he is to grow in holiness. Many of those who had repented as a result of John's preaching, as well as many who had responded to Jesus' call to repentance, had rapidly fallen away, for they had not brought forth 'fruits meet for repentance'. Moreover, to have seen the Messiah and 'tasted the good word of God' that fell from His lips; to have experienced, in however small a degree, the reign of God He had come to bring; and then to reject Him, rendered Jesus' generation a *wicked generation*, more evil than it had been before He came; and the demand for 'a sign' was itself a sign of its wickedness and unfaithfulness. The words *Even so shall it be also unto this wicked generation* are found only in Matthew; they make the preceding sayings relevant to the spiritual condition of Israel as a whole. In Luke xi. 24–26 the same sayings are recorded immediately after the Beelzebub incident, and refer to the unsatisfactory methods of Jewish exorcists.

Additional Notes

xii. 38. RV inserts 'him' after *answered* following the reading of many ancient MSS. The later MSS omit 'him' and by so doing give a better sense. No question has been put to Jesus, and the incident is not closely connected in time with what has gone before. For the significance of *Then* see note on xii. 22, and for that of *answered* see note on xi. 25.

39. *Adulterous* is used here in the peculiarly biblical sense of 'unfaithful' as Knox here translates. For this meaning cf. James iv. 4. To demand the kind of sign that the Pharisees were demanding was evidence of a lack of trust that God could, and would, reveal Himself and His purposes, when He willed, and in the way He willed.

Seeketh translates *epizētei* which means not just 'is looking for' but 'is demanding as a necessary preliminary to belief'.

40. *In the heart of the earth* does not mean 'in the grave', for the body of Jesus was not given earth burial but laid in a tomb hewn out of the rock. The expression indicates 'the nether-regions' or 'the abode of the dead'.

41, 42. The translation *a greater* in these two verses fails to bring out that the word being translated, *meizon*, is neuter; and here there is no variant in the masculine as in xii. 6. RSV, rightly, translates 'something greater'. The preaching of repentance by a prophet such as Jonah to a heathen city, and the enunciation of profound sayings by a wise man such as Solomon, were inferior to the establishment of God's kingdom by the Messiah.

42. *The queen of the south* is a somewhat curious synonym for 'the queen of Sheba', whose story is told in 1 Kings x. 1 13.

43. *Dry places* are mentioned because the desert was popularly considered to be the special haunt of demons.

i. The new family of Jesus (xii. 46–50; cf. Mk. iii. 31–35 and Lk. viii. 19–21)

Matthew inserts the story of the visit to Jesus of His mother and brothers at this point in his narrative to make it clear that not the whole of Jesus' generation was evil. On the contrary, there were some who responded to Jesus and in so doing showed that they were obedient to the will of His Father. By their faith they were brought into so close a relationship with Himself that they could be said to constitute His family. Matthew's silence about the purpose of the visit of Jesus' mother and brothers, which is made clear in Mark iii. 21, throws into clearer relief the truth which he desires to emphasize.

Additional Notes

xii. 46. For the nature of the relationship between Jesus and

His 'brothers' see the present writer's *Tyndale Commentary on the Epistle of James*, pp. 22–24.

It is usually assumed that the absence of any reference in this passage to the foster-father of Jesus is an indication that Joseph was dead.

47. This verse is omitted in the remarkably strong combination of early witnesses to the text, the Codices Sinaiticus and Vaticanus, the MS representing the earliest Latin version, and the ancient Syriac versions. The possibility must therefore be allowed for that it was a later insertion made to smooth out the otherwise awkward transition from verse 46 to verse 48. On the other hand, Matthew is a very lucid writer, and it is equally possible that the verse was omitted accidentally.

VII. SEVEN PARABLES OF THE KINGDOM OF HEAVEN (xiii. 1-52)

Two of the parables recorded in this chapter are found also in Mark and Luke, viz. the sower and its interpretation (cf. Mk. iv. 1–9 and 13–20 and Lk. viii. 5–15); and the mustard seed (cf. Mk. iv. 30–32 and Lk. xiii. 18, 19). One parable is found also in Luke, viz. the leaven (cf. Lk. xiii. 20, 21); and four only in Matthew, viz. the tares and its interpretation, the hidden treasure, the pearl of great price, and the drag-net. Matthew also records in a very explicit manner the teaching of Jesus as to why He spake in parables, which is also found in Mark iv. 10–12, 33, 34 and Luke viii. 9, 10. And he inserts in verses 16, 17 a saying about the blessedness of the disciples found in a different context in Luke x. 23, 24.

Perhaps the most important and distinctive feature of this chapter is that the evangelist, by the words of Jesus that he records in verses 10–15, makes it clear, as the other evangelists do not, that Jesus deliberately adopted the parabolic method of teaching at a particular stage in His ministry for the purpose of withholding further truth about Himself and the kingdom of heaven from the crowds, who had proved themselves to be deaf to His claims and irresponsive to His demands. Hitherto,

He had used parables as illustrations, whose meaning was self-evident from the context in which they were spoken (e.g. vi. 24–27). From now onwards, when addressing the unbelieving multitude He speaks only in parables (34), which He interprets to His disciples in private. Matthew alone tells us that the disciples, apparently surprised at this new development in His policy, asked Him *Why speakest thou unto them in parables?* The answer they received was that there were *mysteries of the kingdom of heaven* which could not be understood by those who, He said, using language similar to that used by Isaiah about his contemporaries (see Is. vi. 9, 10), looked upon Him with their eyes but never understood the significance of His Person, and heard His teaching with their ears but remained deaf to its implications. When such people heard a parable about the kingdom it would therefore be for them an interesting but pointless story conveying no revelation of divine truth. The disciples, on the other hand, had already grasped something of the supernatural character of their Master and of the kingdom He came to inaugurate. To them therefore He could explain the truth embodied in these parables, as in fact He did in the interpretations here recorded of the parables of the sower and the tares. The result was that their powers of spiritual understanding developed and the mysteries of the kingdom became clearer to them; and in their case there was another illustration of the proverbial truth that *whosoever hath, to him shall be given, and he shall have more abundance*; just as in the case of the crowds the complementary truth was also being demonstrated that *whosoever hath not, from him shall be taken away even that he hath.* The disciples therefore could be described, as Jesus describes them in verse 17, as a happy company who saw and heard what prophets and saints in Israel had long desired to see and hear, but had in fact never seen and heard, because they had died before the age of fulfilment came and the kingdom of God was a reality.

Liberal critics have been persistently unwilling to think that Jesus could have adopted this policy, and they have almost invariably refused to accept this section of Matthew at its face value. As Chapman pertinently remarked (p. 260):

'Moderns prefer to say that all this is an invention of Matthew and Mark, and that our Lord's parables were intended to be understood by the people in the very simplest sense, which the evangelists were (I suppose) too complicated to seize. Really I think the extraordinary and unexpected reason given by Matthew for the teaching in parables must appear more likely than the painfully obvious idea that a parable is meant to be understood! But are parables always understood without explanation? Did David understand Nathan's parable of the ewe lamb? I expect many of the crowds thought our Lord was telling nice stories and did not know what it was all about.' Certainly, the view that the evangelists are all wrong in this matter and that we moderns know better, together with all the negative criticism that it entails, is one that we would do well to reject. It has led scholars, for example, to deny the authenticity of the interpretations of the parables of the sower and the tares, on the ground that they are allegorical, whereas it is arbitrarily assumed that parables of Jesus were always simple illustrations. But, when it is recognized that these explanations of the parables were given, as Matthew expressly states in verses 18 and 36 that they were, to the disciples only, the denial of their authenticity seems arbitrary. Moreover, when once Matthew's account of the general situation is accepted at its face value, there is seen to be no contradiction between Matthew xiii. 13 and Mark iv. 11, 12, as is often maintained by modern commentators. Jesus spoke in parables, as Mark asserts, 'that seeing they may see and not perceive'; and also, as Matthew records, *because they seeing see not; and hearing they hear not, neither do they understand.*

It is clear from this chapter that the parables of the kingdom are not in fact general illustrations of moral and spiritual truths which are easy to understand, even when detached from the life-situation in which they were spoken, but essential elements in the revelation of God which was actually taking place in the Person and work of Jesus the Messiah. As Hoskyns therefore truly remarked, 'Their understanding depends upon the recognition of Jesus as the Messiah and upon the recognition of the kingdom of God which is breaking forth in His ministry.'[1] The literal rendering in our English versions of the words which introduce these parables is apt to be misleading. Jesus does not mean literally that the kingdom is like a farmer who sows his wheat, or a merchant looking for pearls. What He does mean is that there is something in the unique situation which has arisen through the coming of the kingdom of heaven in His own Person and actions, which is analogous to the situation that may occur when a farmer does his sowing or when a merchant is on the search for precious pearls. There are *mysteries* about the kingdom of heaven, and they arise because the kingdom is present but not yet in its fullness, and because its King is at the moment rejected and humiliated so that the glory that belongs inherently to Him and which will one day be visible to all is at present obscured.

The inauguration of the kingdom by Jesus the Messiah has already taken place, but the outward signs of its presence are as yet very few. It is here, but not with irresistible power. Men can and do reject it. Indeed, it can be accepted only by those whose hearts have been made ready to receive it, just as seed can produce a crop only when it is sown in ground prepared for its fertilization. That is the essential point of the parable of the sower (3–9, 18–23). But, because the kingdom has already taken root in some hearts, results are bound to follow. The inevitability of growth from what appears a very small beginning to a result seemingly out of all proportion to it is the truth set forth in the parable of the mustard seed (31, 32). Moreover, the presence of the kingly reign of God is bound to penetrate the evil environment in which it is exercised as effectively as yeast penetrates and transforms the flour into which it is put (33). To be sure, the powers of evil, which will not be finally destroyed till the final judgment, will do all they can to resist the kingdom, but their efforts will ultimately be seen to have been to no purpose. That is the meaning of the parable of the tares (24–30, 36–43). And the complementary truth that, until the consummation comes, there will always be found along with the *bona fide* sons of the kingdom those

[1] E. C. Hoskyns, *The Riddle of the New Testament* (Faber and Faber, 1931), p. 188.

who do not belong to it, is underlined in the parable of the drag-net (47–50). Finally, because the kingdom of heaven is the only lasting reality, and its worth is so incalculably precious, the person who is really eager to obtain its benefits, once he has been confronted by it, will readily and joyfully make the necessary sacrifice, whether it be loss of possessions, friends or even of life itself. That is the teaching of the twin parables of the costly pearl and the hidden treasure (45, 46 and 44).

Additional Notes

xiii. 1. As there has been no specific reference to a house, it is not surprising that the Codex Bezae, some MSS of the Old Latin versions, and the Sinaitic Syriac MS omit *out of the house*. If, as seems probable, the words are genuine, they may be evidence that the one to whom the house belonged, perhaps Matthew himself, is the author of the story (cf. ix. 10 and xvii. 25). They would then carry the meaning 'out of my house', and the evangelist would be recalling with special vividness the day when this particular teaching was given, and how Jesus after deliberately sending the crowds away returned to the house with the disciples (see verse 36), and there expounded to them the parable of the tares.

3. Perhaps the force of the aorist tense in the verb translated *spake* is inceptive, i.e. he began to speak. It was the first time Jesus embarked upon this policy.

7. *Thorns* is more naturally rendered 'thistles'.

15. This passage from Isaiah vi. 9, 10 is also quoted in John xii. 40, and Acts xxviii. 26ff. For its meaning see the present writer's *Tyndale Commentary on St. John's Gospel, ad locum.*

18. In the original, *ye* is emphatic. 'Do *you* (i.e. the disciples, but not the crowds) hear what the parable means?' This is brought out by Knox 'The parable of the sower is for your hearing'.

21. *By and by* fails to bring out for the modern reader that the man at once took offence. So RSV 'immediately'.

Is offended is the usual AV rendering of the difficult word *skandalizetai*. RV translates 'stumbleth'. RSV 'falls away' and Knox's paraphrase 'his faith is shaken' come nearer to the sense. What the word seems to indicate is the sudden shock of finding that the situation is very different from what the man expected.

32. *Herbs* is better rendered 'shrubs' as in RSV.

If the expression *the birds of the air* is more than a corroborative detail, it may be an allusion to the comprehensive character of the kingdom. Gentiles as well as Jews will be included. So Knox seems to imply by his translation 'all the birds'; cf. Daniel's interpretation of Nebuchadnezzar's dream of the tree 'upon whose branches the fowls of the heaven had their habitation' (Dn. iv. 21).

35. *That it might be fulfilled* does not mean that the sole or even primary purpose Jesus had in mind in speaking to the crowds in parables was the fulfilment of this prophecy from Psalm lxxviii. 2. The sense is brought out by Knox 'so fulfilling'. The evangelist notes as a matter of interest that these words found their fulfilment in what Jesus was doing.

The fact that the Greek word *parabolē*, here rendered *parable*, is the LXX translation of the Hebrew *mashal* meaning 'a difficult or enigmatic saying' corroborates the view that the word does not mean in this chapter 'a simple illustration'.

44. *For joy thereof* construes *autou* as an objective genitive, 'for joy at it'. RV regards the genitive as subjective, 'his joy'. Both meanings are implied.

46. *All* is in the neuter in the Greek, which makes it clear that the man sold all his possessions, and not merely all his other pearls, as the Greek word for pearls is masculine.

48. *Bad* is misleading. As the fish were just caught they could not have been rotten. They may however have been 'useless' (so Knox) because of their size, etc.

51. By *them* the disciples are clearly indicated, since in answering the question put to them they call Jesus, *Lord*.

52. In the somewhat difficult saying of Jesus with which Matthew brings the present collection of parables to a close, the word *scribe* would seem not to have its usual meaning of a Pharisaic teacher of the law; for that would make the saying somewhat irrelevant to the context. The reference would appear to be to the disciple of Jesus who has learned the truths of the kingdom of heaven (the *these things* of verse 51) about which Jesus has been giving instruction. Such a 'scribe' as a teacher of 'the law of Christ' has a rich store of knowledge from which he can draw truth which can be described as both *new and old*. It is *new* in the sense that only with the coming of the Messiah has it been clearly revealed; it is *old* because it is concerned with *mysteries* that have been present in the mind of God but *kept secret from the foundation of the world* (35). Moreover, while the Pharisaic scribe interpreted the Mosaic law as an end in itself, the Christian 'scribe' interprets it in the light of the fulfilment it has received in the life and teaching of Jesus.

VIII. THE REJECTION OF JESUS AT NAZARETH AND THE MARTYRDOM OF JOHN THE BAPTIST (xiii. 53-xiv. 12; cf. Mk. vi. 1-6, 14-29 and Lk. ix. 7-9)

The disappointment of the populace that Jesus was not the kind of Messiah they were looking for, and their lack of insight into the nature of His Person and work, led Jesus, as the evangelist has noted, to adopt the parabolic method of teaching when confronted by crowds, and to confine His direct teaching to His disciples. Matthew now proceeds to show that it was His final rejection at Nazareth, spoken of as *his own country*, and the fear aroused in Herod Antipas the tetrarch of Galilee that in Jesus he was confronted once again with John the Baptist, of whom he imagined that he had been rid for ever when he had him beheaded, that led Jesus to withdraw from the domain of Herod and concentrate His attention, for the most part, upon the instruction of His disciples.

Jesus had opened His Galilaean ministry in the synagogue at Nazareth and had been forcibly ejected (see Lk. iv. 16–30). On His present return after a long interval, His teaching intensified the curiosity of His listeners but failed to win their confidence. It would appear from Matthew's account of this visit that Jesus had been known to the villagers probably from His boyhood as *the carpenter's son*; and the fact that Mark at this point uses the expression 'the carpenter' indicates that in due course, probably after the death of Joseph, Jesus had taken over the business. It seemed very strange to those who had known Him all His life that One who had been trained solely as a carpenter, and who had had no further education, should be not only teaching as though He were a qualified rabbi, but displaying what was clearly supernatural power. They imagined that they knew all that there was to know about Him, but they were mistaken. There was in fact a hidden source of knowledge and a secret reservoir of power available for Him, of which they were wholly unaware. Jesus does not attempt to justify Himself to them, as He had done on the earlier visit. He understands that their prejudice is an impenetrable barrier to belief. Nor does He perform any mighty work in their presence, for He has always resisted the temptation to use His miraculous power to force belief in those who seemed incapable of it. He merely points out to them that their attitude is not surprising to those familiar with the proverb often quoted by writers in the ancient world, *A prophet is not without honour, save in his own country, and in his own house.*

Chronologically, xiv. 13 follows directly upon xiv. 2. What Jesus is said to have heard, in verse 13, is not the news of the death and burial of John the Baptist, but the news of the assessment of Him that had been made by Herod. It was this that led to His departure *by ship into a desert place apart*. In fact, the martyrdom of John had taken place much earlier, but Matthew's particular way of grouping his material had not afforded him an opportunity hitherto of recording it. The mention of Herod's reference to Jesus as John *risen from the dead* enables him to make good the omission. Verses 3–12 should therefore be regarded as a parenthesis.

Additional Notes

xiii. 54, 55. *This* in the original is contemptuous, 'this fellow'.

57. In one of the sayings of Jesus found at Oxyrynchus the proverb is found in the form 'A prophet is not acceptable in his own country, nor is a physician able to cure those who are well known to him'.

xiv. 2. *Therefore.* Herod had had no evidence that John was a miracle-worker. But if, as he supposed, John had been raised from the dead, it would be inevitable, Herod felt, that he should possess supernatural power.

4. The illegality was twofold, for not only was Herodias married to Philip, but Herod Antipas was the husband of the daughter of Aretas mentioned in 2 Corinthians xi. 32. The verb translated *said* is in the imperfect tense indicating that John was constantly pointing out the illegality to Herod.

5. *When he would* translates a concessive participle (*thelōn*), and is better rendered 'though he wanted' as in RSV.

8. *Charger* is archaic English for 'a large flat dish'. By derivation, it denotes something on which a 'charge' or load could be placed. RSV 'platter' is also archaic except in the U.S.A.

9. McNeile remarks that the reference to the sorrow of Herod is inexplicable if what has been said in verse 5 was true. But it may have been that, though Herod desired to do away with John because of the hold that the 'fanatical' prophet seemed to have over some of his subjects, nevertheless, when the necessity for doing so arose, he was *sorry* (Knox, 'stricken with remorse') that the light-hearted promise he had made to a dancing-girl should have forced him to issue the order for John's execution. In his heart he knew, as Mark records, that John was 'a righteous and holy man'. Herod, it would seem, had the streak of weakness often found in a cruel nature.

IX. WITHDRAWAL OF JESUS FROM HEROD'S DOMINION (xiv. 13–xvii. 27)

a. The feeding of the five thousand and the walking on the lake (xiv. 13–36; cf. Mk. vi. 31–56; Lk. ix. 10–17; Jn. vi. 1–21)

It has already been pointed out that the sequence of Matthew's narrative implies that the primary object of Jesus' withdrawal in xiv. 13 was to escape from the dominion of Herod. Mark also asserts that Jesus crossed the lake with His disciples to *a desert place apart* to avoid the thronging crowds, and so presumably to have the necessary leisure for continuing the task of instructing them. But when Jesus disembarked on the north-eastern shore of the lake, near Bethsaida as it would appear from Luke ix. 10, He discovered that the crowds from Capernaum and other towns had gone on ahead of Him on foot and were awaiting His arrival. He was *moved with compassion toward them*, Matthew asserts, especially as they had brought with them some of their sick folk. Jesus therefore felt constrained to continue His gracious work of healing. Matthew does not state, as do Mark and Luke, that He also continued His teaching, though it is impossible to distinguish too sharply between the words and actions of Jesus. As the day wore on, the disciples urged Him to discontinue His healing activity and to send the crowds away to obtain provisions before it was too late. Jesus, still moved with compassion for the hungry, shepherdless throng that surrounded Him, decides to use His miraculous power to satisfy their needs. But first He brings home to His disciples indirectly the fundamental truth that He has called them to be shepherds of the new Israel which constitute the Messiah's flock, but that they will never be able to discharge that function in their own strength. All the power necessary for 'feeding the sheep' comes from Him, the chief Shepherd of the flock, and from Him alone. Such would seem to be the significance of Jesus' words *They need not depart; give ye them to eat*. When they point out that their available supplies, *but five loaves, and two fishes*, are totally inadequate for a catering task of such magnitude, He bids them bring their resources to

Him; and in His hands they become so wonderfully multiplied that when the disciples receive them back from Him and distribute the broken pieces to the people they are found to be more than adequate for the entire company.

This action of Jesus was sacramental. He intended it to convey the truth that the benefits that He as Messiah had come to bestow upon God's people were *spiritual* and not merely material. But it is clear that the disciples did not understand this truth all at once (see xvi. 9 and Mk. viii. 17–21). And as for the crowds, John vi states explicitly that they were ready to accept Jesus as a prophet like unto Moses, who had given the people bread from heaven to eat in the wilderness, and also perhaps, though this is not stated, as another Elisha, who had fed a hundred men with twenty loaves of barley so that some of the food was left over after they had eaten (see 2 Ki. iv. 42–44); but they remained totally unaware that they had other needs than the physical, and that those other needs Jesus alone could satisfy. They would gladly accept Jesus as their king, but only because He would use His miraculous powers, they thought, to supply their material wants. It is not therefore surprising to read in verse 22 that the reaction of Jesus to their attitude was to compel His disciples to leave by boat at once, while He Himself dismissed the crowds, and then withdrew to the hills to pray in solitude.

Matthew states in verse 22 that the disciples were bidden to go before Jesus to *the other side* (*eis to peran*), which *prima facie* might mean the western side of the lake. But, as that would have brought them back again into Herod's dominion, and the primary object of the journey mentioned in verse 13 was to get away from that district, it is unlikely that this interpretation is right. In Mark, the words 'unto Bethsaida' are added after *to the other side*, but according to Luke Jesus had already come to Bethsaida before the feeding took place. McNeile remarks that unless there were two Bethsaidas, which is improbable, 'the accounts must be harmonized by supposing that "the desert place" was close to Bethsaida, but separated from it by a bay, across which (*eis to peran*) the disciples were to sail, and they would think that Jesus intended to walk round the shore; but the contrary wind drove them back to Gennesaret (verse 34).'

Although the boat in which the disciples were making the crossing was some way off shore, Jesus when He rose from prayer was able to see from the hillside that it was making heavy weather in a rough sea against a head-wind; and between three and six o'clock in the morning He Himself came towards them walking over the sea. The narrative assumes that Jesus as God's Messiah shares the power of God as the Lord of creation, and that the wind and the sea obey Him. The disciples, however, do not yet understand that He possesses such power, and cry out in terror when they see Him 'It is a ghost!' (26, RSV), but they are reassured when they hear Him at once reply *Be of good cheer; it is I; be not afraid.*

Mark tells us that Jesus' intention had been to show Himself to the disciples but not to enter the boat. 'He would have passed them by.' Presumably He wanted them to learn that, even though He would not always be in close physical proximity to them, He would always be near them spiritually. Circumstances arose, however, which led Him to rejoin them in the boat. Only Matthew tells us what those circumstances were. Peter, hearing Jesus' voice, but also noticing that He did not seem to be intending to enter the boat, asks for the power to come to Him over the water and presumably walk with Him to the shore. To be able to exercise that power would indeed be a privilege. Jesus bids him do so, but as soon as Peter leaves the boat and starts to try to walk over the water, his courage fails him owing to the strength of the gale, and with the desperation of a drowning man he cries out *Lord, save me.* Jesus then takes hold of him, chiding him for his lack of faith, and both are taken into the boat. The wind drops at once; and Jesus is now seen by His disciples to be indeed the Lord of wind and water; and they fall down in adoration before Him exclaiming *Of a truth thou art the Son of God.*

It is, strictly speaking, inaccurate to speak of Peter 'walking on the sea'. The narrative in its original form almost certainly does not imply that Peter even for a brief moment exercised the power which his Master possessed. *Walked*, in verse 29, translates *periepatēsen*, which should be construed as an inceptive aorist 'began to walk'. Moreover, in the same verse, the original reading *elthein* translated *to go* in AV, 'to come' in RV, and 'to reach' by Knox, is an infinitive of purpose. It was altered at an early date to the less well-attested *kai ēlthen* 'and (he) came', which is the reading followed by RSV.

The fact that the Gospel of Mark, traditionally based on Peter's reminiscences, is silent about the incident is no argument against its historicity. Peter, who came to learn humility, most probably deliberately avoided alluding to it. Mark's narrative is less detailed at this point, no explanation being given why Jesus who wanted to pass the disciples by eventually entered the boat. Matthew's story, on the other hand, is wholly coherent. (See Chapman, p. 46.)

When Jesus and His disciples eventually came to land at Gennesaret, He was recognized by the inhabitants who spread the news of His arrival over the countryside with the result that Jesus was once more confronted by a crowd of sick folk. They had such confidence that He could heal them that they asked to be allowed only to *touch the hem of his garment*; and their faith did not go unrewarded.

Additional Notes

xiv. 14. *Went forth*, i.e. disembarked.

15. *The time is now past* probably means 'the time for the evening meal has now passed'.

19. *Blessed* (*eulogēsen*) means 'said the blessing', i.e. offered praise to God. The English versions imply this by placing a comma after *blessed*. Knox's rendering, 'blessed and broke the loaves', erroneously gives the impression that the loaves were blessed. No spiritual quality was infused into the bread of the miraculous feedings any more than it was infused into the bread set apart at the Last Supper.

23. *A mountain* renders the original *to oros* as though there was no definite article. The expression *to oros* does not however mean 'the mountain' but is a colloquial expression for 'the hill-country'.

24. *In the midst of the sea* does not necessarily imply more than 'out on the sea' as it is rendered in RSV mg. There is a variant reading, followed in later editions of RSV and by NEB, which would appear to mean 'some furlongs from the shore'.

25. *In the fourth watch,* i.e. between 3 and 6 a.m., the Romans dividing the night into four watches of three hours each, beginning at 6 p.m.

34. The oldest witnesses for the text should be translated as RSV 'landed at Gennesaret'; *came to the land of Gennesaret* translates the text of the later MSS.

b. Controversy about 'cleanliness'; the healing of the Canaanite woman's daughter (xv. 1-28; cf. Mk. vii. 1-30 and Lk. xi. 37-41)

The quiet that Jesus sought for Himself and His disciples when He crossed the lake (xiv. 13) had been unobtainable because of the necessity which gave rise to the feeding of the five thousand and its consequences, and also because of the renewed demands that were made upon the Messiah's powers of healing after He had returned to Gennesaret. It is now further prevented by the appearance of some Pharisees and lawyers from Jerusalem, who engage Jesus in controversy about the nature of 'cleanliness'. Washing the hands before meals was not required by the Old Testament, but it had become an essential part of *the tradition* of the Pharisees, which they regarded as possessing the same authority as the law itself. They insisted upon this washing not for sanitary but religious reasons. To them it was the means by which any ritual defilement they might have incurred by coming into contact with people or things that were legally 'unclean' could be removed. The Pharisees by such traditions as these had added so many complicated rules and regulations to the law, that in Jesus' view they had not merely obscured, but were trying to defeat the purpose for which God had given the law to His people. He therefore counters their provocative question *Why do thy disciples transgress the tradition of the elders?* with the direct and pertinent retort *Why do ye also transgress the commandment of God by your tradition?* He then illustrates what He has in mind by showing that one of their man-made traditions had virtually *made . . . of none effect* the unqualified divine injunction that men should honour their parents under all circumstances.

In verses 5 and 6, AV gives a very clumsy and obscure rendering of the text found in the later MSS, which insert *and* before *honour not* in verse 6, and spell the verb translated *honour* so that it is in the subjunctive mood. This makes it necessary to regard the first clause of verse 6 beginning *and honour not* as a continuation of the relative clause begun in verse 5 with the words *Whosoever shall say*. As a result, the sentence has no principal clause; and that defect is supplied by AV in the words *he shall be free*. RV follows the text of the older MSS which omit the word *and*, and have the word *honour* in the indicative mood. The sentence now has a principal clause, and is rendered 'Whosoever shall say to his father or his mother, That wherewith thou mightest have been profited by me is given *to God*; he shall not honour his father'. The words *to God*, however, are added to the original, which has simply 'a gift', a Greek equivalent for the Aramaic word *Korban* found in Mark. 'Korban', writes Levertoff, 'was a sort of vow or curse which legally meant that a man's goods were prohibited from benefiting the one against whom he uttered it. If a man said "My goods are *Korban* to all people", he could not give anything away at all. If he placed such a *Korban* on his father he might not even give him a crust of bread. He does not intend to give it to God, i.e. to the Temple, either.' RV 'he *shall* not honour' is better than RSV 'he *need* not honour', for the point is that the man was legally prohibited from doing so.

Insistence by the Pharisees upon strict obedience to their *tradition*, Jesus now asserts, renders the words used by Isaiah with reference to some of the hypocritical worshippers of his day strictly applicable to the Pharisees He is now addressing;

and He quotes Isaiah xxix. 13 as a direct prophecy of them. Moreover, so destructive does He regard their teaching, that He deliberately calls the crowd to Him and bids them ponder upon the enigmatic aphorism recorded in verse 11: *Not that which goeth into the mouth defileth a man; but that which cometh out of the mouth, this defileth a man.* Matthew does not state, as Mark does, that the interpretation which Jesus gave to this 'parable' was in effect a pronouncement that all food was 'clean' (see Mk. vii. 19, RV). It may well be that our evangelist did not suppose that Jesus intended the saying of verse 11 to have the implication that all the food laws of Leviticus could now be disregarded, but that He was emphatically asserting that the evil that comes out of the mouth is far greater than any evil that could enter it by the eating of food that was ritually unclean. This was the point that the Pharisees seemed incapable of understanding. Accordingly, when Jesus learns from His disciples that this saying gave offence to the Pharisees, so far from qualifying it, He points out to His disciples that the Pharisees were not only discredited as exponents of the divine will, but were outside the kingdom of God altogether. They were 'plants' which the heavenly Father had not planted, and which He would eventually have to uproot. They should therefore be left to go their own way. They might claim to be guides to the blind (see Rom. ii. 19), but in fact they were themselves blind; and if blind men try to lead others who are blind, disaster is bound to follow.

When Peter bids Jesus explain the *parable* of verse 11 more fully, Jesus expresses surprise that His disciples should still be as dull as the others who had heard it (the probable meaning of the words *akmēn kai* rendered *also yet*), and He explains that by *out of the mouth* He meant in effect 'out of the heart'. The words of a man are often expressions of the murderous, adulterous, dishonest and slanderous thoughts which are the mainspring of his evil actions. How then in the face of such uncleanness as this could eating with unwashed hands be regarded as defilement?

To avoid further interruption either from the Galilaean

crowds or the Pharisaic legalists, Jesus now journeys with His disciples towards the Phoenician coastal towns of Tyre and Sidon. As He implied in the saying recorded in xi. 21, these heathen cities were not the places where messianic works were destined to be performed; and the healing recorded by Matthew in this section is no exception to this general principle. For, as this evangelist deliberately states, the Canaanite woman left her native heathen territory and came to meet Jesus. As she drew near, she uttered a persistent and pathetic cry, the cry of all human cries most calculated to arouse pity in those who hear it, the cry of a mother pleading for an afflicted child. In view of all that has been stated in the previous narrative about the compassion of Jesus, we might perhaps have expected that He would have at once given the woman the help she needed. But the remarkable thing about the story is that He did not do so. On the contrary, He seems almost reluctant to yield to her request, for when she cried *Have mercy on me, O Lord, thou son of David; my daughter is grievously vexed with a devil . . . he answered her not a word.* Whereupon the disciples, either because they wrongly supposed that He was annoyed at being troubled by the woman, or because they were themselves irritated at the disturbance she was causing, bade Him dismiss her. *Send her away*, they said, *for she crieth after us*. But whether this request was prompted by misunderstanding or impatience, Jesus pays no attention to it. He seems preoccupied with His own vocation and the manner in which it should be fulfilled. *I am not sent*, He replies, *but unto the lost sheep of the house of Israel.*

It would seem that Jesus wished the woman to understand that His activities were circumscribed not only by the inevitable limitations of His manhood, but by the specific part that He had been called to play during His brief earthly life. He was indeed the Christ of Jewish prophecy, as she had herself admitted when she addressed Him as *thou son of David*. His mission therefore was exclusively to God's chosen people Israel. Precisely because He was *sent unto the lost sheep of the house of Israel*, He could not be at the beck and call of everyone, however deserving their requests might be. The privileges of the kingdom of God must be offered to the people of God, the children of the covenant. It was indeed true that He was not a slave to a particular programme. There were occasions when He was willing to depart from it, as when He healed the servant of a Roman centurion, a Gentile whose faith was greater than any He had found in Israel (see viii. 5-13). It was also true that, if Israel as a whole rejected the offer of the kingdom, as eventually it did, the offer of it would be extended to a nation bringing forth the fruit thereof (see xxi. 43). But till the final rejection came, He would accept the limitations imposed upon Him by His vocation; and He would make no exception in the case of this Canaanite woman, until He was convinced that she understood fully what that vocation was, and until He had overwhelming evidence of her faith.

He did not however have long to wait before the essential worth of this woman was made clear to Him. With heartfelt shamelessness she repeats her cry, in a shorter and more poignant form *Lord, help me*, as she flings herself almost desperately upon His pity. And when He reminds her, very gently and almost playfully, of the familiar saying that *it is not meet to take the children's bread, and to cast it to dogs*, although she well knows that she, a heathen woman, is as unclean in the eyes of a Jew as one of the pariah dogs which prowled around ancient eastern cities, without a home and without an owner, feeding on the filth and refuse of the streets, she does not contradict what Jesus is saying. On the contrary, she accepts the implied allusion to herself, and in the very humility of such acceptance she reveals her faith. 'Yes, Lord,' she says in effect, 'what you say is true. It is *not* right to take the children's bread and throw it to dogs; and yet even the dogs eat the crumbs that fall from their masters' table.' She does not stay to argue that her claims are as good as anyone else's. She does not discuss whether Jew is better than Gentile, or Gentile as good as Jew. She does not dispute the justice of the mysterious ways by which God works out His divine purpose, choosing one race and rejecting another. All she knows is that her daughter is grievously tormented, that she needs supernatural help, and that here in the person of the *Lord*, the *son of David* is One who is able to give her that help; and she is confident that even if she is not entitled to sit down as a guest at the Messiah's table, Gentile 'dog' that she is, yet at least she may be allowed to receive a crumb of the uncovenanted mercies of God. And such humility and faith draw forth the healing power of the Messiah. *O woman, great is thy faith: be it unto thee even as thou wilt.*

Additional Notes

xv. 4. *Die the death* is an attempt to render a Greek equivalent for a Hebrew idiom expressing emphasis. The meaning is better brought out by RSV 'let him surely die' and Knox 'dies without hope of reprieve'.

14. *Let them alone.* The Greek *aphete autous* might mean 'let them do what they will' or 'leave them to their own fate'.

15. *Declare* is better rendered 'explain' (so RSV and Knox).

22. *A woman of Canaan.* In describing the woman by the name of the ancient heathen population of Palestine, Matthew, as McNeile notes, 'shows his biblical and archaeological interest'.

26. By omitting the words 'let the children first be fed', found in the parallel passage in Mark vii. 27, Matthew emphasizes that Jesus envisaged His earthly ministry as confined, with a few exceptions, to Israel.

c. Return to the lake; the feeding of the four thousand; a further request for a sign (xv. 29–xvi. 12; cf. Mk. viii. 1–26)

The detour into Phoenicia and the return to the Sea of Galilee from Tyre through Sidon (see Mk. vii. 31) must have lasted several weeks, if not months; and no doubt it afforded Jesus the opportunity of giving further instruction to His disciples in private, which is unrecorded. News of His arrival at the south-eastern shore of the lake was broadcast throughout the hellenized district known as the Decapolis in the tetrarchy of Herod Philip (see Mk. vii. 31); and great crowds soon followed Jesus up the hillside bringing with them a company of afflicted folk, whom He felt constrained to heal. Matthew does not indicate directly the district in which these cures took place, but that Jesus was now in predominantly non-Jewish territory is implicit in the statement that the praise offered by those who experienced Jesus' healing power was ascribed to *the God of Israel*.

This further extension of the beneficent activity of Jesus was another exception to the 'rule' that He was sent only to the lost sheep of the house of Israel, and it is probable that the disciples, who would be inclined to be prejudiced against the Gentiles, were somewhat bewildered by it. At any rate, it is significant that in the following account of the feeding of the four thousand the disciples do not point out to Jesus the plight of the crowd after three days' absence from their homes, as they had done before the miracle of the feeding of the five thousand. On this occasion Jesus Himself gives expression to His compassionate concern for the people. Then, disregarding the somewhat petulant reaction of the disciples, who complain that it was unreasonable to expect them to have sufficient supplies to feed so large a company in so remote a spot, He again makes use of their slender resources, so that multiplied under His hand they prove more than adequate to satisfy the needs of four thousand men apart from the women and children.

Many scholars have assumed that the stories of the two miraculous feedings are in fact duplicate accounts of a single incident. But it would seem extremely unlikely that the evangelists Matthew and Mark, who both record the two stories, would have taken up valuable space in the necessarily limited papyrus rolls on which they wrote their Gospels, by giving two versions of the same incident. Moreover, the different numbers in the records of the people fed, of the loaves available, and of the baskets containing the fragments left over; the careful specification of the different type of basket used on each occasion; and the fact that later Jesus drew attention to these differences (see xvi. 9, 10) are indications that two different events are being described. Not only is the scene of the two feedings totally different, but, as has already been suggested, the spiritual lessons which Jesus seems to have wished His disciples to learn from them are different. Although both miracles are performed in the same way, and are signs that Jesus possesses supernatural power over created things, in the first story He seems to be concerned that the disciples should understand how utterly dependent upon Him they must always be, if they are to do what He would have them do, and in the second story He seems to be indirectly reproving them for their lack of sympathy with the needs of the Gentile world. They have to learn what the woman of Canaan seemed instinctively to understand, not only that 'no true household can exist unless it provides for more than its own children',[1] but that the field in which the kingdom of God will eventually have to be proclaimed cannot be less than the world itself (see xiii. 38, xxviii. 19), for nothing smaller than the world is the object of His love (see Jn. iii. 16).

After returning to the western shore of the lake Jesus is tempted once again to perform a sign in the sky, which will compel men to believe. On this occasion, however, the Pharisees are joined by *the Sadducees*, as Matthew records but not Mark. It is the presence of the Sadducees, together with the reproach recorded in xvi. 2, 3, that differentiates the present demand for a sign from that recorded in xii. 38–40. Some scholars maintain that verses 2 and 3, which are omitted in some important early witnesses to the text such as Codex Sinaiticus, Codex Vaticanus, and the old Syriac version, should be regarded as a later insertion. McNeile goes so far as to say 'The MS authority is decisive against the genuineness of the passage'. More recently, however, Butler (pp. 141, 142) has given cogent reasons for supposing that it is probably authentic. Following Lagrange, he says 'Nothing can explain the addition by a copyist of this penetrating and delicately ironical observation. The *same sign* (redness in the sky) foretells at one time fine weather, and at another time rain. The Pharisees and the Sadducees have the perspicacity to

[1] T. W. Manson, *Jesus and the non-Jews* (Athlone Press, 1955), p. 17.

interpret it correctly at these different times—yet they cannot interpret "the signs of the times!" ' Further, this passage about signs in *the sky* links up with the *sign from heaven* demanded in verse 1, but not designated in xii. 38. The use of the plural in the expression *the times* is found once again in Matthew, but not in the other evangelists. In a word, if these verses are omitted, then with the exception of *the Sadducees* the paragraph is 'a sheer and otiose repeat of xii. 38f.' It is also surely not without significance that an observation of the kind contained in these verses should have been addressed to the worldly-wise Sadducees. On the assumption that the passage is genuine, its omission in some MSS could be readily explained by an early copyist retaining in his memory what he had written in xii. 38, 39, and jumping without thinking from xvi. 1 to xvi. 4 (see Torrey, p. 294). Verse 4 is a cross reference to xii. 39, for it would seem to be no different and unexplained *sign of the prophet Jonas* that is here mentioned. The evangelist, it is true, does not repeat the explanation of the sign given in xii. 40, but that the sign is still in the future is indicated by *shall . . . be given*; and the reader of this Gospel would naturally conclude that the reference is to the resurrection of Jesus as in the previous passage. As the Sadducees disbelieved in any form of resurrection, while the Pharisees believed in a final resurrection of the righteous only, mention of this 'sign' would be particularly appropriate.

Later, when Jesus warns the disciples against *the leaven of the Pharisees and the Sadducees*, they are much troubled because they have brought no bread. It is possible, as has been suggested, that 'they imagined that He was annoyed with them for not taking with them the bread in the seven baskets because they thought it was "defiled", since it had been handled by Gentiles' (Levertoff, p. 51). Jesus rebukes them, however, not for their lack of charity, but for the anxiety born of their lack of faith. He recalls the details of the feeding incidents and implies that He could feed them in the same way that He had twice fed the multitudes. He then explains, as Matthew makes explicit but as Mark does not, that by *the leaven of the Pharisees and the Sadducees* He meant their *teaching*, the rigid legalism and the casuistical sophistry of the Pharisees, and the political opportunism and the worldly materialism of the Sadducees.

Additional Notes

xv. 29. 'Passed along' (RSV) is a more accurate rendering of *ēlthen para* than *came nigh unto*; and 'the hills' (RSV) interprets *to oros* better than *a mountain*.

30. *Cast*. Although the verb in the original *eripsan* is a strong one, and usually means 'hurl' or 'fling', it would seem to be used here in a weaker sense. So RSV 'put'.

32. Contrast *Jesus called his disciples unto him* with *The disciples came to him* in. xiv. 15 (see commentary).

37. The English versions do not make it clear that *basket* in this incident translates *sphuris*, 'a flexible mat basket employed for carrying fish or fruit', while *basket* in xiv. 20 renders *kophinos*, 'a stout wicker basket used mostly for agricultural purposes' (so McNeile).

39. The oldest MSS have 'Magada', an unknown place, for which the well-known *Magdala* came to be substituted. From the nature of the incident next recorded it is assumed that it was on the western shore of the lake.

xvi. 11. AV translating the reading *prosechein* (infinitive) gives the clumsy rendering *that ye should beware* and *I spake it not to you concerning bread*. RV following the older reading *prosechete* (imperative) *de* renders 'But beware'.

d. Peter's confession and the first prediction of the passion (xvi. 13-28; cf. Mk. viii. 27-ix. 1 and Lk. ix. 18-27)

The arrival of Jesus with His disciples in the district of Caesarea Philippi, where they were free from the danger of interference from the partisans of Herod, afforded Him a suitable opportunity for obtaining from them an answer to two questions. What views were held about Him by people in general? And who did the disciples themselves think that He really was? In reply to the first question they gave three specimen answers, typical no doubt of the more thoughtful and less superficial views that were current—John the Baptist risen from the dead, a second Elijah, another Jeremiah. All three suggestions had two things at least in common. They all identified Jesus with a figure of the past instead of acknowledging Him as unique. And they all contained dangerous and misleading half-truths; for, though Jesus possessed some of the characteristics of each of these three great men, He transcended them all.

Certainly, as has already been made clear in this Gospel, there was some likeness between John and Jesus. Both were children of the divine wisdom, and both had vital parts to play in the working out of God's plan for man's salvation. But the difference was far greater. John could *prepare* men to receive the reign of God in their hearts, but he could not *enable* them to receive it. He stood on the threshold of the kingdom of God, but Jesus was the door through whom alone men could enter it. There were also real parallels between Elijah and Jesus. Both were men of prayer, both performed supernatural works of healing, and both waged triumphant war against false religion. But the victories of Elijah were won by physical force, while the victory of Jesus was destined to be won, not by the shedding of the blood of others, but by allowing His own blood to be shed. Elijah, moreover, wavered in his vocation, but Jesus set Himself constantly and steadfastly to accomplish the work He had come into the world to do. The third estimate was perhaps nearer the truth than the other two. For of all the historical characters of the Old Testament Jeremiah approximates most closely to Jesus as an outstanding example of patient endurance of undeserved suffering. But for all the nobility of his character, Jeremiah remained a prophet and no more. He foretold the new covenant, by which men with their sins forgiven would be given a direct knowledge of God, but neither he nor any prophet like him could ever bring it into being.

The only adequate answer to the question put by Jesus was given by Peter in the words *Thou art the Christ, the Son of the living God*. Peter knew that Jesus was not just another in the long line of prophets to whom the living God had spoken in many and various ways in the past, but the Son of that living God who knew, as only such a Son could know, the mind and purposes of His Father. Jesus was well aware that this great confession was not made by Peter on the spur of the moment as if he had been 'stung by the splendour of a sudden thought'. Nor was he voicing a second-hand opinion learned from some other creature of flesh and blood. On the contrary, ever since the day when he stood before Jesus and felt compelled to say 'Depart from me; for I am a sinful man, O Lord', and yet in spite of that reluctance had found himself irresistibly led to respond to Jesus' call and leave his nets and follow Him, during all the time that he had witnessed his Master's mighty works and listened to the words of eternal life that fell daily from His lips, *the living God*, the God who acts and intervenes in the affairs of men, had been leading him to see that Jesus was indeed His Son. Jesus therefore pronounced him highly favoured, addressed him directly as Peter, the man of rock, and made it clear that the faith that was expressed by him was the rock upon which He would build His Church, the Church of the living God, which the forces of death would never be able to overcome. Within that Church Peter would have a unique part to play in the early critical days of its history. He would be entrusted by his Master with the 'keys' of authority. He would possess the power of 'binding and loosing', i.e. of saying what conduct was and what conduct was not worthy of those who were subject to the rule of God, and 'the law of Christ', and his decisions would carry a divine sanction. This latter power was also vested in the other apostles (see xviii. 18); and there is no suggestion that Peter's successors in the centre of Christendom where he would ultimately work would enjoy the same privileges and have the same spiritual authority as Peter himself.

It is often said that the words of Peter's confession as recorded by Matthew are a later theological expansion of the simpler and more historical 'Thou art the Christ' of Mark viii. 29. Many liberal reconstructions of the life of Jesus assume, moreover, that at Caesarea Philippi Peter was expressing *for the first time* the apostles' belief in the Messiahship of Jesus. If this is true, then much in the earlier narratives in the Gospel of John must be regarded as unhistorical, for there we read that Andrew when he first found Peter said '*We* have found the Messiah', and a similar belief is expressed a little later by Philip and Nathanael (see Jn. i. 41, 45, 49). But this is a most unsatisfactory and unnecessary conclusion. For, as Chapman pertinently remarked (p. 47), 'If the closer disciples had not thought Jesus to be the Christ when He preached the kingdom of God, what did they think? And what did they take the Baptist to mean?' It would seem clear, as the same writer goes on to say, that it is the confession by Peter of Jesus as *the Son of the living God*, repeating the witness of the heavenly voice at the baptism and re-echoing the words of the disciples after the walking on the sea (see iii. 17 and xiv. 33), that is now accepted by our Lord as a revelation, coming from the lips of Peter but inspired by the Father, that the time has now come for Him to initiate them into the mystery of His forth-coming passion and resurrection. This confession of Peter had been made quietly and deliberately in answer to a specific question, and in this respect it was different from the words uttered perhaps somewhat impulsively by the disciples in a tense situation after Jesus had come to them walking on the sea.

That this exegesis is correct would seem clear from the fact that Matthew's explicit statement in verse 21, *From that time forth began* (ērxato emphatic) *Jesus to shew unto his disciples, how that he must go unto Jerusalem*, etc. makes it much clearer than Mark's 'And he began (ērxato, not usually emphatic in Mark) to teach them, that the Son of man must suffer many things', etc., that a new stage in the self-revelation of Jesus has now been reached, which is not adequately explained by supposing that Peter merely gave expression once again to what the disciples already believed, viz. that Jesus was the Messiah. The distinctive feature of Peter's confession is that he ack-nowledges that the man Jesus, a son of man even though 'the (unique) Son of man', is also *the Son of the living God*—not a risen John the Baptist, nor a second Elijah, nor another Jeremiah. And it is *the Son of the living God* who will journey to Jerusalem to *be killed, and be raised again*. History is not going to repeat itself, for it is not 'one of the prophets' who is destined to be martyred by Jerusalem 'the slayer of the prophets'. History is going to be *made*, for the forthcoming death and resurrection of *Christ, the Son of the living God*, has no precedent, and nothing like it can ever happen again.

But, though Jesus is not going to die as a prophet, He has prophetic insight into all that is coming to Him. He knows that, though all the roads leading *from* Jerusalem lie open before Him, it is the road *to* Jerusalem that He must tread, and that in that 'holy' city He must suffer indignities and injustice at the hands of the religious authorities, be put to death, and raised again on the third day. This detailed and gruesome forecast of the sufferings that await his Master strikes horror into the heart of Peter. That the living God should submit His Son to such humiliation and cruelty is more than he can bear. So he draws Jesus aside, and gives expression to his indignation and resentment in words which literally mean 'God be kind to you, Master; this shall never happen to you'. Peter's outburst was no doubt well meant, but it revealed such utter misunderstanding of Jesus' vocation that, had He heeded it, Jesus would have been doing precisely what the devil had tempted Him to do in the wilderness. So He turned upon the man, whom He had recently pronounced so highly-favoured, and addressed him as He had addressed the tempter on that occasion, *Get thee behind me, Satan*. When Peter spoke as he had just spoken he was no longer God-inspired but diabolically-possessed. The Rock had become a stone of stumbling and a rock of offence.

It is often held by critics that the commendation of Peter contained in verses 17–19, because it is absent from Mark and Luke, is a later unhistorical addition made in some part of the Church where an exalted position was given to Peter. It is too deeply embedded, however, in the narrative of Matthew for it to be dismissed in such arbitrary fashion. Butler has drawn attention to the artistic symmetry of the whole passage. It is against the verses which record Peter's confession of faith and his subsequent commendation that the verses relating his incredulity and his subsequent reproof would seem to be most clearly set. *Blessed art thou, Simon Bar-jona* is opposed by *Get thee behind me, Satan. Flesh and blood hath not revealed it unto thee, but my Father which is in heaven* becomes by contrast *thou savourest* (RV 'mindest') *not the things that be of God, but those that be of men. Upon this rock I will build my church* is now *thou art an offence*, i.e. 'a rock of offence', *unto me*. (See Butler, pp. 131–133 and Chapman, p. 48.) The differences between the accounts of Peter's confession and its aftermath in the Gospels of Matthew and Mark are best explained on the assumption that Peter, whose teaching is embodied in Mark, deliberately under-emphasized the part that He played on this momentous occasion. Consequently, the narrative of Mark tends to give the impression that there was nothing very distinctive about Peter's confession; it omits the praise he received for it; and it accentuates the rebuke that was subsequently addressed to him by stating that it was deliberately made in the presence of all the disciples (see Mk. viii. 33).

The painful lesson that Peter and all the apostles had now to learn was that to follow Jesus meant to follow a *crucified* Jesus. Jesus accordingly turns to His disciples (verse 24) and explains to them what discipleship involves in the sphere of conduct. It means saying 'No' to the imperious sinful ego, which not only puts self first, but makes 'safety first' its primary aim. It means being prepared to suffer in the company of Christ the indignities that a condemned man has to suffer. But when the old sinful self has been thus repudiated, great though the cost involved in such repudiation will undoubtedly be, a man's true self will be discovered; and for such a discovery no price can be too high. For, unless the true self is discovered, and a man ceases to be self-centred and becomes God-centred, he may gain possession of the whole world, but will remain in all essentials a beggar without any hope of reward when the final day of reckoning comes and the Son of man returns in glory. At the moment, the Son of man has to tread the path of humiliation. He is already on the way to be crucified, that His disciples may be crucified with Him, in the sense that they may have the power to die to their old selves and rise again new men in Christ. For the humiliation of the Son of man in death will be followed by His resurrection; and raised from the dead, He will begin to exercise a world-wide dominion, and in a very real sense come *in his kingdom*; and that coming many who were now listening to Jesus would be alive to see (see xxviii. 18).

Additional Notes

xvi. 13. *Caesarea Philippi* is so named to distinguish it from the more important Caesarea on the coast of Samaria which was in the Province of Judaea and under the procurator Pontius Pilate.

For *I the Son of man am*, the reading of the later MSS, RV following the older MSS, has 'the Son of man is'. Whichever reading is adopted, it is clear that Jesus is referring to Himself as 'the Son of man'.

17. *Flesh and blood* signifies here 'a human person' as in Galatians i. 16. In 1 Corinthians xv. 50, 'flesh and blood cannot inherit the kingdom of God', it refers to the material element in man.

18. The only way to make clear to the English reader that there is a play of words in the Greek, *Peter* transliterating *petros* and *rock* translating *petra*, is to insert 'the man of rock' after Peter. If Peter, either in virtue of himself or any office he might hold, rather than by reason of the faith he professed, had been indicated by the words *this rock*, the sentence would probably have run 'and upon *you* I will build my church'.

The gates of hell translates *pulai hadou* which means in all probability not 'the powers of evil' but 'the powers of death' (so RSV).

19. As McNeile points out, *the keys* are envisaged as in the possession not of a door keeper, who uses them to admit to and exclude from the church, but of a chief steward who has been entrusted with them by their real owner, viz. Christ Himself.

21. The *elders*, the *chief priests* and *scribes* were the three constituent parts of the Jewish Sanhedrin.

25, 26. The same Greek word *psuchē* is translated *life* in verse 25, and *soul* in verse 26. RV and RSV have 'life' in both verses. In verse 25 *his life* means 'his physical life', and in verse 26 *his own soul* means 'his higher self'.

28. The reference to *the Son of man coming in his kingdom* is not to the parousia (as in xxiv. 30 and xxv. 31), for none of those who accompanied Jesus lived to see His return on the clouds of heaven, but probably to His coming back from the dead after the resurrection, when a new era began both for Himself and His disciples (see Stonehouse, pp. 238-240).

e. The transfiguration; and the cure of the epileptic boy (xvii. 1-21; cf. Mk. ix. 2-29 and Lk. ix. 28-43)

All the first three evangelists record that Jesus was accompanied on the occasion of the transfiguration six days after Peter's confession at Caesarea Philippi by Peter, John and James; just as when Moses went up to the holy mountain he took with him Aaron, Nadab and Abihu (Ex. xxiv. 1). Matthew however brings into clearer relief than the other evangelists both the resemblance and the contrast of the scene at the transfiguration to the scene on Sinai. Moses saw the glory of the Lord and 'the skin of his face shone by reason of his speaking with him' (Ex. xxxiv. 29, RV). At the transfiguration the face of the greater than Moses shone not with a reflected glory but with an unborrowed glory similar to the rays of the sun. Matthew alone records that the face of Jesus shone *as the sun*, and that His garments became white *as the light*, and that a *bright cloud* (lit. 'a cloud of light') overshadowed them. But, as at Sinai, it is the divine voice speaking out of the cloud, in itself a sign of the divine presence, that strikes fear into the hearts of the apostles. *When the disciples heard it, they fell on their face, and were sore afraid.*

This divine voice confirms both the confession made by Peter, and also by implication the acceptance of that confession by Jesus as the sign that the time had come for Him to initiate His disciples into the truth that the Son of man must suffer. Jesus, it asserts, is indeed God's beloved Son, the supreme object of the divine favour; and He is to be listened to, even when He speaks, as He has already begun to speak, about the necessity for His death. That this last truth is implied in the words *hear ye him* may be deduced from Luke's explicit statement that Moses and Elijah 'appeared in glory, and spake of his decease which he should accomplish at Jerusalem' (Lk. ix. 31). The disciples may well have thought that their Master would be exempt from the experience of death as Elijah had been (2 Ki. ii. 11). They had now to learn that it was only through death that Jesus could enter into His glory.

Matthew, however, does not draw attention to this particular object of the presence of Moses and Elijah on the mount. The truth underlined in his narrative would seem to be that Moses and Elijah, the first great lawgiver and the first great prophet of Israel, now unite in recognizing in Jesus the One who is the fulfilment of all that is embodied in the Law and the Prophets. Moses, Elijah and Jesus do *not* possess *equal* authority as revealers of the divine will; and now that the perfect has come in the Person of the Son of the living God, that which is in part is done away, in the sense that it is fulfilled. Luke tells us that it was while Moses and Elijah were moving away from Jesus to leave Him that Peter made his offer to build three shelters so that the stay of the distinguished guests might be prolonged. Luke also adds that Peter did not really know what he was saying. As Knox has remarked, 'it was one of those half-rambling remarks which are forced up from the unconscious by the stimulus of a great emotion'. But, whatever Peter's motive may have been, his offer could certainly not be accepted, for the primary purpose of the appearance of Moses and Elijah was to salute their divine

Successor, and then to leave Him alone in His unchallenged supremacy, the sole object of His disciples' veneration. Accordingly, before Peter had finished what he had to say, the cloud descends upon the three main figures; out of it the divine voice gives its authoritative testimony to the uniqueness of Jesus; and under the cover of it Moses and Elijah vanish. The terror-struck disciples are aroused by the reassuring touch of their Master, and by the welcome sound of words they had heard so often from His lips *be not afraid*; and when they raised their eyes once again from the ground, *they saw no man, save Jesus only.*

On the way down from the mountain Jesus tells His disciples not to relate what they had seen to anyone till the Son of man had risen from the dead. At the moment, if the knowledge of it became widespread, Jesus would be surrounded once again by excitable and idly-curious crowds, at a time when He wanted to concentrate His attention upon the training of His disciples. The mention of the resurrection causes Peter, James and John to express to their Master a difficulty of which they had probably been conscious for some time past. They were very sure that the Messiah had come in the Person of Jesus, but at the same time they were aware that the scribes were teaching that Elijah would return before Messiah came, and restore everything to its original perfection. Where was that Elijah? And had all things undergone such a restoration? This scribal teaching was in fact nothing more than a wholly conjectural elaboration of the prophecy of Malachi, 'I will send you Elijah the prophet before the coming of the great and dreadful day of the Lord, and he shall turn the fathers to the children, and the heart of the children to their fathers' (Mal. iv. 5, 6). This was scarcely the restoration of all things! The words of Jesus in verse 11 are best understood as a recognition by Him that what the disciples have said is a true statement of what the scribes were teaching. They are not an indication that He agrees with it. On the contrary, in verse 12 He implies that the scribal tradition is wrong. He accepts of course the teaching of Malachi that another Elijah would come as God's messenger sent to prepare the way for the Messiah (see Mal.

iii. 1), but He insists that this second Elijah has in fact already come. In verse 13, the evangelist makes it clear that the disciples now understood that Jesus identified this Elijah with John the Baptist; and they no doubt remembered that Jesus had suggested once before that they also should make this identification (see xi. 14). Verses 11 and 12 are well paraphrased by McNeile: 'It is true that the scribes teach that Elijah cometh, etc., but I say he has already come, but so far from restoring all things they did unto him whatever they wished.' If the immediate forerunner of the Messiah, Jesus now goes on to say, was treated in this way, how could the Messiah expect anything different for Himself?

While the faith of Peter, John and James is being strengthened on the mount of transfiguration, the other nine apostles on the plain below are totally unable, through a temporary absence of faith, to cure an epileptic boy. A comparison between Matthew's and Mark's version of this incident shows that Matthew's aim is to throw into relief the lack of faith of these apostles. In Matthew's account the father of the boy comes directly to Jesus, kneels before Him, and requests Him to take pity on his afflicted child, a lunatic with suicidal tendencies, whom Jesus' disciples, the father points out, have been unable to cure. Mark gives a more elaborate description of the scene. In his narrative the scribes are disputing with the disciples in the presence of a large crowd, which hastens to greet Jesus when He is seen descending from the mountain; and it is only when Jesus asks what the dispute is all about that the father of the epileptic brings to His notice the failure of the disciples to heal his son. Later, Mark records another conversation between Jesus and the father, in which the boy's symptoms are further elaborated, and in which the initial scepticism of the father and his subsequent confession of faith are emphasized; and when the disciples ask Jesus afterwards the reason for this failure, the only answer is 'This kind can come forth by nothing, but by prayer and fasting' (Mk. ix. 29). Matthew's narrative, on the other hand, very pointedly leads up to a severe indictment by Jesus of the disciples for their lack of faith. It is not even, He tells them, as big as a grain of mustard seed! Even the apostles, it is clear, were capable of the spiritual impotence that results from loss of faith. As Chrysostom says, in a comment recorded by McNeile, 'they were not always the same'.

Attention has been drawn to the difference between Matthew and Mark at this point, for it is often said, to the disparagement of Matthew, that he 'lets the apostles down lightly' by minimizing or failing to mention the stupidity and the faithlessness of the apostles. In the present instance at least such an inference is wholly unwarranted. The truth would appear to be that Mark's narrative reflects Peter's unwillingness to draw attention to his colleagues' lack of faith. As Chapman very appositely remarks (p. 45), 'Matthew was one of the nine Apostles who did not go up the mountain, and had failed to accomplish a miracle; so he records the words *because of your unbelief*, which condemn himself and the rest. Peter never spares the unbelief of the Apostles *when he is included in their number*; but he had come down from the mountain with his Master. He omits the words which tell Matthew and eight others that they have not faith as a grain of mustard seed, and gives instead an excuse "This kind goeth not out but by prayer and fasting".' These last words, which constitute verse 21 in AV, should almost certainly be omitted from the text of Matthew (as in RV and RSV) on the authority of Codex Sinaiticus, Codex Vaticanus, and the ancient Syriac and Egyptian versions. They would seem to have been imported from Mark ix. 29 in the interest of harmonization.

Additional Notes

xvii. 1. *The mountain* of the transfiguration is usually regarded as Mount Hermon, which lay a little to the north of Caesarea Philippi and outside Palestine proper.

4. *Answered* indicates that this was Peter's reaction to the situation.

Let us make is an assimilation to the text of Mark, and probably reflects Peter's deliberate avoidance in his preaching of egotistical references to himself. The reading 'I will make' (RV) is well attested and almost certainly correct.

9. The rendering *the vision* (*to horama*) is not very happy, as it might give the impression that the transfiguration experience was in the nature of a dream. 'What you have seen' is better.

11. In the most ancient MSS *first* is omitted and the word *come* is in the present tense. The interpretation given by the scribes to Malachi's prophecy is here quoted by Jesus from the viewpoint of the prophet himself. 'Elijah is going to come (prophetic present) and will restore all things.' John did not restore all things, but what he did do was a direct fulfilment of Malachi's prophecy about Elijah, as is made clear in the words addressed by the angel to Zacharias before John's birth (see Lk. i. 16, 17), and as Jesus here recognizes.

12. *Knew him not*, i.e. did not see in him the Elijah of Malachi iv. 5.

15. *He falleth* probably indicates that the boy had an urge to burn or drown himself.

17. The scene of confusion and human inadequacy which confronted Jesus at the foot of the mountain, described more vividly in Mark than in Matthew, no doubt reminded Jesus of the faithlessness of the Israelites when Moses descended from Mount Sinai (see Ex. xxxii). The 'greater than Moses' addresses the men and women of His generation in words similar to those used by Moses to describe his contemporaries (see Dt. xxxii. 5).

20. *As a grain*, i.e. 'as small as a grain'.
This mountain. Jesus was speaking metaphorically, though pointing to Mount Hermon as He spoke. To 'remove mountains' meant in Jewish idiom 'to remove difficulties'. The meaning of the verse is that strong faith can accomplish the apparently impossible, for the man of faith is drawing upon divine resources.

f. The second prediction of the passion; and the temple tax (xvii. 22-27; cf. Mk. ix. 30-32 and Lk. ix. 44, 45)

Jesus and His disciples now return to the dominion of Herod Antipas (but, as Mark states, secretly) and visit Capernaum for the last time. In verse 22, AV and RV translate the reading *anastrephomenōn, while they abode.* RSV adopts the more difficult but probably original *sustrephomenōn*, 'as they were gathering'. If this reading, found in Codex Sinaiticus, Codex Vaticanus, several MSS of the Old Latin version, and the ancient Syriac version, is correct, the meaning would seem to be that the disciples of Jesus, including others in addition to the Twelve, were beginning to assemble in groups in preparation for the journey to Jerusalem. Before this passover pilgrimage begins Jesus tells His disciples once again how fateful this visit will be for Himself. According to AV, He now predicts what He had not mentioned before, that the Son of man will be *betrayed* into the hands of men; and it may be that it was this mention of betrayal, presumably by one of His friends, that caused the disciples the great sorrow that the evangelist mentions in verse 23. The verb *paradidosthai* however may not mean more than 'be handed over to' and it is taken in this sense by RV and RSV. It is clear from Matthew's narrative that, whatever the precise reason may have been, the reaction of the disciples to this second prediction of the passion was not to make an indignant protest as Peter had done on the previous occasion; nor to accept it because it was in accordance with the divine will, for as Mark relates they did not really understand it, and were afraid to question Jesus further about it; but to be plunged into grief at the prospect of a forthcoming personal bereavement, which was unmitigated by the promise that Jesus would be raised from the dead. This sorrow never left them, and Jesus referred to it, and said much to transform it, when He spoke to them in the upper room on the last night of His earthly life (see Jn. xvi. 6).

But, although the thoughts of Jesus were mostly occupied at this time with the passion which He as the Messiah of the new Israel must soon endure, He was not irresponsive to the legitimate demands which His own membership of the old

Israel laid upon Him. Though Son of God, He was also Son of man, a child of the Jewish race, born under the law and subject to that law. And as the Temple at Jerusalem was the centre of Jewish worship, Jesus had visited this central shrine for the great festivals ever since He was a child. The maintenance of the Temple was costly. So in accordance with the instructions given to Moses in Exodus xxx. 11–16, a tax was levied upon every male Jew above the age of nineteen for the upkeep of the temple services. This tax consisted of half-a-shekel, called a *didrachma* or 'double-drachma' in verse 24, where it is translated *tribute money* in AV and 'half-shekel' in RV. But as the *didrachma* was not in current coinage, it was customary for two persons to combine and pay a full shekel, called a *statēr* in verse 27, where it is translated *a piece of money* in AV and 'a shekel' in RV. It would seem from verse 27 that Jesus suggested that Peter should pay a shekel to cover the dues of them both.

The tax-collectors in the present story, which is found only in Matthew, may have accosted Peter, because Jesus, having been away from Capernaum for a considerable time, was somewhat behind with His payment. Peter therefore assures them that Jesus is no tax-dodger; and he clearly intends to bring the matter to his Master's attention at the earliest opportunity. But, as soon as they enter *the house*, by which may be meant Matthew's house, before Peter has time to broach the subject, Jesus points out to him that in fact neither He nor Peter are under any moral obligation to pay the temple tax any longer. Earthly kings, so His argument runs, do not collect taxes and tolls from their own families; *a fortiori* therefore the heavenly King does not tax His own children. But who are His 'children'? No longer all members of the Jewish race, but the *new* Israel, the disciples of Jesus the Messiah. They are now the 'Temple' in which the Father is pleased to dwell. For them, in consequence, the Jerusalem Temple is superseded. But Jesus does not wish to cause difficulty to those who have not yet understood that discipleship of Himself means in effect a break with the Temple and its services. He therefore agrees that the tax should be paid by Peter and

Himself on this occasion, though they are in fact now *strangers* as far as the Temple is concerned.

Verse 27 is often called 'the miracle of the stater in the fish's mouth', but it should perhaps be noted that the absence of any such phrase as 'and he went and found the money as Jesus said' means that this is the only miracle-story which leaves the reader to *infer* that the miracle occurred. This has led some commentators to question whether Jesus ever intended the suggestion to be taken seriously by Peter ànd they point out that our Lord's humanity must have included, as all true humanity does, a sense of humour. These writers urge that a miracle performed for such a comparatively trivial object, and in such a seemingly light-hearted way, would be wholly different in character from any of His other miracles, and more akin to the 'wonder-working' which is such a feature of the apocryphal Gospels. It is also argued that to solve the problem of the temple tax in this way would be inconsistent with our Lord's rejection of the temptations in the wilderness.

If this is the case, however, it is not easy to see why the evangelist took the trouble to record such an unimportant incident. Moreover, the clear statement of Jesus' intention may not unreasonably be regarded as an indication that He expected Peter to take His command seriously. His aim was to avoid giving offence (or 'causing difficulty', NEB) to the tax-collectors (verse 27), and not to provide 'easy money' for paying a debt, responsibility for which He in any case emphatically disowns in verse 26.

Additional Notes

xvii. 24. Many early Christian writers draw attention to the fact that Peter's primacy seems to be recognized here by the tax-collector; and they also, rightly or wrongly, conclude that it was jealousy on the part of the other disciples, arising from this recognition, that led them to ask Jesus the question 'Who is the greatest in the kingdom of heaven?' (xviii. 1).

It is impossible, and unnecessary, to attempt to give modern equivalents to ancient coinage particularly in days when the value of money is constantly changing. In this matter the makers of the AV, in this passage at any rate, were wiser than the Revisers.

25. *Custom* translates *telē*, which were indirect local taxes collected at custom-houses by *telōnai* (the 'publicans' of the AV).

Tribute renders *kēnsos*, which was a direct capitation tax levied on persons and paid direct to the imperial treasury. It is the latter word that is used in the 'tribute unto Caesar' passage in xxii. 17. For the payment of this tax a roll was kept of people subject to it (see Lk. ii. 1, RSV); and here we have the origin of the English word 'census'.

27. It is not clear whether by *them* is meant the collectors of the tax who were discharging what they believed to be their duty, or the wider group of those who did not understand the implications of Jesus' Messiahship.

X. LIFE IN THE MESSIANIC COMMUNITY

(xviii. 1–35; cf. Mk. ix. 33–37, 43–48 and Lk. ix. 46–48)

In this chapter the evangelist has collected the teaching of Jesus most directly concerned with the conduct of His disciples as members of the new society brought into being by Himself— the messianic community. The kingdom of heaven has values essentially different from those that characterize earthly institutions and worldly organizations. In that kingdom the humble, not the self-assertive, are the truly great (1–4). In that kingdom the lowliest and most inconspicuous subject who is faithful and loyal to his King has an infinite worth. In consequence, the supreme offence of those who are stronger and more domineering is to make the discipleship of the weaker and more sensitive brethren more difficult (6, 7). To show contempt for any of Christ's brethren, however unimportant, however young, and however spiritually immature they may be, is in fact to despise those who have direct access to the

King and are the permanent objects of His love (11). He wills that they should never perish, and His own concern for them must be reflected in other members of the messianic community. If one of them is wandering from the fold, no effort must be spared to bring about his safe return (12–14).

The temptation to be overbearing and over-self-confident, and the natural desire to enjoy life to the full regardless of moral considerations, are so strong in those not yet made perfect in love, that severe self-discipline is demanded from all who would remain members of the kingdom of heaven and enjoy the eternal life which such membership makes possible. In the interests of healthy growth and development a deliberate, and, if necessary, a ruthless, narrowing of the sphere in which this or that faculty of their nature may find opportunity for expression, must be considered preferable to the unhealthy and indeed mortal condition which results if every faculty is afforded the means of uncontrolled activity (7, 8).

It is possible, however, for some to gain access to the company of the Messiah's followers who are not really the sheep of His pasture. When therefore there is unmistakable evidence that such do not belong to the kingdom of heaven, the other members of the community, acting with a full sense of mutual responsibility and in no spirit of self-righteousness, must regard them as outside the fellowship. Great care must be taken, however, not to treat every erring brother as a reprobate; and every opportunity must be given to the offender to show that his offence is only a temporary lapse from grace (15–17). Although the new Israel differs from the old in that it is not under law but under grace, nevertheless, because it is a society, it must be subject to rules; and upon those called to exercise authority within it there rests not only the privilege but the duty of 'binding' and 'loosing', i.e. of saying what is permitted and what is disallowed. But such disciples must understand that their decisions must never be arbitrary expressions of personal opinion, but convictions reached after united prayer has been offered to the heavenly Father. Only so will they have eternal sanction (18–20).

The messianic community is first and foremost the community of the redeemed. It owes its very existence to the forgiveness made possible by the Messiah's death. It is the fellowship of the men and women for whom Christ died. There is therefore laid upon every member the paramount duty, of which he must be always conscious and never tire, of forgiving the personal wrong that may be done to him. Once the willingness to forgive is abandoned, the *raison d'être* of the Christian fellowship is lost. The society of the forgiven has no meaning if those who are forgiven are themselves unforgiving (21, 22). It is not therefore surprising that Matthew should conclude this section of Christ's teaching with the story, found only in his Gospel, of the unmerciful debtor, with its moral 'forgive and you will be forgiven'. This parable addressed to the disciples has no mystery about it. It emphasizes in no uncertain manner both the urgency of the duty of forgiveness, and the heinousness and serious consequences of the failure to discharge it. Any human king, Jesus points out, would very naturally and very justifiably feel anger towards and demand the punishment of a subject who, after he had himself been mercifully and graciously forgiven by his sovereign a debt so large that it could never be repaid, subsequently showed such a cruel and unforgiving spirit that he ruthlessly and forcibly demanded repayment by one of his fellows of a debt that by comparison with his own was infinitesimally small. *So likewise*, says Jesus in the solemn pronouncement with which this section ends, *shall my heavenly Father do also unto you, if ye from your hearts forgive not every one his brother*.

Additional Notes

xviii. 1. *At the same time* renders the reading which is more literally construed 'In that hour' by RV. It is probable that the expression was meant to be vague, for it is the evangelist's introduction to a collection of the sayings of Jesus which were not all spoken on the same occasion. A variant reading 'on that day' found in some ancient witnesses to the text connects the teaching contained in the first part of this chapter with the incident of the tribute money at the end of the previous chapter. As has been suggested, the recognition of the 'primacy' of Peter by the tax-collectors may have caused jealousy among the other disciples, who, so Mark tells us, had been arguing about the question of precedence.

3. It is noticeable that Jesus does not answer the disciples' question directly, but draws their attention to the conditions that have to be satisfied before it becomes relevant. It would be idle to discuss who is greatest in the kingdom of heaven, while there is still uncertainty about the qualifications for entering it.

For *be converted* RV and RSV have 'turn'. It would seem best however to construe the Greek *straphēte* as a strict passive, for the change that is necessary before a man becomes as a little child is not something that he can bring about by himself. It is in fact a new birth, which we are told in John iii. 3–6 is supernatural.

And before *become* is consequential 'and *so* become as little children'. Jesus is not saying here that children are outstanding examples of humility, or of any other virtue. He is pointing out that arrogant men and women can only possess the humility necessary for entrance into the kingdom of heaven if they are prepared to be insignificant, as little children were in the ancient world. It is important to notice that He does not say 'Except ye become as little children' but *Except ye be converted and become as little children.*

4. The sense is not 'humbles himself as this little child humbles himself' but 'humbles himself until he is like this little child'. A little child has no idea that he is great, and so in the kingdom of heaven the greatest is he who is least conscious of being great.

5. *In my name* probably means 'for my sake'. Jesus had an affectionate regard for children which is unique among teachers and writers of the ancient world; and He regarded service rendered to them by His disciples as service rendered to Himself.

6. Both in this verse and in verses 8 and 9, the difficult word *skandalizō* is rendered by AV *offend* and by RV and RSV 'cause . . . to *stumble*'. Knox rightly varies the translation to suit the different contexts. In this verse he translates 'hurts the conscience of' and in verses 8 and 9 'is an occasion of falling'.

It is clear from the addition of the words *which believe in me* that *little ones* in this verse refer to a wider company than children.

RV inserts the epithet 'great' before *millstone* to make it clear that in the original the millstone is described as a large one worked by an ass, and not the smaller one worked by human hands.

8, 9. These verses are a repetition of v. 29, 30, though the order in which the offending members are mentioned is different. In the present context this passage interrupts the verses dealing with 'the little ones'. It would seem that the evangelist, while recording Jesus' teaching about the sin of offending *others*, wishes to remind his readers of what Jesus had said about the importance of not giving offence to *oneself*. As Butler interestingly remarks (p. 99), 'The author shares the ancient inconvenience of not being able to subjoin cross-references in footnotes. He therefore employs the simple device of appending in the text itself the passage to which he wishes to call the readers' attention. It will be observed that the omission of verses 8 and 9 leaves a perfect connection between verses 6, 7 and 10.'

10. *Their angels* are 'their counterparts', or 'their spiritual doubles', who have access at all times to the Father's presence, the meaning of *do always behold the face of my Father*.

11. This verse is rightly left out by RV and RSV. It is omitted in most of the ancient witnesses to the Greek text, and would seem to have been inserted later into the text of Matthew from Luke xix. 10. The 'lost' sheep in verses 12 and 13 is not completely lost, but *gone astray*.

12. Both AV and RV, translating the reading of the later MSS, construe the words *epi ta orē* as *into the mountains* and insert them after *goeth*. In the reading of the more ancient

MSS, translated by RSV, it is clear that the *ninety and nine* sheep are left *on* the hills, while the owner goes in search of the one that has strayed.

14. The MSS vary between 'my father' (so RSV) and *your Father* (so AV and RV). 'Your' may have been changed later to 'my' under the influence of verse 10. On the whole 'your' suits the present context best. As all the sheep are the property of one owner, so all the members of the kingdom of heaven are the children of the same Father.

15. The words *against thee* are omitted by Codex Sinaiticus and Codex Vaticanus and a few other MSS. But even if they are not original, they rightly interpret the text; and they are retained by RV and RSV. It is not every kind of sin that is here under consideration, but the personal wrong done by one brother to another.

16. The reference in this verse is to Deuteronomy xix. 15, where it is stated that 'at the mouth of two or three witnesses every *matter* shall be established'. As the Hebrew word *dabhar* can mean either 'matter' or 'word', it is probable that the Greek word *rhēma* which translates it should here be rendered 'every fact'.

17. On the sole authority of some MSS of the Old Latin version, the makers of AV left out *kai* ('also' or 'even') before the second mention of *the church*. RV renders 'the church also' and RSV 'even the church'.

By *the church* is meant the local congregation.

20. As McNeile remarks, 'The agreement of two is not a magic which forces God to answer, but it implies that they have met as *disciples* which involves the making only of such requests as the Master will endorse.'

The Jews believed that the Shekinah or divine presence rested upon those who were occupied in the study of the law. Christians are here given the assurance that Christ is present with those who are diligently concerned with understanding His mind and will.

21. The significance of the numbers here mentioned is that Christ's followers must be merciful, as Lamech in Genesis iv. 24 threatened to be unmerciful, 490 times instead of 7!

23, 24. *Take account of* is better rendered by RSV 'settle accounts with'.

The servants in the parable were high-placed officials in the service of the emperor, some of whom would often have occasion to borrow large sums from the imperial exchequer. In this story the amount of the first debt is deliberately exaggerated so as to make the contrast with the second debt more vivid. Nothing is gained by trying to find exact equivalents in modern English or American coinage for the sums mentioned. The sense would be adequately conveyed by thinking of the first debt as 'two or three million pounds' and of the second as 'two or three hundred pounds'.

26. As has often been pointed out, debtors are optimistic. If only they are given enough time they are convinced the means of repayment will be found.

Fell down, and worshipped is too strong a translation of *pesōn prosekunei*. RSV more accurately renders 'fell on his knees, imploring him'. The Latin versions translated *prosekunei* by *orabat* or *rogabat*.

28. *Went out, and found.* The meaning probably is 'no sooner had he left the king's presence than he found'. This cruel wretch was still basking in the sunshine of the royal mercy, when he dealt with his fellow-servant so unmercifully.

29. The best reading omits *all* in this verse. It would seem to have been added later to make the parallel with verse 26 exact. Though the second debtor's liability is so small compared with the first's, his promise to repay is not made with such bombastic assurance. He will make *some* payment at any rate.

32–34. The king now revokes his former decision. The order that the debtor should be sold gives way to the order that he should be delivered to the torturers till he should pay, even as he himself had his own debtor jailed till *he* should pay.

Debtors were submitted to torture to make them disclose unacknowledged sources of revenue. In this case, however, the torture was solely penal, as the victim would never have the means of paying.

35. Forgiveness must be granted not in a grudging spirit, but *ex corde*.

XI. THE JOURNEY TO JERUSALEM (xix. 1–xx. 34)

a. The question of divorce (xix. 1–12; cf. Mk. x. 1–12)

Jesus now leaves Galilee and journeys to the Judaean district east of the Jordan. Here numerous sick folk make further demands upon His compassion, and the Pharisees endeavour once again to find some means of discrediting both Him and His teaching.

This passage about divorce is so difficult, and there have been so many diverse interpretations given by individual scholars and different sections of the Christian Church, that a commentator may well feel reluctant to express any opinion at all about it, lest he should be guilty of adding to the exegetical and ecclesiastical confusion. It is therefore with great diffidence, and in the full knowledge that what he has to say may not be acceptable to many, who may be more learned and more spiritual than himself, that the present author puts forward some of his own reflections upon this section.

It is clear that the Pharisees were attempting to place Jesus in a dilemma by forcing Him to say something which would imply that He took either too lax or too strict a view on the notoriously difficult and much debated subject of divorce. He is, however, well aware of their intentions. Their question *Is it lawful for a man to put away his wife for every cause?* is not immediately or very directly answered; but the subsequent narrative implies that in effect the answer of Jesus is 'If you mean for *any* cause, My answer is Yes; if you mean for *every* cause, My answer is No'. First, He reminds them of the truth known to every reader of Scripture that the purpose of the creation of *two* sexes was that the solidarity, the continuance

179

and the happiness of the human race might have as its foundation the physical union of man and woman. Such union is an essential part of the Creator's plan, and attempts to thwart it, either by indulging in promiscuous sexual intercourse, or by asceticism and enforced celibacy, or by unnatural vice, or by attempts to break up marriages where the unity that God has in mind is being realized, are all contrary to the divine will (6).

At this point, the Pharisees ask a supplementary question (7) suggesting that, if all this is really so, it would seem that Moses was guilty of an infringement of God's purpose by ordering a husband to present his wife with a certificate of divorce if 'he hath found some uncleanness in her' (Dt. xxiv. 1). Is not this self-appointed Messiah speaking contrary to the law by questioning Moses' decision? In verse 8, Jesus retorts that, on the contrary, Moses was in fact upholding the divine purpose, for at the time when this legislation was enacted many so-called 'marriages' were in fact not achieving but preventing that unity of man and woman which was the reason why God created mankind 'male and female'. The Mosaic injunction did much to bring this ideal of unity nearer realization. Hitherto, in fact *from the beginning*, the situation had been much less satisfactory. Polygamy had been prevalent, and men had regarded themselves as free to put away their wives whenever, and for whatever reason, however trivial, they might wish. This was the natural outcome of man's fallen nature, his *hardness of heart*. And so long as that *hardness of heart* prevails, there will always be, both within and outside marriage, 'unions' between men and women, which, because they are not real unions at all, cannot be said to have been *joined together by God*. In these cases it may be in the interest of the divine purpose that they should be dissolved. Jesus therefore accepts the interpretation put upon the Mosaic legislation by the contemporary school of Shammai, which allowed divorce in the case of fornication, as the best way of seeking to interpret the divine will in this matter in the circumstances prevailing at that particular time. *I say unto you, Whosoever shall put away his wife, except it be for fornication, and shall marry another, committeth*

adultery. It would be not only an act of adultery, but an act
of cruelty, for a man to dismiss an *innocent* wife, in order that he
might marry someone else, for the divorced wife, under the
social conditions of those days, would more often than not be
forced into a life of adultery herself. This is implied in the
reading 'makes her to become an adulteress' found in some
MSS in place of *committeth adultery*. The avoidance, or the
mitigation of cruelty, it is here implied, must be uppermost
in the minds of all who are concerned with divorce legislation.
But Jesus is not laying down in these words addressed to *the
Pharisees* any fixed rule which must be followed by *his disciples*
at all times in the future. It is strange that Christians, who have
been ready enough to see that Jesus, in dealing with other
matters of conduct, is not legislating, have often been reluctant
to bring the same consideration to their interpretation of His
teaching on marriage and divorce. But in Palestine in the
first century, to mention only one all-important consideration,
the social and economic status of women was vastly different
from what it was destined in divine providence to become.
No fixed rules therefore about divorce could possibly have
been given which were equally capable of being applied to
Christians in the first and in the twentieth centuries. The only
static factors are first that the divine ideal for the relationship
of men and women remains the same, and secondly, that men
and women remain the same frail creatures who often find it
extremely difficult to achieve in a particular marriage relationship the unity which could alone be truthfully described
as 'a joining together by God'. Jesus, we may surely believe,
expects His followers, far from perfect themselves, to recognize
this frailty, and to treat it with sympathy; and it may well be
that all who fail to do so have not yet fully learned the lesson
of the story of Jesus and the woman taken in adultery found in
John viii. 1–11.

It is difficult, then, to feel that this section of Matthew's
Gospel gives us any ground for supposing that Jesus expected
His Church to become an 'anti-divorce society', which would
make no provision for 'the hardness of men's hearts' or would
debar from communion those, often more sinned against than

sinning, whose marriages have been dissolved. Nor have we any reason to think that He would approve of the somewhat naïve assumption made by some sacramentalists, that any marriage that happens to have begun with a religious ceremony is *ipso facto* a union which *God* has created. Nor is it defensible, on scholarly considerations, to justify a rigorous attitude to divorce by ruling out the words *except it be for fornication* as an interpolation on the ground that they are not found in the parallel passage in Mark; for it is an arbitrary canon of criticism to assume that, where there are differences between Matthew and Mark, Matthew must always be in error. This was, however, the position taken by the very influential Anglican, Bishop Charles Gore; and it has been one of the factors which has led to a hardening of many modern Anglican churchmen on the subject of divorce which would have surprised and distressed many of their predecessors. As Hastings Rashdall wrote in 1916, 'The attitude of both Roman Catholicism and High Anglicanism on this subject is indefensible. Orthodoxy cannot refuse to admit the authority of the actual text of any one Gospel, and the text of Matthew distinctly allows the divorce *a vinculo matrimonii*. We cannot condemn the practice of half Christendom[1] on the strength of what is after all only a conjectural emendation of our Lord's recorded utterance.' We may conclude a necessarily brief commentary on this section with some further words of Dr. Rashdall, in which he summarized, surely rightly, what would seem to be here laid down for our guidance in this most difficult subject. 'That the ideal is permanent monogamous marriage is undoubtedly the principle which Jesus taught; and that idea still appeals to all the higher ethical feeling of our time. By what detailed enactments, however, the ideal may be best promoted, and which is the less of two evils when that ideal has been violated and made impossible, is a question which must be settled by the moral consciousness, the ex-

---

[1] The writer was thinking of the Eastern Orthodox Church and many Protestant churches on the continent. Roman Catholicism allows separation *a mensa et thoro*, but not divorce, though it often makes generous provision for the annulment of marriages.

perience, and the practical judgment of the present.'[1] And no one branch of Christendom, we may add, has a monopoly of the Christian conscience in this matter.

In verse 10, some of the *disciples* who have overheard Jesus' remarks to the Pharisees, intervene with the reflection that in view of the difficulties which seem to be inseparable from marriage it would be better to abstain from marriage altogether. This is the voice of the perfectionist, and the ascetic, who because the best is unlikely to be attained would avoid the second-best. Jesus, though unmarried Himself, is opposed to this attitude. He takes His stand firmly on the expression of the divine will in the creation stories of Genesis; and it is to that utterance that He refers in *this saying* in verse 11. It is true, He asserts, that some are prevented from making the attempt to achieve the unity between man and woman which demands the physical union of marriage. Some *cannot* do so because they are physically defective from birth, or have been made so by man's inhumanity to man, while others have deliberately *refused* to do so, in order to give themselves unreservedly to the service of the kingdom of God. But in no other circumstances, He implies, is it right to say 'it is not expedient to marry' (RV); and all who can *receive* the principle asserted in Genesis should do so.

Additional Notes

xix. 1. *The coasts* translates *ta horia*, which is literally construed by RV 'the borders', and more idiomatically rendered 'the region' in RSV.

4. Jesus *answered*, as He so often did, by asking a counter-question.

At the beginning is more accurately rendered 'from the beginning' in RV and RSV.

5. Probably the question mark ought to be put at the end of verse 4, in which Jesus is referring to Genesis i. 27 'male and female created he them'. *And said* at the beginning of verse 5

[1] Hastings Rashdall, *Conscience and Christ* (Duckworth, 1916), pp. 105, 106.

would then mean not that the Creator said, but that Jesus went on to quote the words of Genesis ii. 24 in which the implication of the creation of the two sexes is set forth.

8. The words *but from the beginning it was not so* do not mean that Jesus thought that the moral situation was *better* before the Mosaic injunction, but that it was *worse*.

9. The word *porneia* translated *fornication* is a comprehensive word, including adultery, fornication and unnatural vice. RSV renders 'unchastity'. Jesus does not insist that there must be divorce in these cases, for He is not legislating, but that these, and not trivial considerations, are the kind of things for which divorce may rightly be granted. RSV omits, probably rightly, the clause *and whoso marrieth her which is put away doth commit adultery*. It would seem to be a later insertion into the text of some MSS to bring the passage into line with Mark x. 12.

10. As has been suggested in the commentary, the disciples are not stating, as some commentators suppose, that celibacy is preferable in view of the limited opportunities for divorce, but because of the difficulties of reaching 'perfection' in the married state.

11. *This saying* does not refer to the disciples' statement in verse 10, but to the Genesis passage quoted in verse 5.

b. 'Suffer little children' (xix. 13–15; cf. Mk. x. 13–16 and Lk. xviii. 15–17)

It may or may not be significant that in Matthew and Mark, tnough not in Luke, this beautiful story is placed directly after the passage about divorce. In any case, the welfare of children must always be a primary concern of Christians in coming to decisions about divorce. More probably, however, this incident took place on a different occasion. Matthew's *then* (*tote*) does not necessarily mean 'at that particular time'.

Those who brought these little children to Jesus were very sure that they would receive a blessing if He laid His hands upon them and prayed for them. But, for some unspecified reason, the disciples tried to prevent them gaining access to their Master; and so, before Jesus touched them, He used the opportunity to teach the disciples in a unique and vivid way a vital truth about the character of the members of the kingdom of God.

It has already been noticed in the commentary upon xi. 16–19 that Jesus was not sentimental about children, but was fully aware of their frailties. Nevertheless, He undoubtedly believed that, though far from innocent, they were more sensitive than adults tend to be to the supernatural world (see the commentary on xviii. 10). It is easier for them to think in terms of primary, rather than secondary causes, and in consequence to see God's hand directly at work in His creation, and not least in what adults tend to regard as ordinary things but which to children are matters of great significance. Jesus is not of course encouraging His disciples to be childish. The Peter Pans of the world may have a whimsical attractiveness but they remain irresponsible and ill-adjusted to reality. Jesus would rather have His disciples regain and retain those child-like qualities which are not incompatible with maturity. The kingdom of God, He implies, belongs to those who are trustful, receptive and friendly, and who remain unsullied by the difficulties and disillusionments, the cynicism and the pessimism, the compromises and the subterfuges which so often depress and disfigure adult life.

It is evidence of the essential goodness of Jesus that in an age when children were regarded as insignificant and unimportant, they should have been irresistibly drawn to Him, as He stretched out His arms to welcome them in His embrace. This incident, we cannot doubt, played an important part in the training of the original disciples; and the fact that Jesus suffered little children to come unto Him has had an incalculable influence upon the attitude of subsequent Christians to children. Though this passage is not in fact a justification for infant baptism, as the Book of Common Prayer seems to regard it, it was very natural that attention should be drawn in the service for infant baptism to what Jesus did on this occasion.

c. The rich young ruler; and the disciples' reward (xix. 16–30; cf. Mk. x. 17–31 and Lk. xviii. 18–30)

It has often been held that in this nineteenth chapter of Matthew we have indications that Jesus taught what is called 'a double standard' of morality. For the spiritually *élite* a counsel of perfection lay open consisting of absolute chastity, complete poverty, and unreserved obedience. It has already been noticed that so far as the relevant passage on chastity is concerned (verses 10–12) it is improbable that any ideal of asceticism is taught. It would also seem true that in the present section there is no emphasis upon complete renunciation of possessions as a counsel of perfection for those who are able to make it. Only by detaching verse 21 entirely from its context could such a view have any degree of plausibility. It is therefore important to study this incident as a whole, as Matthew's very clear account enables us to do even better than the versions of the other evangelists.

It is clear that this particular questioner, called a *young man* in verse 20 and 'a ruler' in Luke xviii. 18, thought that the attainment of eternal life lay in the performance of some specifically heroic act, when in fact, as the subsequent narrative makes clear, it lies in the persistent obedience to a number of commandments embracing man's duty to God and to his neighbour. The AV in verse 17 follows the reading of the later MSS which assimilate the text to the corresponding passages in Mark and Luke. There is no doubt, however, that the correct reading in Matthew is not *Why callest thou me good?*, but, as in RV, 'Why askest thou me concerning that which is good?' The emphasis in the Greek is upon the word *me*. Jesus is in effect saying 'You are asking *me* for information about the good life, as though you did not already possess, as a well-instructed Jew, divine revelation upon the subject. God alone is perfectly good; and so He alone can instruct man about good conduct, and that is what He has already done. If therefore you would enter into life, keep the divinely-ordained commandments.' The man's reaction to this, made clear in Matthew's account, is very self-revealing. By asking *Which?* he not only implies that in his view some of the commandments are less important than others, but indirectly confesses that there are some, or perhaps one in particular, which he has altogether failed to keep. Jesus, who knows what is in man, is aware of this, for in answering the young man's question He specifies the divine injunctions against murder, theft, and false-witness; draws attention to the duty of filial obedience to parents; and then, deliberately omitting, it would seem, the tenth commandment 'Thou shalt not covet', passes rapidly to the summing-up of the second half of the decalogue contained in Leviticus xix. 18 *Thou shalt love thy neighbour as thyself.* At this point the young man interrupts. Avoiding the implications of this last comprehensive command, he points out that the other commandments enumerated by Jesus he has in fact kept, and yet still he knows himself to be outside the gate that would open the way for him to eternal life. His conscience is troubling him; and the reason seems to be that he is aware that he has altogether failed to keep the tenth commandment. This is why he lacks joy and has no zest in his life. His riches have increased, and he has set his heart upon them. He has become a slave to his possessions. There is much wealth in his house, but leanness in his soul. There is therefore much pathos in his question *What lack I yet?* Jesus is aware of this, and tells him that if he would be *perfect (teleios)*, not in the sense of being better than others, but of reaching the goal at which he was aiming, he must make a direct assault upon the covetousness which holds him enthralled. He must sell all his possessions, and give the proceeds to the poor; for only by such complete surrender will it be possible for him to enjoy the heavenly riches; and only *after* that surrender can he respond to the invitation to become a follower of Jesus. It is clear that this command of Jesus in verse 21 is an *ad hoc* command, addressed on a particular occasion to a particular individual, a victim of the covetousness, equated by Paul with idolatry, which drives men relentlessly on to amass great wealth and to cling to it with grim tenacity. To regard this injunction as a counsel of perfection leading to a higher degree of holiness is unjustifiable.

That it was on these lines that this story was interpreted in the early Church receives some corroboration from the fact that in the elaboration of it in the apocryphal Gospel of the Hebrews, as quoted by Origen in his *Commentary on Matthew*, we read that, when Jesus bade the man make so great a renunciation, 'he began to scratch his head, and it did not please him; and the Lord said to him "How sayest thou I have kept the law and the prophets, since it is written in the law that thou shalt love thy neighbour as thyself, and behold many of thy brethren, sons of Abraham, are clothed in filth and dying of hunger, and thy house is full of many good things, and nothing goes out from it to them" '.

The failure of the young man to extricate himself from the clutches of his covetousness leads Jesus to make the solemn assertion to His disciples 'it is hard for a rich man to enter into the kingdom of heaven' (RV), and to drive the point home by semi-humorously suggesting that the difficulty was even greater than a camel, that most clumsy and ungainly of animals, would experience trying to penetrate the eye of a needle! Jesus does not say that it is *impossible* for a rich man to enter God's kingdom; and from Zacchaeus onwards there has been a long line of rich men who have devoted their wealth to the service of God and their fellow men. But, because great wealth enables a man to shut himself away from his fellows, if he so desires, and to make himself increasingly independent of them; and because it tends to make him value exclusively the things that money can buy, and to feel the need of nothing better, it is more difficult for him than for others to enter the narrow gateway leading to eternal life. As the Jews were apt to regard material prosperity as a mark of divine favour, and the possession of riches as a kind of virtue, it is not as surprising as it might otherwise appear that the disciples' reaction to this statement of Jesus was stark amazement. *Who then*, they asked, *can be saved?* Jesus looked them straight in the eyes and gave them the only possible answer 'No-one, without the power of God'.

When Peter saw the young man walk sorrowfully away unable to respond to the Master's challenge, he took the opportunity to point out that he and his fellow apostles (the *we* in verse 27 is emphatic) had surrendered everything to become disciples of Jesus. It was an unnecessary and rather self-complacent intervention on Peter's part; and Matthew, so far from letting him down lightly, as critics comparing his work with Mark so often suppose, underlines the self-complacency by recording, alone of the evangelists, that Peter went on to ask the very mercenary question *What shall we have therefore?* Jesus' reply, however, is not a rebuke. On the contrary, He makes it clear that Peter and the other apostles of the Messiah (*ye* in verse 28 is emphatic, answering the *we* of verse 27) will have a special place of honour as His co-assessors when, after the old world has passed away, He will be enthroned in glory and minister justice to the entire Israel of God. But, though a certain primacy belongs to *them*, Jesus immediately adds that among the company of God's people who will enjoy the Messiah's reign and the eternal life that it will ensure, will be found *everyone* that has made personal and material sacrifices for His sake during his or her earthly pilgrimage. And the last verse of the section indicates that late-comers into the kingdom of God will be treated on an equality with those who have come in first, a truth which Jesus proceeds to illustrate in the parable which follows.

Additional Notes

xix. 16, 17. RV, following the most ancient textual evidence, omits *good* before *Master* in verse 16, and *God* after *but one* in verse 17. These additions were probably made to bring the passage into line with the other Gospels.

20. The words *from my youth up* are not found in the most ancient witnesses to the text, and are almost certainly an insertion into Matthew from the other Gospels. The tradition of the story that found expression in Mark and Luke does not imply, what Matthew definitely states, that the man was *young*; for a young man would not have used the expression 'from my youth up'.

27. The force of *answered* is well brought out by Knox 'took occasion to say'.

29. *Receive an hundredfold*, i.e. 'will be paid back a hundred times over'. Some MSS have 'many fold', i.e. 'many times over'.

d. The parable of the labourers in the vineyard (xx. 1–16)

Jesus has made it clear that there will be rewards for all who respond to the call to discipleship and accept the sacrifices it involves. But the fact that Peter could ask such a question as *What shall we have?* was evidence that he had not fully grasped that God promises rewards to those who obey Him without thought of reward, for in the kingdom of God all reward is the result of God's grace and not of human merit. This is why Jesus at once told the story of the labourers in the vineyard, recorded only by Matthew. It is essentially a parable of the kingdom of God, where the grace of God is the predominant factor, and where commercial conceptions of morality are wholly irrelevant. Jesus is not therefore attempting to throw light upon the question of how labourers should be paid, or upon other economic problems with which the modern man is so preoccupied; and any attempt to interpret the parable along these lines is doomed to failure.

The high light of the story is that there was something akin to the goodness and generosity of God in the action of this imaginary employer of labour, who out of sheer pity for the workless sent more labourers into his vineyard than he really needed, and paid them all a full day's wage, even though some of them had not rendered a full day's service. The benefits of the kingdom of God, Jesus is here saying, are the same for all who become subject to the rule of its king, whenever they may come under His dominion. Jews have no precedence in this matter over Gentiles; and the man converted early in life is not for that reason entitled to better treatment from God than the man who is much older when he experiences the new birth, for all alike receive the best of treatment. As has been well said, 'this parable is in fact the gospel of the penitent thief'. The same paradise awaits both the man who has experienced divine grace in the last hour of his life, and him who was first called to be Christ's disciple. Because salvation is entirely a matter of God's grace, God is free *to do what* (He) *will with* (His) *own* (15). The grumble of those who had toiled all day long in the blazing sun was akin to the complaint of the elder brother in the parable of the prodigal son. These malcontents were not fretting under a sense of injustice, but were the victims of jealousy. The employer had in fact kept the agreement he had made; and the prodigal's elder brother enjoyed all that his father possessed. The labourers did not protest because they were not paid more, but simply because those hired later were given equal pay. In a word, they begrudged the employer's generosity, as RSV well translates verse 15.

It is interesting to notice that it was only with those who were sent into the vineyard in the early morning that the employer made an agreement. Those who were sent at the third, sixth, and ninth hours were told that they would be given a fair wage, the amount being unspecified. And those who were called at the eleventh hour were not told that they would be paid at all; for the words at the end of verse 7 *whatsoever is right, that shall ye receive,* omitted from RV, are not found in most ancient witnesses to the text. The significance of these details should probably not be pressed, but they serve to throw into relief both the employer's persistent concern for the unemployed, and the conviction of those who went into the vineyard last that he would do his best for them. In the same way, when God's saving grace is offered to mankind, the response He desires is implicit trust.

Additional Notes

xx. 2, 9, 13. *A penny* of course sounds ridiculous to modern ears; but it is equally unilluminating merely to transliterate 'a denarius' (RSV). The important point is that the employer agreed to pay the usual full day's wage. Knox's 'a silver piece for the day's wage' is sufficiently lucid without attempting to be specific.

3, 5, 6. The *third, sixth, ninth* and *eleventh* hours are 9 a.m., noon, 3 p.m., and an hour before sunset, respectively.

8. Payment had to be made according to Jewish law at sunset, i.e. 6 p.m. when the day ended; cf. Leviticus xix. 13 'the wages of him that is hired shall not abide all night with thee until the morning'.

The fact that the steward was told to pay the last-called first has no particular significance. It was necessary for the story that the first-called should witness the payment of those called last.

12. *Wrought . . . one hour.* Both Greek and English use the expression 'done an hour' to signify 'completed an hour's work'.

15. *With mine own* is better rendered 'with what belongs to me' (RSV).

An *evil eye* was a common Jewish expression for a jealous or grudging spirit (see Dt. xv. 9).

16. *So* looks back to xix. 30. 'This is the kind of thing I meant when I said *Many that are first shall be last; and the last shall be first.*' Other examples of this Semitic device of *inclusio*, the repetition at the end of a paragraph of the words that introduce it, are vii. 16 picked up at vii. 20, and xxiv. 42 repeated at xxv. 13. According to Butler there are eleven certain uses of it in Matthew.

The words *for many be called, but few chosen* are rightly omitted from RV. They are not found in many ancient MSS, and they are ill-suited to the present context, for *all* the labourers sent into the vineyard were 'chosen'. The phrase was inserted from xxii. 14 where it is strictly relevant.

e. The third prediction of the passion (xx. 17–19; cf. Mk. x. 32–34 and Lk. xviii. 31–34)

Jesus now foretells once again the three salient experiences which await Him at Jerusalem; His treatment at the hands of the Jewish authorities, here amplified by the information that He will be handed over to the Gentiles (i.e. the Roman soldiers) to be mocked and scourged; His crucifixion; and

His resurrection. On this third occasion He introduces the prophecy with the solemn words *Behold, we go up to Jerusalem.* This, as McNeile well points out, 'expresses the resolve He had made; they knew already they were going to the capital for the passover, but they could not know the struggle it had caused Him.'

f. The request of the sons of Zebedee (xx. 20-28; cf. Mk. x. 35-45 and Lk. xxii. 24-27)

In Mark, the request that James and John might be permitted to occupy places of honour on either side of Jesus when He sat on the throne of His glory is made by the two brothers themselves. In Matthew, their mother gives utterance to it. It is often assumed by critics that Matthew has here deliberately altered Mark's narrative in order to spare the apostles by throwing the onus on their mother! We agree with Butler that 'this is a falsification that we may hope the evangelist would have eschewed'. It is clear that, in fact, the request emanated from the brothers themselves, for the remaining ten apostles, when they hear about it, do not in Matthew's narrative any more than in Mark's turn in indignation upon the mother but upon her sons. This Jewish mother, like many other mothers, may have been ambitious for her sons, but on this occasion she was nothing more than their spokeswoman.

In this incident James and John reveal both the strength and the weakness of their discipleship. On the one hand, it is clear that they have not yet grasped the true nature of the kingdom of God, and that they are not content with the assurance Jesus has already given them that all His apostles will share in His ultimate triumph. They wish to extract from Him a further promise that they themselves will occupy special seats of honour when He finally reigns in glory. On the other hand, their loyalty to their Master is so strong that they feel confident that they will be able to endure suffering, shame and persecution for His sake. *In the end* they were indeed found ready for such ordeals, as Jesus prophesies they would be. James was martyred by Herod Agrippa I at Jerusalem (Acts

xii. 2); and John, though spared a martyr's death, spent the remainder of his long life in devoted service to his Master. But *in the immediate future*, on the eve of His agony, when He was called upon to drink His cup of sorrow and suffering, both of them deserted Him with the others. Jesus had therefore to drink that cup alone; and, had He failed to drink it, there would have been no throne for Him to share with His apostles. But exactly how they would be seated round Him on that throne Jesus states that He Himself is ignorant. The omniscient Father alone knew who would be closest to His Son when He should reign in triumph.

All this anxiety about pride of place in the kingdom was evidence of a deep-seated misunderstanding on the part of James and John of the sense in which the term 'greatness' should be applied to 'the glorious company of the apostles'. Jesus therefore contrasts for their special benefit the two ways in which authority can be exercised and power manifested. In societies composed of sinful men and women, the possession of power almost invariably corrupts, and rulers easily become tyrants and oppressors; nevertheless, all such potentates are styled 'great'. In the kingdom of God, because the King is Himself a servant, the title 'great' is reserved for those who, inspired by His example, spend themselves freely and gladly in the service of others. The sign of Christ's kingdom is the criminal's cross, on which He crowned a ministry of loving service by surrendering His life in a penal death, thereby paying the costly price that had to be paid if mankind was to be redeemed from the guilt and power of sin.

Luke tells us that on the last night of Jesus' earthly life, in the upper room at Jerusalem, 'there was also a strife among (the apostles), which of them should be accounted the greatest', and that Jesus then spoke to them words very similar to those recorded in verses 25–27 of this present section. The greatest lessons in life are not learned all at once; and the good teacher has patiently to persevere in driving his lesson home. By repeating His teaching in this way, Jesus was making it possible for His disciples to prove themselves after His resurrection devoted 'servants of Christ'.

Additional Notes

xx. 21. For *in thy kingdom* Mark has 'in thy glory'. The sense therefore is 'when you reign in glory'.

22. *I shall drink.* The original is not a simple future, but *mellō pinein*, which is better rendered 'I am to drink' (Knox). There is a divine necessity about it.

22, 23. The clauses about 'being baptized' in these two verses are rightly omitted from RV, as they are found only in the later MSS. They were inserted later from the corresponding passage in Mark. The 'cup' and the 'baptism' clauses have virtually the same meaning.

23. *It is prepared* translates a perfect indicative passive. So 'it hath been prepared' (RV) is a better rendering. The places have already been assigned.

24. The verb translated *moved with indignation* (*ēganaktēsan*) implies that they *expressed* their indignation. They in fact 'turned on' the two brothers. They seem to have been prompted by jealousy, for it is not only to James and John that Jesus addresses the following words, but to all of them.

25. The Greek words translated *exercise dominion* (*katakurieuousi*) and *exercise authority* (*katexousiazousi*) are strong compounds and convey more than AV suggests. It is of course right and proper that those in authority should exercise it, but not in a domineering or oppressive manner. Knox well renders the Latin equivalent for the first word *dominantur* 'lord it over', and the Latin equivalent for the second word *exercent potestatem* 'vaunt their power over'. In colloquial English we speak disdainfully in this connection of those who 'throw their weight about'.

26. *It shall not* represents a strong imperatival future. Knox brings this out 'with you it must be otherwise'.

26, 27. *Your minister* means 'your willing servant' and *your servant* 'your willing slave'.

28. *A ransom for many* translates *lutron anti pollōn*, which conveys the idea of substitution. Christ was to die in the place of (*anti*) many the death which they, but not He, deserved. The word *lutron* occurs nowhere else in the New Testament, but the cognate word *antilutron* is found in 1 Timothy ii. 6.

g. Two blind men at Jericho (xx. 29–34; cf. Mk. x. 46–52 and Lk. xviii. 35–43)

The corresponding passages in Mark and Luke mention only one blind man, and Mark refers to him by his name Bartimaeus and states that he was a beggar. It is often held by critics that Matthew is here deliberately 'falsifying' the narrative, either because of a supposed fondness for 'pairs', or because he desires to make compensation for omitting the story of the gradual restoration of sight to a blind man at Bethsaida recorded in Mark viii. 22–26. The latter conjecture is said to be strengthened by the observation that the word used for 'eyes' in Mark viii. 23, *ommata*, is also used here in verse 34, but nowhere else in the New Testament. It is however equally probable that two men were in fact given back their sight, but that the Petrine tradition of the story known to Mark concentrated attention solely upon one of the beneficiaries, who may have been personally known to Peter.

Matthew alone records in verse 33 that Jesus gave a token of His compassion by touching the blind men's eyes; and there is an interesting textual variant in the same verse, found only in the Curetonian MS of the Old Syriac version, which adds the words 'and that we may see thee' after *that our eyes may be opened*. We can, at any rate, well imagine how intense the desire of these afflicted men must have been to set eyes upon Him whom they greeted with such enthusiasm as the *son of David*, refusing to be bludgeoned into silence.

XII. THE MESSIAH'S CHALLENGE TO
JERUSALEM (xxi. 1-xxii. 46)

a. The triumphal entry (xxi. 1-11; cf. Mk. xi. 1-10; Lk. xix. 29, 40; Jn. xii. 12-19)

Jesus entered Jerusalem for the last time in a manner which showed that He was none other than the Messiah, the Son of David, who was coming to Sion to claim the city as His own. He was coming to make Jerusalem what God had intended it to be, but what it had never yet been, 'the joy of the whole earth', from which streams of mercy and salvation would flow for all mankind. It was indeed a *strange* coming, but in its very strangeness it was the fulfilment of ancient prophecy. Jesus deliberately arranged that He should ride into the city, not arrayed in the outward pomp of royalty, not mounted as an earthly warrior-king on horse and chariot, but, as the prophet had foretold, *meek, and sitting upon an ass*. That Jesus was influenced by the words of Zechariah ix. 9, in which the prophet bade the daughter of Sion rejoice greatly, because her king was coming to her 'just and having salvation; lowly, and riding upon an ass', is evident from the fact that He made arrangements for an ass to be available at the entrance to the village of Bethphage when He might decide that the moment had arrived for Him to make use of it. It is also possible that verses 4 and 5 should be read as a contribution of His words to His disciples rather than as an addition of the evangelist himself, as is usually supposed. *All this was done* is not an accurate translation of the original *touto de gegonen*, which is better rendered in RV 'Now this is come to pass'. Precisely the same wording is used in i. 22 and xxvi. 56, where the commentator is confronted by similar difficulty. Knox, who throughout his translation deliberately shuns the use of marks of quotation so as to avoid the necessity of having to be unambiguous where the original has some ambiguity, translates 'All this was so ordained to fulfil the words spoken by the prophet', and his readers are free to suppose either that Jesus deliberately mounted the ass in fulfilment of prophecy *and said so*, or that the evangelist, seeing the congruity of what actually happened with the prophecy, felt compelled to draw his readers' attention to it.

Mark states that the arrangement was that *one* animal, described by him as a foal (*pōlos*), which does not necessarily mean a donkey, should be fetched. In consequence, the scholars who assume that Mark is always primary and Matthew secondary where they disagree in details, argue that Matthew has here deliberately altered the narrative in order to adjust it to the quotation. But, in all probability, the quotation is an example of parallelism, a common feature of Hebrew poetry, so that only one animal is indicated. The right translation of the closing words of the quotation should therefore be 'on an ass, *even* on the foal of a beast of burden'. When Matthew states that the foal was brought with her dam he is recording a fact, and not rather unintelligently adapting his material in the interest of a literal fulfilment of prophecy. We may reasonably suppose that it would have been much easier for the disciples to bring the foal with her dam than by herself. Jesus, however, actually rode upon the foal, which Mark tells us was 'unbroken' and had never yet been ridden. The words translated *thereon* in verse 7 are in the plural *epanō autōn*, and we are surely at liberty to suppose that the evangelist meant them to refer to the *clothes* and not to both animals! There is good textual evidence for supposing that *on them* in verse 7 should be 'on it' (*ep auton* for *ep autōn*), i.e. 'on the foal'. In any case, the alteration of an *omikron* to an *omega*, and vice versa, is such a frequent occurrence in copying Greek MSS, that the presence of one rather than the other should not be made the basis of unintelligent exposition. The authors of Scripture did not write nonsense, and Jesus did not ride on two animals at once!

Matthew alone tells us that *all the city was moved* at the sight of the strange procession as it wended its way down the Mount of Olives. Mixed feelings of surprise, indignation, expectation and contempt prompted the question *Who is this?* It is not clear whether *the multitude* mentioned in verse 11 refers to the company of Galilaean pilgrims who preceded the procession (cf. verse 9), or to the crowds in Jerusalem itself, familiar by now with Jesus as the well-known prophet of Nazareth, for, as the Gospel of John makes explicit, He had often visited the city.

Additional Notes

xxi. 3. The expression *The Lord* indicated that the owner of the animals was a disciple of Jesus, as also does the statement of Jesus that the owner would immediately comply with the disciples' request.

7. Instead of *they set him thereon*, RV, following the more widely-attested reading, has 'he sat thereon'.

8. To 'spread garments in the way', to be trodden on and then picked up again, was a royal honour. After Jehu had been anointed king, we read 'they hasted, and took every man his garment, and put it under him on the top of the stairs, and blew with the trumpets, saying, Jehu is king' (2 Ki. ix. 13).

9. In Mark, *Hosanna* is a sentence in itself meaning 'Save us, we pray thee' as in Psalm cxviii. 25. In Matthew, it is a shout of praise, followed first by *to the son of David* and then by *in the highest*. The implication would seem to be 'Glory be to the Son of David in heaven and on earth'. Luke gives a paraphrase of the words which echoes the song of the angels at Jesus' birth 'Peace in heaven, and glory in the highest'.

In the name of the Lord, i.e. 'as the Lord's representative, God's Messiah'. In the original (Ps. cxviii. 26) it is the pilgrim approaching the Jerusalem Temple who is stated to be *blessed*.

b. The cleansing of the Temple (xxi. 12–17; cf. Mk. xi. 15–19 and Lk. xix. 45, 46)

It was as Messiah that Jesus entered Jerusalem, and it was as Messiah that He 'cleansed' the Temple. What He said and did on this momentous occasion was a trenchant denunciation of the way in which worshippers from abroad were being cheated by excessive rates of exchange and by the exorbitant cost of animals necessary for sacrifice. But He was also, in effect, passing judgment upon the sacrificial system as it was then practised. It had become so commercialized, and regarded so much as an end in itself, that it was proving an obstacle to harmonious relationships between Jews themselves, and making it increasingly impossible for the prophet's words ever to find fulfilment within the setting of the Jewish Temple: 'The sons of the stranger, that join themselves unto the Lord, ... them will I bring to my holy mountain, and make them joyful in my house of prayer . . . for mine house shall be called an house of prayer for all people' (Is. lvi. 6, 7). In the symbolic actions described in verse 12 Jesus gave forcible expression to the truth that no external piety practised within the supposed sanctity of a sacred building can ever render unrepentant sinners immune from divine judgment. When cheats imagined they could salve their consciences by the mechanical offering of sacrifices without any change of heart they were in fact turning *the house of prayer* into *a den of thieves*.

Service rendered to the afflicted is worship more acceptable to God than multitudes of sacrifices, a truth brought out in Matthew's narrative, when he, alone of the evangelists, records that Jesus miraculously healed the blind and the lame that came to Him in the Temple. That this is true religion was instinctively recognized by the children present. Jesus had previously expressed His gratitude that truth hidden from the wise and sophisticated had been revealed to 'babes'; and He now rejoices to hear children repeat the greeting they had heard when He entered Jerusalem *Hosanna to the son of David*. The chief priests and scribes were highly indignant that He should take no notice of this display of 'irreverence' within the temple precincts, as though the manner in which trade was being conducted within the same precincts did not itself constitute irreverence! Jesus in consequence made it clear that in fact the praises sounded by the children were in the nature of a rebuke to their religious 'superiors', and He drew their attention to the truth expressed by the psalmist, that God had caused children and infants at the breast to sound aloud His praises.

Additional Notes

xxi. 12. By *the temple* the Court of the Gentiles is here meant.

13. Mark completes the quotation from Isaiah lvi. 7 by adding 'for all the nations' (Mk. xi. 17, RSV).

16. The quotation from Psalm viii. 2 follows the LXX. The Hebrew has 'strength' for *praise*. The translation *perfected* is influenced by the Vulgate *perfecisti*. The Greek *katērtisō* is in the middle voice, and means 'provided thyself with'.

c. The withering of the fig tree (xxi. 18–22; cf. Mk. xi. 12–14, 20–25)

Just as the 'cleansing' of the Temple was a symbolic denunciation by the Messiah of the worship of the old Israel, so the withering of the fig tree was a symbolic denunciation by Him of the Jewish nation as the privileged people of God. The fig tree that confronted Jesus on His return to Jerusalem from Bethany early the following morning had all the appearance of being able to satisfy His hunger. As *some* fruit usually appeared on a fig tree *before* the leaves, when a tree was in full leaf, those who approached it would very naturally expect to find it bearing a crop. Similarly, the Jewish nation held out before the world the promise that it was rich in spiritual fruit; it could still show many outward signs of being religious; but it was being rendered unfruitful by barren legalism and perfunctory ceremonialism. Such a fruitless tree, even though seemingly alive, was in fact dying; and Jesus foretells its destruction. The words translated *Let no fruit grow on thee henceforward for ever* are in the original perhaps more of a prediction than a curse. 'You will never again bear any fruit.' To the amazement of the disciples the prediction was fulfilled at once, for *presently* in verse 20 is used in the sense, now archaic, of 'directly'. RV renders 'immediately'. When the disciples question Jesus as to how it was that the tree had withered so *soon*, He points out to them that in the supernatural world ordinary time-processes are often irrelevant. In consequence, the praying disciple gifted with the supernatural power of faith can achieve with apparent suddenness results which apart from faith and prayer would be wholly beyond his reach. The sudden withering, and therefore removal, of the fig tree by supernatural means is therefore further regarded by Jesus as an acted symbol of the removal by the same means of apparently insurmountable difficulties, here spoken of metaphorically by Him as 'mountains'.

d. The authority of John and Jesus (xxi. 23–32; cf. Mk. xi. 27–33 and Lk. xx. 1–8)

The triumphant entry of Jesus into Jerusalem, His interference with the customary procedure of those who supplied the needs of worshippers in the Court of the Gentiles, and His acceptance without protest of the acclamation of the children in the Temple who shouted their hosannas to Him as the Son of David, not unnaturally caused great indignation to those members of the Sanhedrin who were present. These are called *the chief priests and the scribes* in verse 15 and *the chief priests and elders of the people* in verse 23. It is not surprising that these three influential groups, the spiritual hierarchy, the representatives of the congregation, and the exponents of the written law and the oral tradition, should have challenged Jesus directly the next time they found Him teaching in the Temple to tell them *by what authority* He was behaving as He did. Jesus met this peremptory request, not by giving a direct answer to their specific question, but by a counter-challenge, which revealed indirectly the authority by which He was acting. This counter-challenge consisted of a pertinent question about the source of John's authority, to which they found it impossible to give an answer, followed by three parables, in which a sustained attack is made upon their worthiness to be members of the kingdom of God.

The authority of Jesus was closely connected with the authority of John His forerunner, whose baptism of repentance unto the remission of sins had found a ready response among the ordinary people and the tax-collectors, but had been rejected for the most part by the Pharisees and the lawyers (see Lk. vii. 29, 30). The latter could not therefore reply to Jesus' counter-question by stating that John's authority was divine, without laying themselves open to the obvious retort *Why did ye not then believe him?* And if they answered that John was discharging a merely human ministry, they would be in danger of adding fuel to the fire of a popular 'pro-Baptist' movement which might endanger their own position. Their failure to give any answer at all to Jesus' question meant that the initiative in the debate about authority now passed to Him, and He used it first by uttering the parable of the two sons, which showed up the so-called religious leaders of Israel in a very unfavourable light, as far as the kingdom of God was concerned, in comparison with the tax-collectors and prostitutes.

In this parable, recorded only by Matthew, the first son who says he will not go and work in his father's vineyard, but afterwards changes his mind and goes, corresponds to the publicans and sinners, who though at first they were very far from righteous, later repented as a result of the preaching of John the Baptist. The second son, who as soon as he receives the order promises with a good deal of gush that he will go and work, but who in the end never goes at all, stands for the professedly religious, whose self-righteousness prevents them from responding to any call to repentance. Unconscious of the need for forgiveness they are among those satirized elsewhere by Jesus as 'the ninety and nine just persons, which need no repentance'. Verse 32 connects the parable closely with the earlier question about the nature of John's authority. In it the religious leaders of Israel are castigated first for having seen that John came to them *in the way of righteousness*, i.e. showing men how they ought to behave (see Lk. iii. 10-14), and yet not believing him, and secondly for not having changed their attitude when they saw the response that was being given to John's message by many who heard it.

e. The parable of the wicked husbandmen (xxi. 33-46; cf. Mk. xii. 1-12 and Lk. xx. 9-19)

Matthew, by the introductory words *Hear another parable*, makes it clear that this parable is the second of a trilogy, and that it was spoken directly after the parable of the two sons and addressed to the same audience. The parable is in the nature of an allegory. The vineyard is Israel, and is described in language taken from Isaiah v. 1, 2; its owner is God; the vinegrowers, or tenant-farmers, are the religious leaders of Israel; the servants who are sent to gather the fruit are the prophets; and the son of the owner is Jesus the Messiah. Those critics who assume that the parables of Jesus in their original form were never allegories, regard these allusions as later allegorical interpolations made by the Church in the interests of Christology. But if we approach the text with no such arbitrary assumptions, the parable is seen to be of the greatest importance for the light it throws both on Jesus' own understanding of His Person, and on His certainty as to the destiny that awaited Him at the hands of Israel. Moreover, when it is interpreted in this way, it forms a natural sequel to the parable that precedes it. The former story implies that John was a true prophet and forerunner of the Messiah, and that his baptism was in consequence from heaven. In the present parable, Jesus indirectly, but none the less certainly, teaches that He is the Messiah acting by divine authority and destined in obedience to the divine will to be slain outside the vineyard of Israel. Because of this rejection of Jesus the Messiah, which came as the climax of a long series of rejections of the prophets God had sent to it (35, 36), the old Israel as such would forfeit the right to receive the blessings appertaining to the kingdom of God. These blessings would in consequence be made available to a less exclusive people of God which would contain men of all races and nations (43); and the murderers of God's Son would themselves be destroyed (41).

The metaphor of the rejected stone which became the head stone of the corner, which the writer of Psalm cxviii. 22, 23 originally used about Israel as the nation so often restored by God to its unique and honourable position, is stated by Jesus to be especially applicable to Himself, the embodiment of the true Israel. Though destined to be rejected by men He would become the chief corner-stone of a new Temple in which God would be worshipped in spirit and in truth. Thrown aside at His crucifixion He would come back again to take His rightful place after His resurrection. And to this resurrection of the Messiah the words, with which the psalmist concluded his parable of the stone rejected and restored, would be equally applicable; *this is the Lord's doing, and it is marvellous in our eyes* (42).

Additional Notes

xxi. 33. The *tower* was a watch-tower; the *husbandmen* (*geōrgoi*) were tenant-farmers who paid a proportion of the crops each year as their rent; and the word rendered *went into a far country* (*apedēmēsen*) means simply 'went abroad'.

35, 36. There are differences in detail between the Gospels as regards the number of the servants sent and the exact manner in which they were treated; but these differences, the natural consequence of oral tradition, in no way affect the meaning of the parable. In verse 35 *killed* is well rendered by Knox 'killed outright' to differentiate it from what could have been a slower method of death by stoning.

39. Matthew's version makes it clear that Jesus died *outside* Jerusalem, a detail of considerable interest to the author of the Epistle to the Hebrews (see Heb. xiii. 12).

41. In Matthew's narrative the chief priests and the Pharisees utter their own condemnation, just as in the previous parable Jesus calls forth from them to their self-condemnation the decision as to which of the two sons did his father's will (see verse 31).

43. This verse is omitted from Mark and Luke, but this is not an indication that it is a later interpolation. Matthew is anxious to show his readers that Jesus was concerned with the problem of the rejection of the Messiah by Israel, and the emergence in consequence of a new Israel. In commenting on the omission of the passage from Mark, Chapman writes (p. 56): 'Peter would leave out the words, for he does not preach at Rome about the rejection of the Jews; and were not the Romans sure to jump to the unfortunate conclusion that they themselves were "the nation" which should get the forfeited kingdom?'

44. This verse is omitted by the important combination of witnesses to the text, Codex Bezae, many Old Latin MSS, and the Sinaitic MS of the Old Syriac version. Most modern editors (e.g. RSV) regard it as a later insertion into the text of Matthew from Luke xx. 18.

f. The parable of the wedding-guests (xxii. 1-14; cf. Lk. xiv. 16-24)

Many commentators regard this parable as another version of the similar story recorded in Luke xiv. 16-24. This may be so, but as the differences are as numerous as the agreements, it is perhaps more probable that Jesus used the same theme, that of giving a feast, to teach different aspects of truth on what were entirely different occasions. The present parable is concerned with the extension of the offer of the kingdom of God, here thought of as a royal wedding feast, to others than those who were originally invited, because the latter when the moment arrived were unwilling to come. That the Gentiles were to be included in the people of God because the original Israel had for the most part rejected Jesus the Messiah, is a dominant theme of the Gospel of Matthew. The parable is in fact a further elucidation of the statement contained in xxi. 43.

Verses 6 and 7 interrupt the story and are unnecessary for the exposition of the main truth it enshrines. They may therefore have been added in the margin of an early copy of the Gospel after the fall of Jerusalem by someone who wished to bring the parable into line with the previous story (xxii. 6 being seemingly parallel to xxi. 35, 36), and to draw attention to the judgment inflicted upon Israel in the destruction of Jerusalem because it had persecuted the Christian apostles and evangelists. Subsequently, this marginal addition became embodied in the text. Several considerations lead us to conclude that it is unlikely that Jesus would have introduced details so lacking in verisimilitude into an otherwise simple and straightforward story. In the first place, there is no *real* parallel between the killing by the vinegrowers of the servants of the owner of the vineyard and the murder of the king's servants who came to inform the invited guests that the wedding feast was now ready. The vinegrowers wished to keep the produce for themselves, and hoped eventually to gain possession of the vineyard; the ungracious guests merely refused what was being offered them. Secondly, it would be very strange behaviour for any king on the eve of his son's wedding to call out his armies, put to death the murderers of his servants, destroy by fire the city where they lived, the same city presumably in which the wedding was to be held, and then issue further invitations because the other invited guests had proved unworthy of the honour done to them. There is, to be sure, ample evidence that Jesus foretold that Israel would suffer punishment for its rejection of the Messiah, and that He predicted in detail the destruction of Jerusalem, but that He did so in the manner here recorded cannot be regarded as probable. A parable must be a consistent story and contain a semblance of actuality, however difficult it may be for the uninitiated to grasp fully the spiritual truth it embodies.

Verses 11–13 were probably not originally spoken as a continuation of the previous passage, for the guests brought in hurriedly from the highways could scarcely have been expected to arrive suitably dressed, yet only one apparently is without a wedding garment, and he is punished with what would seem to be excessive severity. The view that the garment was provided by the royal host was a guess of Augustine, but it is unsupported by any evidence. These verses are best explained on the assumption that they originally formed the conclusion of another parable, which was concerned, so it would seem, with the qualifications necessary for final inclusion in the kingdom of God. Matthew may be giving his readers a hint that verses 1–14 are in fact not a single parable by his introductory words *Jesus spake again to them by parables*.

The wedding garment is usually interpreted by Protestant exegetes as a reference to the robe of righteousness—Christ's righteousness which the Christian can put on by faith. Catholic commentators are generally of the opinion that it represents charity, for, as Paul said, 'though I have all faith, so that I could remove mountains, and have not charity, I am nothing' (1 Cor. xiii. 2).

Additional Notes

xxii. 7. *His armies* evokes the query 'Would Jesus have implied that the Roman legions which destroyed Jerusalem were *God's* armies?'

8. *Were not worthy*, as McNeile notices, 'seems a very inadequate description of the murderers of the servants'. But if it refers to those who made light of the invitation, mentioned in verse 5, it is very appropriate.

10. *Both bad and good* shows that the concept of the kingdom of God is here similar to that envisaged in the parable of the tares, and different from that presupposed in verses 11–14.

The wedding translates *numphōn* which probably refers here, as in ix. 15, to the room where the wedding feast was held (so RSV).

Furnished (*eplēsthē*) is rendered 'filled' in RV and RSV. Knox felicitously translates 'had its full tale of guests'.

12. It is at first sight strange that the king should address as *friend* (*hetaire*, 'comrade') one whom he is about to sentence to such severe punishment. Perhaps in the context in which verses 11–14 were originally uttered, Jesus had Judas directly in view as the disciple who was in the kingdom of God under false pretences. At any rate it is significant that Jesus addresses Judas in Gethsemane by the same word (xxvi. 50), found elsewhere in the New Testament only in xx. 13.

How camest thou in hither? i.e. 'how did you presume to come here?' Knox renders 'how is it that you come to be here?'

g. A series of questions (xxii. 15–46; cf. Mk. xii. 13–37 and Lk. xx. 20–44)

The spiritual leaders of Israel, against whom the parables of the two sons, the wicked husbandmen and the royal marriage feast have been directed, now indulge in more subtle tactics in an attempt to regain the initiative in the conflict between themselves and Jesus. First, the Pharisees endeavour to force Him to make some definite statement which could be used in evidence against Him. For this purpose they allied themselves with some partisans of Herod Antipas who had journeyed from Galilee to Jerusalem for the festival. It was a strange alliance, and the matter on which they tried to make Jesus commit Himself was one on which the Pharisees and the Herodians held different views; but it was dangerous for Jesus to be confronted by such a combination of ecclesiastical and secular power. The question they put to Him was introduced by ingratiating words of flattery. Jesus was an honest teacher, they said, who taught about the conduct that God required in men without fear or favour. Who therefore was better able than He to give a ruling upon the matter they would submit to His judgment? Their question was so framed that in their view it admitted of no answer except a direct 'Yes' or 'No'. And if Jesus said that it *was* lawful to pay tribute to the occupying foreign power, His answer, though not displeasing to the Herodians, would enable the Pharisees to arouse public opinion against Him, for the ordinary people regarded the Romans as their oppressors. If, on the other hand, He said that it was *not* lawful, the Pharisees would welcome the answer, but the Herodians would readily seize on it as grounds for a charge of sedition, for these courtiers knew well enough that Herod owed his position to the imperial power, and was entrusted by it with the general supervision of taxation.

But Jesus was deceived neither by the flattery of His questioners nor by the form their question took. He knew that their intentions were mischievous, and that they were concerned not with what they were or were not permitted to do in this matter, but with the quickest way by which they could catch Him out. Herein lay their hypocrisy. Instead therefore of answering 'Yes' or 'No', He bids them bring one of the silver coins in which the tax was paid, and then, holding it in His hand, asks the counter-question 'Whose likeness and inscription is this?' (RSV), to which there was only one possible answer 'Caesar's'. He then instructs them not to *give* tribute to Caesar, but to *give back* to Caesar what belongs to him, and at the same time to give back to God what belongs to God. The payment of a tax, He insists, is not a gift to him who levies it, but a debt owing to him for benefits received. Both Caesar and God have their rights; therefore to pay taxes to one is not to rob the other of His due. This all-important pronouncement of Jesus shows that He distinguished without dividing the secular and the sacred, and that He united without unifying the two spheres in which His disciples have to live. They are citizens of two cities, the earthly and the heavenly, and they have duties to discharge in both. The answer of Jesus took the Pharisees by surprise, and they made a temporary retreat.

All three Synoptic Gospels record the question put by the Sadducees to Jesus about the resurrection directly after the Pharisees' question, but Matthew alone states that it was asked on the same day, which was indeed a day of questions. The aim of the Sadducees was to discredit Jesus as a theologian by showing the logical absurdity of the orthodox Pharisaic doctrine of the resurrection, which they assumed that Jesus accepted. Their logic was based, however, upon the false premise that the material is the only reality, and that, in consequence, in the resurrection life the same conditions must prevail as in the earthly. On this assumption, if a woman, six times left a widow, was married in succession to seven brothers in order to try and obtain a physical descendant, the question *In the resurrection whose wife shall she be . . .?* would indeed be relevant, for on the resurrection day she would be faced with seven living husbands at once! But the question becomes wholly irrelevant once it is allowed that the eternal world is spiritual and immaterial. It was precisely this that the Sadducees were unwilling to accept, for they believed in neither resurrection, nor angels, nor spirit (see Acts xxiii. 8). Jesus attacks their limited view of what constitutes reality, on the ground that it is unscriptural and unduly circumscribes the power of God.

The Sadducees regarded the Pentateuch as the most important part of Scripture, and they quote the Mosaic law about levirate marriage contained in Deuteronomy xxv. 5. From this they infer that Moses could not have believed in a future life, for on their assumption that the life to come could only be a continuation of the life that now is, absurd results might follow from the law's observance, as in the case of a woman known to them, to which they draw attention. Jesus points out in reply that marriage and the propagation of the race, which it is one of the objects of marriage to secure, are supremely necessary in a world where death is a permanent factor; but they are completely unnecessary in an existence whose main characteristic is that it is deathless. He also directs their attention to another passage in the Pentateuch, the divine utterance in Exodus iii. 6, where God speaks of Himself as having a permanent relationship to the patriarchs of Israel who had long since been dead. The Sadducees had appealed to logic; so does Jesus. 'God is the God of the living only,' He argues, 'but He describes Himself as the God of Abraham, therefore Abraham is living.' It is interesting to notice that the deduction drawn by Jesus from this text depends upon the genitives being construed subjectively. 'The God of Abraham' means 'the God to whom Abraham belongs'. If the genitives are taken objectively, the same words could mean 'The God whom Abraham worshipped'. It has often been pointed out that even when the genitives are regarded as subjective, the passage does not of itself establish the doctrine of the resurrection, but only the doctrine of immortality. But Jesus, as a Jew, regards it as axiomatic that immortality implies the resurrection of the body.

The Pharisees, who were among the crowd mentioned in verse 33, were no doubt delighted that Jesus had reduced the

Sadducees to silence; but they came together not merely to gloat over the discomfiture of their opponents but to conspire further against Jesus. It is significant that the language used in verse 34 is similar to that found in the LXX of Psalm ii. 2 'the rulers (*were gathered together*) . . . against his anointed'.

The question put to Jesus by one of these Pharisees was a *test* question because, it would seem, they hoped that Jesus in His reply would say something unorthodox and startling, which would render Him liable to a charge of blasphemy. But, if this was so, the questioner was destined to be sadly disappointed, for the answer given by Jesus proved to be orthodoxy itself. He says in effect, 'The greatest commandment in the law is the one that comes first in the law, and is found in Deuteronomy vi. 5. It states that God is to be loved unreservedly with every faculty of your being. But there is a second commandment, which is a corollary to the first and akin to it, for it too makes love the dominant motive. It is written in Leviticus xix. 18 *Thou shalt love thy neighbour as thyself*. A man cannot love God in any real sense without also loving his neighbour made in God's image like himself. Every other religious or moral precept laid down in the law, or inculcated by the prophets, has divine sanction precisely because it is based on one or other of these fundamental principles.' Matthew does not record the questioner's reaction to this reply of Jesus, but there can be no doubt that he went away much discomforted.

The parallel passages in Mark xii. 28–34 and Luke x. 25–37 contain verbal similarities to this section of Matthew but also great differences. In the Marcan narrative, though the context is the same, the point of the story lies *not*, as in Matthew, in the answer given by Jesus to the lawyer's question, but in the lawyer's agreement with it and amplification of it, which evokes the approving comment 'Thou art not far from the kingdom of God'. In Luke's narrative, the context is entirely different; the lawyer asks what he shall do to inherit eternal life and himself quotes the two great commandments in reply to Jesus' question 'What is written in the law?', and the incident leads up to and concludes with the parable of the good Samaritan. In neither Mark nor Luke is the lawyer said to be *tempting* Jesus, as he is in Matthew. All efforts to solve these differences synoptically by literary source-criticism have proved unsuccessful, and it would seem best to conclude that we are dealing here with three different traditions. Each narrative is self-consistent and has the marks of verisimilitude.

The fourth of the series of questions contained in this section is put by Jesus Himself to the Pharisees. By the nature of His question He seems to imply that the questions the Pharisees and Sadducees have asked Him pale into insignificance before the all-important question 'What is *your* view of the Messiah?' It was fundamentally because they had the wrong conception of the Messiah, thinking of Him as a human warrior rather than as a divine Saviour, that they failed to see Him in Jesus. They were looking for a Son of David who would inherit the military prowess of his sire. Jesus therefore reminds them, using a type of scriptural exegesis with which they were familiar, that if David himself in an inspired utterance in Psalm cx. 1 speaks of the Messiah as *Lord*, then the Messiah must be more than David's physical descendant, who would be a national leader, greater perhaps, but similar to David himself. In other words, the Messiah, though of Davidic descent, is also of divine origin. David's Son is David's God. Such a logical exposition of one of the key psalms reduced the Pharisees to silence. Their attempts, moreover, to trap Jesus in what He said had also failed, and, as the evangelist notes in conclusion, were now abandoned.

Additional Notes

xxii. 16. *Herodians* was probably a nickname for Herod's supporters. They are mentioned elsewhere in the New Testament only in Mark iii. 6.

Neither carest thou for any man: for thou regardest not the person of men is archaic. The meaning is better conveyed in Knox 'thou holdest no-one in awe, making no distinction between man and man'.

17. *Tribute* renders *kēnson* (the Latin *census*), which was a poll-tax levied on all adult persons and paid directly to the imperial exchequer. It is distinguished from *telē*, the word used for indirect taxes levied through the customs.

19. *Penny* was a silver *denarius* specially minted for taxation purposes. Knox brings this out by translating 'Show me the coinage in which the tax is paid'.

21. *Render* translates *apodote*, 'pay back', which is in contrast to *give (dounai)* in verse 17.

23. *The Sadducees* were the priestly aristocracy of Israel and very influential with the wealthy classes. They were not resentful of Gentile influences and were anxious above all else to maintain the political *status quo*, for under the Romans they felt themselves to be secure. This is the only *direct* encounter Jesus had with the Sadducees.

Which say. The best attested reading is 'saying'. If this is adopted, the Sadducees were stating their denial of the resurrection as a prelude to their question.

24. The law referred to here was called the law of levirate marriage from the Latin *levir*, a brother-in-law.

25. The words *with us* are found in Matthew only. The narratives of Mark and Luke allow the reader to conclude that the Sadducees were giving an imaginary illustration.

31. The words *unto you* are peculiar to Matthew, and show that Jesus regarded the utterances of God recorded in Scripture as relevant for men of every age.

34. *Were gathered together.* As the aorist tense in the original is probably inceptive, the translation should be 'came together' (RSV) or 'met together' (Knox). A less well-attested reading has 'round him' instead of *together (eis auton* for *eis auto)*.

35. A small but important combination of textual authorities omit *lawyer (nomikos)*. As Matthew never uses this word but usually speaks of 'scribe' (*grammateus*), and as Luke constantly substitutes 'lawyer' for 'scribe', it is probable that *lawyer* should be omitted in this verse.

36. Although *the great* is the literal rendering of the original, the positive is often used in Hellenistic Greek for the other degrees of comparison, and the probable meaning here is 'the greatest'.

37. These words were known to the Jews as the *Shema* from the Hebrew root meaning 'hear'. The introductory words in Deuteronomy vi. 4 are 'Hear, O Israel; the Lord our God is one Lord'. The *Shema* was recited twice daily.

38. *First and great.* The most ancient MSS have these words in reverse order, which perhaps makes better sense (see the commentary).

39. It is probable, though not certain, that Jesus was the first to draw together in this way Deuteronomy vi. 5 and Leviticus xix. 18.

41. *Were gathered together.* The sense is probably rightly brought out in Knox's rendering 'were still gathered about him'.

XIII. DENUNCIATION OF THE SCRIBES AND PHARISEES (xxiii. 1–39; cf. Mk. xii. 38–40; Lk. xi. 39–50, xiii. 34, 35)

It would seem evident that in this chapter Matthew has assembled sayings uttered by Jesus on various occasions against those scribes and Pharisees, whose elaboration of the law had become burdensome to ordinary people, and whose practice often belied their teaching. It is important to remember in reading this chapter that not *all* the Pharisees came under the condemnation of Jesus, and that there were good and bad Pharisees just as there have always been, and still are, good and bad Christians. In fact, the failings exposed in this section tend to be the failings of all whose zeal for religion is untempered by charity, mercy and commonsense. This discourse, addressed to *the multitudes* as well as *to his disciples*, is the last *public* utterance of Jesus recorded by this evangelist; and it may be (though the point cannot be pressed) that Matthew, who seems to have envisaged Jesus the Messiah as the second and greater Moses, was influenced in the way in which he has arranged his material by the pattern of Deuteronomy xxxii. 1–40. In Levertoff's words 'In the so-called "Song of Moses", the first redeemer at the close of his life sang of Israel's ingratitude and lapse into idolatry, and of God's goodness. The poem begins reproachfully; but tenderness and pity prevail above severity, and towards the close the strain rises into one of positive encouragement and promise. Similarly, Jesus, the last Redeemer, in the last days of His ministry, denounces the spiritual leaders of the people with seeming harshness, like all the prophets, and yet with tender pity He laments over Jerusalem.'

At the outset of the discourse Jesus recognizes the rightful claims of the scribes, the legal experts of the Pharisaic party, to be exponents of the law; and so long as they confine themselves to that task, their words, He insists, are to be respected, even if the conduct of some of them is inconsistent with their teaching (2, 3). But when they insist upon a meticulous observance of the minutiae of the law, or unreasonably extend the sphere in which a particular precept is to be regarded as operative, or enjoin new precepts for which there is no authority in the law itself, they become not the guides but the oppressors of mankind (4). Real religion is in essence an inward and unseen relationship between the human soul and God. It is true that this inward experience must find outward expression; but that outward expression must be natural and unselfconscious, and have nothing about it that savours of the religious exhibitionist, who has his eye all the time on his audience and is determined to be recognized and accepted for the religious man that he feels himself to be. Pride of place, the love of power, and the influence over others that the possession of such things as professional and ecclesiastical titles tends to bring with it, were ruining the spiritual influence of many of the Pharisees in the days of Jesus; and they were used by Him as a severe warning to all who would acknowledge Him as Lord and Master, and spend their lives in humble service as children of the one heavenly Father—a warning that only too often has gone unheeded by many who have called themselves by His name (5–12).

In the AV eight 'woes' follow; but it is almost certain that they should be reduced to seven, for the 'woe' contained in verse 14, which is omitted in RV, is not found in the most ancient witnesses to the text, and would seem to have been a later insertion into the text of Matthew from Mark xii. 40 and Luke xx. 47. It is intrinsically probable that our evangelist, with his Jewish fondness for the symbolism of numbers, made a collection of *seven*. These 'woes' are not so much curses as expressions of sorrow, and a better translation would be 'Alas for you' rather than *Woe unto you. Corruptio optimi pessima*, and nothing is sadder or more deleterious in its results than the perversion of religion. Jesus grieves for the harm that these 'hypocritical' scribes and Pharisees are doing to others, and for the inevitable doom that they are bringing upon themselves.

Pharisaic 'hypocrisy' was expressing itself in many ways. In the first place, those who were guilty of it were not accepting the offer of the kingdom of God being made to them by Jesus the Messiah; and by insisting on works of the law as the sole ground of acceptance with God, were standing in the way of others who were willing to accept it on the only two conditions that are essential, repentance and faith (13). Secondly, the Jerusalem scribes were trying to spread their influence in the more liberal synagogues dispersed throughout the Hellenistic world, and were insisting that all converts from paganism should submit to the full yoke of the law as they themselves imposed it. The result was that the *con*verted tended to become the *per*verted (15). Thirdly, the hair-splitting casuistry which sought to differentiate between oaths that were binding and those that were not, was evidence of a wholly inadequate recognition of God as the sole Creator and Governor of the universe (16–22). Fourthly, the lack of a sense of proportion shown in the excessive amplification of the ritual precepts of the law went hand-in-hand with a failure to give priority to the fundamental moral precepts, without which no life could be lived that was pleasing to God (23, 24). Fifthly, the scrupulous attention paid by some of the scribes and Pharisees to the externals of religion, particularly to the careful cleansing of vessels used in ritual observances, made them forget how utterly worthless such externals are if the inward and hidden motives of the heart are not pure and disinterested (25, 26). Sixthly, an outward religious conformity, which gave the appearance of an active spiritual life, only too often concealed an inward corruption that bespoke certain mortality (27, 28). Finally, the leaders of Israel, so far from remaining in the true line of descent from their great spiritual forbears, seemed to have inherited the worst tendencies of their predecessors. The murderous lust that had led to the persecution of so many of God's prophets in the past was still in their blood; and it would not be fully satisfied till the Messiah's own prophets, wise men and scribes had been subjected to a similar fate. But the hour in which that satisfaction would be made would also be the hour of judgment, in which punishment for the sins of all the fathers would be visited on that generation of their children. The destruction of Jerusalem would mark the end of the old Israel (29-36).

This terrible prophecy of Jesus was uttered in no spirit of vindictiveness, but, as the most moving lament over Jerusalem bears eloquent testimony, was truth spoken in love. Luke, who records that Jesus spoke these words as He looked down on the city before He entered it for the last time, states that He spoke with tears in His eyes (Lk. xix. 41). Jesus sorrowed with a patriot's grief for the faithlessness of His fellow-countrymen. He mourned over their failure to reach their high destiny; and He recalled the numerous occasions when He would have sheltered them, if only they had been willing, from the wrath that was coming upon them in the onslaught of the Roman legions, even as a bird shelters her young from the coming storm. But they were rejecting God's Messiah; and because they were abandoning their Saviour, the saving presence of their God would be withdrawn from their city and its Temple. Never again would they see Jesus, until He returned with His glory unveiled and acknowledged by all as God's Representative, the Messiah come in judgment (37-39).

Additional Notes

xxiii. 2. *Sit in Moses' seat*, i.e. they are the proper exponents of the Mosaic law. The rabbis *sat* to teach; hence the metaphorical expression, still current, that speaks of a duly appointed exponent of a subject as occupying a professorial 'chair'.

4. The best attested reading is 'And' instead of *For*. This verse introduces a fresh point and does not give the reason for the assertion at the end of verse 3.

The picture here is of the merciless camel-driver who makes up heavy packs containing ill-assorted articles of all sizes, and then after placing them upon the animal's shoulders stands by and does nothing to adjust the burden.

5. *Phylacteries* translates a Greek word meaning by derivation 'fortified places', which came to be used for 'protective charms'. They were strips of parchment inscribed with portions of the law and enclosed in leather boxes, which were fastened by straps to the left arm and the forehead (see Dt. vi. 4-9, xi. 13-21).

The borders of their garments were fringes attached to the dress, and so arranged that they symbolized the main precepts of the law. Jesus Himself wore such a fringe (see ix. 2). What He condemns is the enlargement of them solely for the purpose of display.

6. *The uppermost rooms.* RV, better, 'the chief place'. The guests reclined on couches, and each place had its own degree of dignity.

The chief seats were those in the highest part of the synagogue facing the congregation.

7. *Greetings.* In the original there is the definite article which probably signifies 'the (accustomed) greetings'.

In the oldest MSS *Rabbi* is only mentioned once. The word means 'my great one'.

8. *Ye* is emphatic in the Greek. '*You* are not to be called Rabbi.'

Master translates *didaskalos*, better rendered 'teacher' as in RV.

Even Christ should be omitted from this verse, as in RV. It is a later insertion from verse 10 where it is genuine.

9. *Father*. The Aramaic equivalent would make it clear that 'spiritual father' is meant. As McNeile says, 'Abba was not commonly a mode of address to a living person, but a title of honour for Rabbis and great ones of the past'. Hence the significance of *upon the earth*.

10. *Master* renders *kathēgētēs* which means a guide, or instructor occupying a position of authority, such as a master at a school or a professor in a university. The word in modern Greek means 'professor'.

13. *Neither go in* is probably a strict present. 'You are not now going in, though the opportunity is being given you.'

15. *The child of hell* is literally 'a son of Gehenna', a Jewish expression meaning 'worthy of suffering punishment in the after-life'. It is well known that those who exchange one religion for another are more likely to show an intemperate zeal for their new religion, than those who have experienced no such drastic change. So the converts of the Pharisees tended to become even more Pharisaic than the Pharisees themselves.

16. The scribes tried to distinguish between oaths made by the Temple or the altar, on the one hand, which could be disregarded, and oaths made by the golden vessels in the Temple or the gifts laid on the altar, on the other hand, which were binding. Jesus reverses their standards of judgment, showing that it is the Temple that hallows the gold, and the altar the gift. He also exposes the folly of those who imagine that inanimate things can witness an oath. God is the primary source of all that is. All oaths therefore are in effect made 'by God'.

17. *Fools and blind*. Stupidity being *wilful* blindness is a moral failing.

18. *Guilty*. RV better 'debtor', i.e. 'bound by his oath'.

23. It is very improbable that Jesus uttered the last words of this verse *these ought ye to have done, and not to leave the other undone*, for they contradict His argument. The point is that the Mosaic law enacted that 'all the tithe of the land, whether of the seed of the land, or of the fruit of the tree, is the Lord's' (Lv. xxvii. 30), and the scribes *wrongly* extended this to the tiniest and commonest herbs. Although there is no MSS evidence for the omission of these words, the rhythm of the passage is against them. There would seem to be a triple rhythm in most of these 'woes'. Compare for example verses 23, 24 on the one hand, and verses 25, 26 on the other in the RV.

i. ye tithe mint and anise and cummin,
ii. and have left undone the weightier matters of the law, judgement, and mercy, and faith.
iii. Ye blind guides, which strain out the gnat, and swallow the camel (23, 24).

i. ye cleanse the outside of the cup and of the platter,
ii. but within they are full from extortion and excess.
iii. Thou blind Pharisee, cleanse first the inside of the cup and of the platter, etc. (25, 26).

We may assume that the suspected words were originally a marginal comment made by a stringent Jewish Christian, which subsequently became inserted in the text.

23. *Faith* here means 'faithfulness'. For *the weightier matters of the law* cf. Micah vi. 8.

24. *Strain at* is a curious mistake for 'strain out' (as RV). The *gnat* is a tiny insect bred during the process of fermentation. The point of this humorous saying lies in the contrast between the size of the two animals mentioned.

25. *Full of extortion and excess* means 'full of produce gained by sweated labour and profiteering'.

27. *Whited sepulchres* probably refer, as McNeile suggests, not to the practice of whitewashing tombs at festival time so that pilgrims might not be contaminated by coming into touch with them, but to the ornamental plastering of the walls of the more ornate sepulchres which would make them appear beautiful.

32. These words are ironical, and mean either 'Make up what was lacking in your fathers' guilt', or 'Go on till you reach the degree of guilt your fathers reached'.

33. *Damnation* (*krisis*) is better rendered 'judgement' in RV.

34. *Wherefore*, better rendered 'therefore' in RV, points forward to *that* at the beginning of verse 35. It is in order that they may have the opportunity of 'filling up the measure of their fathers' guilt, that Christ will send His prophets, wise men and scribes, some of whom, like James and Stephen, will be directly or indirectly murdered by the Jews, and others of whom, such as Paul, will be scourged in the Jewish synagogues and hounded from city to city.

35. The blood of innocent men that is to be unjustly shed by the death of the Messiah and His servants will make it possible for the destruction of Jerusalem in AD 70 to be in effect a judgment upon the murderers of all God's servants whose deaths are recorded in the canonical Scripture. Of these Abel is the first, and Zechariah the priestly son of Jehoiada the last (see Gn. iv. 8 and 2 Ch. xxiv. 20, 21, 2 Chronicles being placed last in the Hebrew Bible). The evangelist has made a slip in referring to *this* Zacharias as *son of Barachias*, as though he was the prophet Zechariah.

38. *Desolate* is omitted in many ancient MSS. Without it, the sense of the passage is 'Your house is left to your own devices, God having withdrawn His presence from it.' If *desolate* is read, the sentence is a prediction of the desolation that would be caused after the destruction of the city by the Romans.

XIV. THE FALL OF JERUSALEM AND THE PAROUSIA OF THE SON OF MAN (xxiv. 1–51; cf. Mk. xiii. 1–32; Lk. xxi. 5–23, xvii. 26, 27, 34, 35, xii. 39–46)

In this very difficult section the evangelist has brought to-gether sayings of Jesus which foretold the downfall of Jerusalem and the final coming of the Son of man in judgment. As the language in which these events is expressed is partly literal and partly symbolic, and as Jesus would seem to have regarded both of them as 'comings' in judgment, scholars have found it extremely difficult to say with any degree of certainty which parts of the chapter contain an answer to the question of the disciples *When shall these things be?* (viz. the destruction of the temple buildings mentioned in verse 2), and which parts are a response to their supplementary question *And what shall be the sign of thy coming, and of the end of the world?*[1]

It would seem that the disciples, by placing these two questions in juxtaposition, associated very closely in their minds the impending fall of Jerusalem and the *coming* of Jesus which would mark the end of the present age. In one sense they were right to do so, for in the fall of Jerusalem judgment would be passed upon the old Israel, so that it would no longer be exclusively the people of God; and at the parousia the Son of man would 'come again to judge both the quick and the dead'. But Jesus seems anxious that the disciples should not suppose that these two 'judgments' would of necessity follow in immediate chronological sequence. Accordingly, in the teaching recorded in verses 5–14 He warns them not to be misled by the deceptive utterances of false Messiahs who would appear from time to time, and not to imagine that events which might seem to be cataclysmic in character, such as wars between nations, earthquakes, and widespread famines, were infallible signs that the end was near. Such happenings would in fact constitute the prolonged birth-pangs of the new age.

[1] For a thorough discussion of the problems raised by this chapter and its parallels in the other Gospels, and for an exhaustive account of the history of the various attempts to solve them, the reader is directed to G. R. Beasley-Murray, *Jesus and the Future* (Macmillan, 1954). The book will be found valuable even by those who cannot accept the author's solution.

The end would only come, as He states explicitly in verse 14, after world-wide evangelism; and that evangelism would be continually hampered by persecutions, martyrdoms, the hatred of the world for those who professed the name of Jesus, loss of faith, the treachery of friends and the failure of love to endure in the face of widespread lawlessness—conditions which would call for the supreme quality of steadfastness (9–13). As Butler has well said (p. 8c):

'Matthew xxiv. 5–14 gives a straightforward anticipation of the whole of future history (in reference to the question about the consummation of the age), warning the disciples that secular catastrophes must not be taken as signs of the imminent end of history; forecasting, briefly, the world's persecution of the Church; and working to a poignant climax which foretells defections from the Church, false prophets and spiritual decay and treason within the Christian body itself, . . . and reaching its culmination in the prophecy of the universal proclamation of the gospel of the kingdom—"and then will come the end".'

Verses 15–28 would seem to refer exclusively to the fall of Jerusalem which would mark the end of one era and the beginning of another. The appearance of *the abomination of desolation* (see additional note) would be an indication that the time had come for the inhabitants of *Judaea* not to seek refuge in Jerusalem, but to escape over the hills immediately and so speedily that there would be no time to salvage their belongings. And because wintry conditions and a strict observance of the law of sabbath-observance would greatly impede such a flight, the disciples were to pray that climatic conditions would be favourable and that it would not have to be made on a sabbath. The oncoming Roman legions would cause distress on a scale unprecedented and restricted only by the merciful intervention of God, who *for the elect's sake* would limit its duration. This distress would be particularly severe for pregnant women and women with children at the breast (15–22).

The chosen people of God would naturally look out expectantly for Christ to return and succour them during the days of this great tribulation. There would therefore be a danger, against which Jesus now warns His disciples, of listening to rumours that the Messiah *had* returned and could be seen in some lonely spot in the Judaean wilderness or in some inner room in the beleaguered city. In fact, however, though false Messiahs and false prophets would deceive many during those days of tension by their pretentious displays, they would be powerless to influence God's chosen, however eager they might be to do so. Nevertheless, the elect would have to endure the anguish of those terrible days alone, for it was not *then*, while the 'eagles' of the Roman army were swooping down upon the 'corpse' of the city, that the Son of man would come to avenge His people. Moreover, of His final coming there would be no preliminary signs. It would be as instantaneous and as universal as a flash of lightning (23–28).

It would seem that the words *Immediately after the tribulation of those days* in verse 29 make it necessary for the reader of this Gospel to assume that the events described in the symbolic language of Jewish prophecy in verses 29–31 would take place directly after the downfall of Jerusalem. If, therefore, reference in those verses is to the final return of the Son of man in judgment, it is necessary to come to the unsatisfactory conclusion that Jesus was mistaken, for His parousia did not come immediately after the catastrophe of AD 70. This conclusion would, moreover, conflict both with verse 27, where the implication is that there will be no preliminary signs to His final return, and also with verse 36, where He is reported as saying that only His Father knew the day and the hour of the consummation of the age. Some scholars do not hesitate to draw this conclusion. But most orthodox commentators have so recoiled from its implications that they have fallen back upon the theory of the 'Little Apocalypse' first put forward by Colani in 1864. This assumes that much of this discourse, and the verses at present under discussion in particular, are drawn from an early Jewish Christian Apocalypse and are not the *ipsissima verba* of Jesus.

But, we may well ask, are these the only possible alternatives? Is it not also possible to regard these verses as a cryptic description in the symbolism of poetry of the Roman conquest of Jerusalem and of the spread of the Christian Church which followed it? The sack of 'the holy city' in which over a million people were slain would inevitably appear to those who witnessed it a world-catastrophe of the greatest magnitude; and only language symbolic of cosmic disturbance, such as the darkening of the sun, the failure of the moon to give light, and stars falling from the sky, was adequate to describe it. In using such language Jesus was following the example of the ancient prophets. As Levertoff remarks (p. 80), 'These are figures, or symbols of divine acts effecting great changes in the world, and are not to be taken literally. The Old Testament prophets employed such imagery in their announcements of God's interventions in the history of nations; cf. Is. xiii. 10, xxxiv. 4; Am. viii. 9; Ezk. xxxii. 7, 8; Joel ii. 28–32.' Indeed, poets all down the ages have used such language to describe the upheaval caused by cataclysmic historical events. Thus in our own day A. E. Housman in his poem *Epitaph on an Army of Mercenaries* refers to the first world war as 'the day when Heaven was falling, the hour when Earth's foundation fled'. It may well be, then, that R. A. Knox is right when he says 'You must understand the portents of verse 29 as an allegorical way of referring to dynastic changes (AD 69–70 was "the year of the four emperors"); and you must identify "the coming of the Son of man" in verse 30 with some verified experience, e.g. the voice which was heard, according to Tacitus, crying out "The gods are departing".'[1] The type of language used by the Roman historian in the passage from which this quotation is taken is certainly instructive. 'Contending hosts were seen meeting in the skies, arms flashed, and suddenly the Temple was illumined with fire from the clouds. Of a sudden the doors of the shrine opened and a superhuman voice cried: "The gods are departing": at the same moment the mighty stir of their going was heard.'[2] The destruction of the Jerusalem Temple was indeed a divine visitation, which one familiar with the language of Jewish prophecy could describe as a coming of the Son of man on *the clouds of heaven with power*

[1] *The Epistles and Gospels*, p. 11.
[2] Tacitus, *History*, 5.13 (Loeb translation).

and great glory. It was in fact only after the old order ended with the destruction of the Temple that world evangelism by the Christian Church, now entirely separate from Judaism, could be conducted in earnest. Not till then could the *trumpet* of the gospel be sounded throughout the world. Not till then could the Son of man, having 'visited' the old Israel in judgment, *send his angels* (i.e. His messengers) to *gather together his elect from the four winds, from one end of heaven to the other*, a result which could be obtained only when the gospel had been preached to the whole world (29–31).

On the assumption that verses describing 'the signs of the times' in this chapter invariably refer to events preceding the downfall of Jerusalem, and not to events heralding the final coming of the Son of man, an assumption which would seem to be justified by verses 27 and 36, it is necessary to regard the illustration drawn from the fig tree and the sayings which accompany it, recorded in verses 32–34, as a reference to the events of AD 69–70. Jesus is here saying in effect that it will be as certain that Jerusalem will fall when *all these things* (i.e. the appearance of the abomination of desolation, and the advent of false Messiahs, etc.) have become apparent, as it is certain that summer will follow when the first leaves are seen on the fig tree's tender branches. Moreover, the generation He is addressing will live to see it all. So sure is He of this, that He affirms that His words on this, as on other subjects, will be shown to possess everlasting power and validity (32–35).

On the other hand, Jesus makes it clear that there is no means of foretelling the precise events which will usher in the end of the age and the final coming of the Son of man, because those events will be as unforeseen and as unexpected as the coming of the flood in the days of Noah, or the breaking into a house by a burglar. Men and women will be engaged upon their usual occupations, cultivating the fields, grinding corn at the mills, enjoying the conviviality of human fellowship, marrying and giving their children in marriage, when in a moment when He is least expected the Son of man will come. The supplementary question of the disciples, recorded in verse 1, *And what shall be the sign of thy coming, and of the end of the world?* is thus shown to be both irrelevant and unanswerable. But there is an all-important moral to be learned from the very fact that it *is* unanswerable. As Jesus makes clear in verses 42–44, His disciples must be prepared for the unexpected; they must not be like a robbed householder who has allowed his home to be broken into because he has failed to realize that burglars do not advertise beforehand the hour of their arrival! Above all, as the following parable of the faithful and unfaithful servants shows, those who have been placed by their Lord in positions of special responsibility, the leaders and teachers of the Christian Church, must be so continuously and faithfully occupied with their work, that when He returns they will be found rendering service to their Lord by 'feeding' the members of His household. On the other hand, should they 'trade upon' the apparent delay in their Lord's return, and bully those committed to their charge, and make the satisfaction of their own appetites their primary concern, their ultimate fate will be no better than that of the hypocritical Pharisees so sternly denounced in the previous chapters (42–51).

Additional Notes

xxiv. 1. *Went out, and departed from the temple.* As the most ancient MSS have *from the temple* after *went out*, and as *departed* in the original is in the imperfect tense, the right translation is 'left the temple and was going away' (RSV).

3. In the present commentary it has been assumed that the answer to the disciples' first question is contained in verses 15–35, and that their second question, to which no definite answer was possible, conditions the subject-matter of verses 4–14 and 36–51.

The word translated *coming, parousia,* is the technical term in the Epistles for what is commonly called the 'second' coming of Jesus. It is found in the Synoptic Gospels only in this chapter. For its significance see the present author's *Tyndale Commentary on the Epistle of James,* pp. 117, 118.

15. The expressions *spoken of by Daniel the prophet* and *stand in the holy place* are peculiar to Matthew; and it is generally agreed that the words *whoso readeth, let him understand*, found also in Mark, are the comments of the evangelists who wish to draw their readers' attention to this further fulfilment of the prophet's words.

The abomination of desolation is a rendering, influenced by the Vulgate *abominationem desolationis*, of the Greek *to bdelugma tēs erēmōseōs*, which is the LXX translation of words which in the Hebrew mean 'the appalling abomination' (see Dn. xi. 31 and xii. 11). The desecration of the Temple by Antiochus Epiphanes who set up a heathen altar within the sacred precincts in 168 BC was such an abomination (see 2 Macc. vi. 1–13). As the emperor Caligula in AD 38 attempted to erect a statue of himself in the Temple, it is often thought that it is this act of impiety which accounts for the language of the present verse. But a reference to some idol or statue erected in the Temple does not seem to be in keeping with the present context, where the appearance of *the abomination of desolation* is regarded as the *first* indication that an attack upon Jerusalem is imminent, and as the sign for the inhabitants in the outlying parts of *Judaea* to take immediately to the hills. Instead of *stand in the holy place*, Mark has 'standing where it ought not' (RV, following the most ancient text, 'where *he* ought not'); while Luke has paraphrased the expression in the words 'when ye shall see Jerusalem compassed with armies'. It would seem highly probable that the clue to the meaning of *the abomination of desolation* is to be found in Luke. And this probability is rendered more certain, when we notice that the words *standing in the holy place* are omitted from Matthew in the very important Sinaitic MS of the Old Syriac version, and that the Syriac tradition as a whole understands the cryptic words from Daniel to mean 'the abominable sign'. It may well be that in this matter the Syriac versions have preserved the meaning of Jesus better than the Greek. The 'abominable sign' would most naturally refer to the ensign carried by the Roman soldiers to which the image of the emperor was attached. There is much evidence that this was most abhorrent to the idol-hating Jews; and the sight of it, as the Roman legions approached Judaea, would readily be accepted as the sign for the flight to begin.

For a comprehensive account of the various ways in which this most difficult verse has been understood reference should be made to G. R. Beasley-Murray, *A Commentary on Mark Thirteen* (Macmillan, 1957), pp. 59–72.

16. When the crisis came the Jewish Christians fled to Pella in Peroea, one of the towns in the Decapolis. To reach this they had to make a journey of some 100 miles across the hills of Judaea and Moab.

18. *Clothes*. In the most ancient MSS this word is found in the singular. So RV 'cloke', i.e. the outer garment which the labourer in the field would throw off while working.

22. The actual siege of Jerusalem began early in the year AD 70, and Titus entered the city about September 12.

28. It may be that this proverbial saying should be interpreted in close connection with verse 27 and therefore with reference to the final judgment. So Levertoff paraphrases (p. 79): 'just as when life has abandoned a body, and it becomes a corpse, the vultures immediately swoop down upon it; so when the world has become rotten with evil, the Son of Man and His angels will come to execute the divine judgment.' On the other hand, as has been suggested in the commentary, Jesus may well have had in mind the eagles carried on the Roman standards, in which case the reference is to the fall of Jerusalem. So Knox comments: 'The lifeless corpse of Judaism will naturally attract to itself the carrion eagles of Rome—attract them to a definite spot' (*The Epistles and Gospels*, p. 278).

30. If this verse refers to the parousia, the translation *all the tribes of the earth*, i.e. 'all the people of the world', is right. But if, as has been suggested in the commentary, the reference is to the conditions prevailing when Jerusalem was being attacked, the translation should be 'all the tribes of the land' (so Knox), i.e. the land of Judaea (cf. Zc. xii. 12).

33. *It is near.* In Matthew and Mark no subject is expressed in the original. In Luke the subject is 'the kingdom of God'. Those who interpret this section with reference to the parousia supply as the subject 'he' (so RV and RSV) or 'the end'. The exegesis in the present commentary assumes that *it* is the right subject (so Knox) and that the reference is to the downfall of Jerusalem.

36. It is very strange that in spite of these words so many have wasted their time in the vain attempt to decide for themselves the date when the parousia may be expected.

42. The best attested reading is 'on what day' (RV) rather than *what hour.*

43. *The goodman of the house* is archaic English for 'the head of the household'.

45. The translation should be '*the* faithful' rather than *a* faithful, as there is the definite article in the original.

XV. THREE PARABLES OF JUDGMENT (xxv. 1-46)
a. The ten virgins (xxv. 1-13; Matthew only, but cf. Lk. xii. 35-37)

Although the first word in verse 1 *Then* (*tote*) is often in this Gospel merely a transitional particle with no chronological significance, it would seem that it should here be construed in a temporal sense, the reference being to the *day* that has played such a large part in the previous section. So Knox rightly renders, 'When that day comes, the kingdom of heaven will be like. . . .' In chapter xxiv, the certainty and the suddenness of the parousia, and the paramount necessity for disciples to be ready for it, have been most solemnly stressed. The parable of the ten virgins is complementary to the parable of the faithful and unfaithful servants which immediately precedes it. In it a further picture is given of the predicament in which disciples will find themselves at the parousia if they have failed to prepare themselves for it. The day of opportunity, they will then discover, will have passed for ever; and the time will have come for a speedy and permanent separation to be effected between those who are prepared to enter into the eternal life made possible for them by Him whom they have accepted as their King, and those who, though nominally subjects of that King, have failed through thoughtlessness, lack of foresight, or irresponsibility to discharge their spiritual obligations. Against the latter the way into the marriage feast, a symbol of the joy of the kingdom of heaven, will be permanently barred. There is a terrible finality about the words *and the door was shut* (10).

This close connection between the parable and the teaching about the parousia in the previous chapter makes it difficult for the reader to envisage the precise feature in the marriage customs of the Jews, which is here being used as an illustration. Normally, in the time of Jesus, there were three stages in matrimonial procedure. First came *the engagement*, when a formal settlement was made by the respective fathers of the bride and bridegroom. This was followed by *the betrothal*, a ceremony held in the house of the bride's parents, when mutual promises were made by the contracting parties before witnesses and presents were given by the bridegroom to his betrothed. 'The man and the woman were bound to one another by the betrothal ceremony, though they were not yet actually man and wife; in fact, so binding was the betrothal that if the man died during the period that it lasted the woman was regarded as a widow; the cancelling of a betrothal was not permitted; if, however, such a thing took place, it was parallel to divorce.'[1] Finally, after the lapse of about a year there was *the marriage*, when the bridegroom accompanied by his friends went to fetch the bride from her father's house and brought her back in procession to his own home where the marriage feast was held. It is most probable that it is *this* procession that the ten girls in the story are pictured as going to meet, though whether as official bridesmaids, servants of the bridegroom, or children of friends and neighbours we have no means of knowing.

[1] W. O. E. Oesterley, *The Gospel Parables in the Light of their Jewish Background* (S.P.C.K., 1936), p. 134.

Because the parable is concerned with the parousia of the Son of man, the bridegroom is the central figure. No mention is made of the bride either in verse 1, or in the call to action in verse 6 *Behold, the bridegroom cometh*, or in the arrival of the marriage party in verse 10. It is true that the words 'and the bride' are found after *the bridegroom* in verse 1 in the Old Latin versions and the Latin Vulgate, in the Greek of the bi-lingual Codex Bezae, and in the Syriac versions, a strong combination of witnesses, but this is probably not the original reading and it is not followed in the English versions. The words were added later, it would seem, to bring the story more into line with Jewish wedding customs. On the other hand, some scholars have argued for their originality on the ground that it is reasonable to suppose that they would have been omitted when it became customary to think of Jesus as the heavenly Bridegroom and of the Church as His bride in the light of Ephesians v. 25. But if the primary purpose of the parable was to stress the importance of being prepared for the final coming of Jesus (a supposition which both the context in which the parable is found and its concluding admonition would seem to compel the reader to make), mention of the bride would have been misleading. It is, moreover, the ten virgins in the story who represent the Church waiting for the return of its Lord. The Church contains, it is implied, both those who are prepared and those who are unprepared, though not necessarily in equal proportion, for the words *five of them were wise, and five were foolish* have a general but not an exact significance.

What differentiates the *foolish* from the *wise* is precisely the failure of the former to face the possibility that the bridegroom, their returning Lord, may come earlier or later than they expect, and that in any case the coming will be so sudden that it will afford no opportunity for making good deficiencies which are then discovered. The statement in verse 7 that all the girls 'grew drowsy and fell asleep' (Knox) is not made by way of recrimination, but to throw into relief the truth that when they were eventually roused there was no time for them to do anything except re-fuel their lamps. Nor could those who had the spare oil in their flasks necessary for this purpose render last-minute assistance to those who had come without it. Saving grace, it is here taught, is a personal possession and untransferable. When the final day of salvation comes none can deliver his brother. Each man is in this respect the arbiter of his own destiny. This truth is underlined in the reply of the wise, when they are asked to share their spare supplies with the foolish, *Not so; lest there be not enough for us and you.* RV and RSV make this reply much more polite but far less decisive: 'peradventure (RSV 'perhaps') there will not be enough for us and you'. But if the reading *mēpote ou mē arkesē* is followed rather than the variant *mēpote ouk arkesē*, the answer *could* be, and perhaps *should* be less polite and more emphatic 'Never! there will certainly not be enough for us and you'. This uncompromising refusal is followed by the semi-ironical injunction *go ye rather to them that sell, and buy for yourselves.* As it was now after midnight it is not surprising that the purchase could not be made in time!

The parable ends with the command to be vigilant and ready, and with a reasoned statement for it which echoes xxiv. 36. The day and the hour of the parousia remain unknown. The explanatory addition *wherein the Son of man cometh* is absent from the most ancient authorities for the text, and should be omitted as in RV.

b. Entrusted wealth (xxv. 14-30; cf. Lk. xix. 11-27)

It is unfortunate that this parable should be generally known as the parable of the talents, for the word 'talent' in contemporary English refers exclusively to the natural aptitude and inherent ability of certain people for certain functions. The parable is in no way concerned, however, with those who are 'talented' in this sense. On the contrary, the *talents* in the parable *belong to someone else*, and are entrusted by him to others to be used not only in their interest but in his.

A business man going abroad hands over to three men in his employment capital sums for them to trade with profitably during his absence. The amount of the sums given to the different men varies in accordance with their proved business ability. The *talent*, of which the parable speaks, was not a coin, but a measure or weight of money, which was sometimes paid in minted coins and sometimes in bars of gold or bullion. It is not in the least necessary for the understanding of the story to try and determine the exact value in modern currency of the talent. The point is simply that different amounts of money were entrusted to the three servants, and that the two who received the larger sums used them in profitable transactions and so doubled their value, while the man who received the smallest sum was so afraid of losing it that he buried it in the ground, where he knew that at least it would be out of the range of burglars and not subject to the hazards of a fluctuating money market.

On the return of their 'chief', the first two men are congratulated by him for the practical evidence of their trustworthiness, given the opportunity for larger enterprises, and allowed to share in his delight. But the third man, who tries to excuse himself, finds that he is himself accused. He is condemned as a lazy ne'er-do-well, and told that even if he had felt inhibited from doing business by a mistaken estimate of the character of his master, he ought at least to have deposited the money with the bankers so that it might have made compound interest. What he *had* done was to treat it as a dead thing, which like all dead things was better buried! But, in fact, money is a living thing, as such expressions as 'current coinage', 'money in circulation', 'money talks', clearly show; and it is interesting to notice in this connection that the Greek word *tokos*, translated *usury* (archaic for 'interest') in verse 27, means 'offspring'. Interest is the 'child' of capital. The over-caution of the third servant is treated as a breach of trust, for he was not dealing with his own money but with someone else's; and the sum committed to him is now transferred to the man who has proved to be the most enterprising and successful. The evangelist bids his readers see in this transference another illustration of some words of Jesus recorded in xiii. 12, and he now quotes them again in verse 29. But it is very doubtful whether they formed part of the parable as originally spoken by Jesus. Not only would verse 30 follow more naturally verse 28, but the saying in verse 29, as McNeile points out, 'cannot be applied to the five talents given to the first servant and the five which he gained; for these are a trust, while *echein* ('to have') describes a real possession, a real condition of heart and life. The true *echein* in the present case is the character shown in faithful diligence, and the increase which could be "given" would be the higher degrees of faithful diligence to which he could advance. But this would be as true of the second servant as of the first.'

The high light of the parable is not therefore to be found in verse 29 but in the sentence passed on the third servant for his timorous and faithless inactivity; and with that the story ends. The moral to be drawn is that, in the interval between the two comings of Jesus, which may be longer than is expected (it was *after a long time*, we notice, that the 'chief' returned to settle accounts with his servants), the disciples must make continuous, practical use by the effort of their wills of those gifts of the Spirit with which they are endowed, whether they be the more conspicuous gifts which vary with different individuals, or the gifts of love, joy, peace, long-suffering, gentleness, goodness and faith, called by Paul 'the fruit of the Spirit' and granted in some degree to every Christian. Failure to *strive* to express these virtues in the practical affairs of life carries with it the penalty that the gifts are withdrawn (*take therefore the talent from him*); and when once they are withdrawn, men and women have nothing that entitles them to *enter . . . into the joy of* (the) *Lord*; the bliss of the kingdom of heaven is denied them; they are useless servants, destined to stay outside in the darkness in the place of *weeping and gnashing of teeth* instead of enjoying the gladdening light of the presence of God.

Additional Notes

xxv. 14-30. The differences between this parable and the parable of the pounds in Luke xix. 11-27 are as great as the similarities, and it is probable that they are independent stories, based on a common theme and spoken on different occasions.

14. *For* indicates that the teaching of this parable is closely related to the previous parable of the ten virgins. Both are concerned with the use to be made by the disciples of the interval before the Lord returns. In both a delay is assumed (cf. verses 5 and 19).

The words *the kingdom of heaven is as* are not in the original, the literal translation of which is 'It is as when a man . . .' (rv).

The word *apodēmōn* rendered *travelling into a far country* simply means 'going abroad'.

Servants (lit. 'slaves') in antiquity managed a great deal of commercial business and were often entrusted, as here, with responsible functions.

23. *I will make thee ruler over many things,* i.e. 'give you a sphere where you will have more scope'

24, 26. The third servant's estimate of his master as a hard money-making Jew who 'enriched himself at the cost of others, gathering gain where he had not spent' (McNeile), was untrue; but the master's point is that the servant, believing as he did that it *was* true, ought to have been all the more concerned to see that he had something more to bring to him on his return from abroad than the one bag of gold he had received! This meaning is best suggested by punctuating verse 26 as a question 'So you knew, did you, that I reap where I have not sowed . . . ?' (So Hort's and Nestle's editions of the Greek Testament and rsv). It is interesting to notice that in verse 26 the master does not quote the servant's reference to himself as *an hard man.*

c. The sheep and the goats (xxv. 31–46)

As has often been pointed out, this is not a parable in the conventional sense. It is a poetic description of the way in which the prophecy of Jesus in xvi. 27 will be fulfilled: 'The Son of man shall come in the glory of his Father with his angels; and then he shall reward every man according to his works.' The Son of man is here pictured enthroned in glory as *King* (34), and exercising His divine prerogative as Judge of *all nations* (32). He is, however, no harsh Judge devoid of sympathy, but one who has been touched with the feelings of our infirmities. In the words of John v. 27, authority has been given Him to execute judgment precisely because he is the Son of man.

As is usual in Hebrew poetry, we have here no varying degrees of light and shade. The picture is painted in sharply-defined contrasts of black and white. All men fall into one or other of two classes, which are as clearly distinguishable as are sheep and goats to a shepherd (32). The *sheep*, identified in verse 37 with *the righteous*, are placed in the favoured position *on his right hand* of the Judge's throne; and *the goats*, who have no other identification, occupy the unfavoured position *on the left*. The former are the elect, now gathered from the four corners of the earth, for the gospel has been proclaimed to all the world. They have made their election sure, not by constantly saying 'Lord, Lord', nor by repeated verbal expressions of their faith, but by numerous acts of self-sacrificing service, rendered unobtrusively to their fellow men. In virtue of the divine compassion and the infinite sympathy shown in His life on earth the Son of man has come to feel the sorrows and afflictions of the children of men as though they were His own. He can, therefore, in a very real sense refer to suffering men and women as His *brethren* (40). Consequently, by feeding the hungry, giving drink to the thirsty, welcoming strangers into their homes, clothing the naked, caring for the sick and visiting the outcasts in prison, *the righteous* have all unwittingly been rendering service to their Lord. By the very spontaneity and unselfconsciousness of their love, by their unaffected goodness, and their perseverance in well-doing, they have proved themselves true sons of their heavenly Father. They are worthy, therefore, both to be addressed by the king as those who are 'blessed by His Father', and also to receive from His lips the gracious invitation to enter into their rightful inheritance, which has been prepared for them from the foundation of the world (34).

In stark contrast, those *on the left hand*, so far from being welcomed into the divine kingdom, are banished from the presence of its King. They are designated *cursed* rather than *blessed*, for they have no place in the family of God, having none of the characteristics of His children; and they are assigned to the conflagration *prepared for the devil and his angels*. They find themselves condemned to this perdition, because they have paid heed to the devil's suggestion that self-interest should be the primary motive in conduct; and, in consequence, they have shut their eyes to the spectacle of human misery, and turned a deaf ear to the cries of their suffering fellows. Devoid of loving-kindness themselves, they cannot receive loving-kindness from their Lord. One of the most striking features in this very striking passage is the way in which those *on the left hand*, in order to excuse themselves for having failed to render service to their Lord on the ground that they had no opportunity to do so, ask in a tone of injured innocence, though in a form more condensed and in a manner more agitated, the same question that *the righteous* had asked in innocent surprise and fully conscious of the implication of every word, in order to disclaim the service with which the Lord had credited them. When verse 44 is compared with verses 37–39, it is seen to contain a parallel with a vast difference. So also does the reply of the Judge to their respective questions. It is virtually the same except for the addition of the vital and determinative word *not*.

As in the previous parables of the ten virgins and of entrusted wealth, so in this picture of the great assize, it is not so much positive wrong-doing that evokes the severest censure, as the utter failure to do good. The sins of omission are seen to be even more damning than the sins of commission. The door is shut against the foolish virgins for their negligence; the unenterprising servant is cast out as a good-for-nothing for doing nothing; and those *on the left hand* are severely punished for failing to notice the many opportunities for showing kindness which had been given them. (See further the note on 'Sins of omission' in the present writer's *Tyndale Commentary on the Epistle of James*, pp. 106–108.)

Additional Notes

xxv. 33. The metaphor of the Judge as Shepherd comes from Ezekiel xxxiv. 17. 'As for you, O my flock, thus saith the Lord God; Behold, I judge between . . . the rams and the he goats.'

34. While Jesus constantly refers to Himself as the Son of man, this is the only place in the Gospels where He speaks of the Son of man as *the King*. He did not disclaim the title, when Pilate asked Him whether He was the King of the Jews, but during His incarnate life there was always the possibility that He would be accepted as a conventional, earthly king, and He had not yet fully entered into His true kingdom; cf. the words of the penitent thief 'Lord, remember me *when thou comest into thy kingdom*' (Lk. xxiii. 42).

41, 46. It is one of the merits of the makers of the AV that they did not always translate the same Greek word by the same English word. Occasionally however their desire for variety, apparently for variety's sake, was destined to have disastrous results. In this verse, the *same* Greek word *aiōnios* is rendered *everlasting* before *punishment*, and *eternal* before *life*; and the reader might draw the erroneous inference that while the punishment of the wicked will last for ever, the life which the blessed are to enjoy will not! In fact, however, *aiōnios* is a qualitative rather than a quantitative word. *Eternal life* is the life that is characteristic of the age (*aiōn*) to come, which is in every way superior to the present, evil age. Similarly, 'eternal punishment' in this context indicates that lack of charity and of loving-kindness, though it may escape punishment in the present age, must and will be punished in the age to come. There is, however, no indication as to how long that punishment will last. The metaphor of 'eternal fire' wrongly rendered *everlasting fire* in verse 41 is meant, we may reasonably presume, to indicate final destruction. It would certainly be difficult to exaggerate the harmful effect of this unfortunate mistranslation, particularly when *fire* is understood in a literal rather than a metaphorical sense.

XVI. THE PASSION NARRATIVE (xxvi. 1–xxvii. 66)

a. The Sanhedrin's decision; the anointing at Bethany; and the betrayal by Judas (xxvi. 1–16; cf. Mk. xiv. 1–11 and Lk. xxii. 1–6)

Matthew makes it clear, as Mark and Luke do not, that Jesus knew that it would be at the coming Passover, due to begin in two days' time, that He would be handed over to the Roman authorities for crucifixion. Moreover, if *then* (*tote*) in verse 3 is given a strictly temporal significance 'at that time', and is not, as it so often is in Matthew, merely transitional, the evangelist would seem to imply that it was while Jesus was making this clear to His disciples, that the Sanhedrin met at the high priest's palace, and decided to have Jesus arrested, not openly but by some act of trickery. As they were anxious to avoid the possibility of rioting by the turbulent Galilaeans, many of whom were in Jerusalem for the festival, they were prepared to wait if necessary till the Passover was over. The situation developed, however, more rapidly than they had anticipated; and when an unexpected offer was made by one of Jesus' closest acquaintances to provide them with information that would enable them to make a surreptitious arrest immediately, they did not hesitate to make use of it, even though it meant taking decisive action during Passover night.

The Gospels do not tell us why Judas was led to take this desperate step, though they draw attention to his avarice and dishonesty. This trait in his character is underlined in the Johannine account of the anointing at Bethany (Jn. xii. 6). It is also emphasized by Matthew, when he states, alone of the evangelists, that Judas put to the priests the revealing question *What will ye give me, and I will deliver him unto unto you?*, with its implication that unless they did give him a substantial *quid pro quo* he would refuse to be their accomplice; and also when he specifies the exact amount of money that the priests made over to Judas there and then (15). Mark relates that they 'promised' and Luke that they 'covenanted' to give him money. It has sometimes been maintained, e.g. by Plummer, in view of the Johannine narrative of the anointing, that what led Judas to betray his Lord for money was his disappointment that the expensive perfume poured on Jesus' head by the woman at Bethany had not been given to Jesus to be sold for the poor, so that Judas, who acted as treasurer, could have purloined all or some of the proceeds of the sale; and that he was determined in consequence to make good his 'loss' in some other way. This is possible, but in view of the lack of any reference to Judas in Matthew's and Mark's account of the anointing it cannot be regarded as more than a conjecture. The motive of Judas remained, it would seem, a mystery to the early Christians; they could only say with Luke that 'Satan entered into him'. It would also seem that Matthew and Mark, by placing in juxtaposition the story of the anointing and the agreement of Judas to betray Jesus, were primarily concerned to throw into clear relief the contrast between this act of treachery by *one of the twelve*, which revealed such ingratitude and lack of understanding, and the generous act of the woman, identified by John with Mary the sister of Martha and Lazarus, which expressed such insight and devotion.

Moreover, by stating, as Matthew does directly and Mark indirectly, that all Jesus' disciples expressed indignation at the extravagance of the woman; by recording Jesus' interpretation of her action in the words *in that she hath poured this ointment on my body, she did it for my burial*; and by adding His prophecy that her action would always be remembered wherever the gospel was proclaimed, these evangelists make it clear that she had an intuitive appreciation of the significance of Jesus' death, which the disciples had as yet failed to grasp. As she gazes across the supper table into the eyes of Jesus, she sees the shadow of the cross lying heavily upon Him, and she penetrates its meaning. She knows that He is ready and willing to die as a supreme act of love for His friends, and she rightly reckons herself and her family among those friends. And so she pours the fragrant perfume, her most costly possession, over His head as though she were anointing a king. Her comparatively small act of sacrifice is symbolic of His much greater sacrifice; and she makes it to show that no gift is too great in response to such a love as His—*divine* love which not only gives everything but is

content to be unrequited. Jesus appreciates the motive that
has prompted her action. He knows that it is no exuberant
expression of vapid sentiment, but eloquent of profound understanding and genuine sympathy. He sees in the broken vase a
picture of His own body soon to be broken on the cross. The
odour of the perfume speaks to Him not of waste and extravagance, but of the preparation of His own crucified body for
burial. He is as indignant with the disciples for their attitude
to the woman, as they had been with her for her attitude to
Him. 'Why do you make trouble for her?' He asks. 'She has
done a grand thing for me. It is true that the poor are always
waiting to be helped, and opportunities for such charity will
never be lacking. You will not, however, always have Me.'
Mary who had sat at Jesus' feet before had once again 'chosen
for herself the best part of all, which shall never be taken away
from her' (Lk. x. 42, Knox).

Additional Notes

xxvi. 1. The evangelist is here indicating that the collection
of the sayings of Jesus recorded in chapters xxiv and xxv is
finished, and that he is now entering upon the narrative of the
passion.

2. *Is betrayed* (*paradidotai*) is rendered by RV 'is delivered up'.
It is possible that the word implies that Judas' action is in
accordance with 'the determinate counsel and foreknowledge of
God' (Acts ii. 23). The present tense is prophetic, 'is to be
betrayed'.

5. *On the feast day*. The Greek *en tē heortē* is better rendered
'during the feast' (RV). The festival lasted eight days.

6. *The leper*. Simon was of course no longer a leper, but he
continued to be known as such to distinguish him from the
many other Simons.

7. *Ointment* suggests too solid a substance. A better translation would be 'oil' or 'perfume'. Similarly *box* should be
rendered 'cruse' (so RV) or in modern English 'bottle'.

10. *Understood it,* i.e. perceived why the disciples were expressing indignation among themselves (see Mk. xiv. 4).

Good translates *kalon,* which implies that the woman's action was not only intrinsically good, but that it had a nobility and an attractiveness which set it in a class by itself.

15. *Covenanted* renders *estēsan,* which may mean either 'set in the scales' (so RV 'weighed unto him' and RSV 'paid him'), or 'set down as the terms of agreement' (so AV *covenanted*). The former seems the meaning here. Judas was paid, in our colloquial expression, 'on the nail'.

For the significance of the *thirty pieces of silver* see xxvii. 9.

b. The Last Supper (xxvi. 17–29; cf. Mk. xiv. 12–25 and Lk. xxii. 7–23)

It is clear that all three Synoptic Gospels regard the Last Supper as the Passover meal; and it is by no means certain that the Gospel of John is in contradiction to the other Gospels on this point, though most modern scholars assume that it is. (See the present writer's *Tyndale Commentary on St. John's Gospel.*) Moreover, features in the Synoptic narratives, which are often regarded as evidence that they are self-contradictory in this matter, have been shown to be congruous with the Passover dating of the Last Supper by Jeremias in his book *The Eucharistic Words of Jesus.*

Although Matthew's narrative has much in common with Mark, it is distinctive in so far as it stresses, even more strongly than Mark, the deliberate intention of Jesus to eat this final Passover meal with His disciples. That Jesus had already made arrangements with a Jerusalem disciple to use a room in his house is clear from the injunction in verse 18, peculiar in this form to Matthew, *Go into the city to such a man.* The Greek word translated *such a man, ton deina,* implies that the person in question, though unnamed, is not unknown. Furthermore, the message that the disciples are bidden by Jesus to convey to him would be unintelligible to a stranger. This message underlines the sense of urgency felt by their Master. He was indeed conscious that He was walking with destiny. His *time*, i.e. His appointed time (*kairos*), as Matthew alone records Him as saying, was *at hand*. He was rapidly approaching the goal to which His earthly life was inevitably moving. And, as the sacrifice that He was about to offer was to be an act of redemption such as was foreshadowed by the redemption of Israel from Egypt, commemorated at every Passover, it was necessary that He should eat the paschal meal with His disciples on the night before He was to die, and in the Passover atmosphere convey to them by word and symbol the significance of His death for themselves and all mankind. The verb rendered *I will keep*, *poiō*, in verse 18 is a prophetic present, and has the meaning 'I am to keep'. Jesus is under an obligation to keep it.

The solemn announcement, in verse 21, that the human agent through whom Jesus would come to His predestined end would be one of His apostles came to them as a staggering blow. Their pained surprise found expression in the question which sprang to the lips of all of them. The form in which this question is put in the original, *mēti egō eimi, kurie*, conveys the meaning 'Can you possibly mean me, Lord?' The reading of the later MSS, *hekastos autōn*, followed by AV *every one of them*, might suggest that they all asked the question together; but the older reading *heis hekastos* makes it clear that they put the question to Jesus 'one after another' (so RSV). The answer of Jesus is deliberately vague, for *all* had dipped their hand with Him in the dish. Matthew alone records, in verse 25, that Judas did not ask the question when the others did, but was led to do so after Jesus had emphasized the necessity for the Son of man to fulfil the role delineated for Him in Scripture, presumably the role of Isaiah's suffering Servant, and had also stressed the ill-fated condition and hapless destiny of the traitor. It may be of some significance, though the point cannot be pressed, that Judas' question is identical with that of the others except for the substitution of *Master* (*rabbi*) for *Lord* (*kurie*). Matthew and Mark give no indication as to when Judas left the upper room. Luke's narrative implies that he was present at the institution of the Holy Communion. John, who does not record the institution, states that Judas left after receiving directly from the Lord a morsel of food after He had dipped it in the bowl (Jn. xiii. 30).

Matthew's account of the institution differs from Mark's in three points. First, he adds the words *for the remission of sins* in verse 28, thereby emphasizing the truth that the covenant Jesus is inaugurating by His death will bring about the happy state envisaged by Jeremiah in his prophecy of the new covenant, 'I will forgive their iniquity, and I will remember their sin no more' (Je. xxxi. 34). The words *for many* (Lk. 'for you') show the sacrificial character of Jesus' death, and echo the words of Isaiah liii. 11, 'my righteous servant (shall) justify many'. Secondly, Matthew adds the word *eat* after *take* in verse 26 to correspond with the invitation to *drink* in verse 27. The most ancient MSS omit *take* in Mark, and instead of an invitation to drink from the cup that evangelist states 'and they all drank of it'. Thirdly, the addition of the words *with you* in verse 29 underlines in different language the promise already made to the apostles in xix. 28 that they will enjoy a still more blessed fellowship, here symbolized by *new* wine, with their Master at the final consummation.

Additional Notes

xxvi. 17. *The feast of unleavened bread* is a synonym for the whole Passover festival. By 'eating *the passover*' is meant 'eating the paschal meal', the most solemn act of remembrance which was made on the first night of the festival.

23. The best attested reading is 'he that dipped' (RV) not *he that dippeth*.

25. *Answered and said*. No question had been put to Judas, but his reaction to the words spoken by Jesus in verse 24 was to repeat the question already asked by the other apostles. Even if Judas spoke the words out loud, as Knox suggests in his translation 'said openly', the reply of Jesus was almost certainly not overheard by the rest—a point Matthew seems to stress by adding the words *unto him*.

Thou hast said is a literal construe of an idiom which indicates that what the questioner has said is correct, and that he has in effect answered his own question. Jesus admits that the situation is as Judas has implied that it is.

26. *Blessed it* is an unfortunate mistranslation. The Greek *eulogēsas* means 'said the blessing'.

This is my body. The original is as ambiguous as this literal translation; and Christendom would have been happier and more Christ-like if theologians had left it so, and refrained from attempting to define what Scripture has left undefined, viz. the manner in which Christ communicates Himself through the medium of bread and wine.

27. The oldest MSS have '*a* cup', presumably one of the cups drunk at the paschal meal.

As *all* is in agreement with the subject of the verb, to avoid ambiguity the clause should be rendered, as in RSV, 'drink of it, all of you'.

28. As there is no reference to the shedding of blood in the new covenant prophecy of Jeremiah, it is probable that the word *new* should be omitted with some of the most ancient MSS (so RV). The expression 'blood of the covenant' is found in Exodus xxiv. 8.

Testament owes its presence in the AV to the Vulgate *testamentum* used to translate *diathēkē*, which is the LXX rendering of the Hebrew word meaning 'covenant'. The latter word is used in all modern English translations.

c. Gethsemane (xxvi. 30–56; cf. Mk. xiv. 26–50 and Lk. xxii. 39–53)

While Jesus was leading His apostles from the upper room to the Mount of Olives, a quiet spot to which, as Luke says He was accustomed to go, He warned them of what the immediate future held in store for them as well as for Himself. Because of what would happen to Him, a point brought out by Matthew who alone inserts *because of me* in verse 31 and *because of thee* in verse 33, they would become disheartened and lose faith before the night had passed. He was their Shepherd and they were His little flock; but the sheep would be temporarily scattered, though with a single exception not finally lost, while the Shepherd laid down His life for them. Jesus knew that this must be so in view of what stood written in the prophet, '*smite the shepherd*, and the sheep shall be scattered' (Zc. xiii. 7): and the subtle change which He makes in this quotation, substituting *I will smite* for 'smite', which is found in both the Hebrew and the LXX, would seem to be due to His desire to emphasize the truth that it was the heavenly Father who was the prime mover in the incidents which constituted the passion of His Son. As Isaiah had foretold, 'it pleased the Lord to bruise him; he hath put him to grief' (Is. liii. 10). But the smiting of the Shepherd would only be temporary. He would be raised again and precede His flock into Galilee, a prophecy which was fulfilled in the incident with which this Gospel closes (xxviii. 9–20), and also in the gathering at the lake-side recorded in the last chapter of the Gospel of John, when Peter was recommissioned by the chief Shepherd as a pastor of His flock.

At this point, Peter insists that he will be an exception to the universal defection of the apostles predicted by Jesus. Never will *he* be found devoid of faith and courage! So cocksure is he of this, that the solemn prophecy of Jesus that before another dawn breaks Peter will three times be found disloyal falls on deaf ears, and with still greater self-assurance he asserts that, even if it means that he will be put to death in company with his Master, he will never disown Him; and his words are echoed by his colleagues who are carried away by his impetuosity.

Matthew's account of what happened in Gethsemane differs only in a few details from Mark's, the most important being the addition of the words *with me* in verses 38 and 40. In this most critical hour in His earthly life the Son of man needed, as every human being needs, the sympathy of others, be it only of a few, for no life that is truly human can be completely independent. Jesus is filled with anguish and dismay as He becomes fully conscious of the weight of the burden He is carrying as the Sin-bearer of mankind. So He leaves the others, and withdraws with Peter and the sons of Zebedee to a more secluded spot in the moon lit garden; and after confiding in them that His heart is at breaking-point with sorrow He requests them to keep awake with Him, for there is nothing else they can do to lessen His grief. But, as McNeile well remarks, 'though needing their company and their sympathy Jesus could not fight His battle in their immediate presence'. The wine-press of the wrath of God had to be trodden *alone* (see Is. lxiii. 3). Accordingly, He goes by Himself further still into the shadows, though remaining within ear shot of His friends; and falling on His face He prays His Father to remove the cup from His lips, 'the cup of my (the Lord's) fury' as Isaiah had called it (Is. li. 22), though He qualifies His request with the determinative and victorious words, eloquent of the obedience and submission of a lifetime, *nevertheless not as I will, but as thou wilt.*

When Jesus rejoins His disciples after this first struggle is over, and finds them asleep, He expresses pained surprise that these three able-bodied fishermen, who had spent many sleepless nights toiling alone on the Sea of Galilee, are so lacking in strength that they cannot keep awake with Him for a single hour; and He bids them once again keep awake and pray, for only so will they emerge triumphant from the testing-time that inevitably awaits them because of their association with Himself. They had all three shown themselves to be eager and impetuous, Peter but a few hours before (see verses 33, 35), and the sons of Zebedee some weeks previously (see xx. 22); but without the discipline and strength of prayer the human spirit, Jesus reminds them, is all too easily overcome by the impulses of the flesh. The second prayer of the Lord during the next phase of His struggle 'shows an advance', as McNeile points out, 'upon the first, as though the Lord had steeled Himself to realize that the cup could not pass from Him'; and this second prayer *O my Father, if this cup may not pass away from me, except I drink it, thy will be done,* was repeated verbatim when He withdrew from His disciples the third time.

The meaning of the words spoken by Jesus to His friends

when He found them once more asleep, as recorded in verse 45, is uncertain. The verbs can be construed either as imperatives or indicatives. AV and RV regard them as imperatives *Sleep on now, and take your rest*. On this interpretation, the words must have been spoken in irony. So McNeile paraphrases 'Sleep on, uninterrupted by further calls to prayer!' But this would not seem to have been a very suitable occasion for irony. Moreover, such an invitation would appear to conflict with the call to action in verse 16. Knox, who is translating the Latin Vulgate, where the words must be taken as imperatives, avoids any suggestion of irony by taking *now* (Gk. *loipon* and Lat. *iam*) not in the sense of 'from now onwards' but 'hereafter'. 'Sleep and take your rest hereafter'; i.e. at some other time, but not now. It is perhaps better to construe the verbs as indicatives and to give the sentence an interrogative form. It then becomes another expression of pained surprise. So RSV 'Are you still sleeping and taking your rest?' In any case, the time for slumber was over. The decisive hour had struck. The traitor was approaching ready to hand over the Son of man to the human agents of the powers of evil, and they must go forward to meet him.

Because the decisive victory had been won when Jesus was praying in Gethsemane, He was now fully prepared to face His passion. He was also well aware that Judas would be the means of His arrest. For this reason, as well as for the grammatical difficulty, it would seem that *wherefore art thou come?* is probably not the right translation of *eph' ho parei* in verse 50. If *ho*, the usual relative pronoun, is here to be regarded as an interrogative, it would be the only instance of this anomaly in the New Testament. The thought in the mind of Jesus, after Judas had hailed Him as *Master* and *kissed* Him, thus giving the assailants the pre-arranged signal, is more likely to have been similar to that which prompted Him to say to Judas, as recorded in the Gospel of John, after he had received the sop, 'that thou doest, do quickly' (Jn. xiii. 27). It is best therefore to assume an ellipse before *eph' ho parei* and to translate with RV and RSV margin 'do that for which thou art come'.

But, though the presence of Judas did not surprise Him,

what did seem strange to Jesus at first was the method adopted by the chief priests and elders to bring about His 'downfall'. Instead of arresting Him earlier and openly in the Temple, where He had been teaching day after day, they had stooped to methods usually taken to bring about the capture of a desperate bandit. According to Matthew and Mark, they had collected a rabble and armed them with swords and cudgels to round Him up. 'Have you come out as against a robber,' He asked them indignantly, 'with swords and clubs to capture me?' (55, RSV). But such amazement was soon transformed into resignation as He remembered that to be treated as a dangerous outlaw, to be 'numbered with the transgressors', was precisely part of the role ordained for Him. So He concluded His protest to His assailants with the words *But all this was done, that the scriptures of the prophets might be fulfilled.* As Matthew alone records in verses 53 and 54, Jesus pointed out to one of those standing near Him, who had drawn his sword in His defence and cut off the ear of the high priest's servant, He could have escaped the shame of such an ignominious arrest by summoning to His aid twelve legions of angels; *but how then*, He exclaimed, *shall the scriptures be fulfilled, that thus it must be?* Instead, He bowed His head submissively before the march of events.

The injunction given by Jesus to His would-be defendant, identified by the fourth evangelist with Peter, to return his sword into its scabbard, because any attempt to offer forceful resistance under the present circumstances would be suicidal, is also recorded only in this Gospel. This precept should be interpreted with reference to the context in which it is found, and not regarded, as Christian pacifists have often regarded it, as a general rule binding upon Christians in all circumstances. It is not in fact true that those who take the sword *always* die by the sword!

When the disciples of Jesus saw that His assailants had Him firmly in their grip, both Matthew and Mark record that they all deserted Him, and presumably for the time being their fellowship was dissolved.

Additional Notes

xxvi. 30. *An hymn* should perhaps be rendered '*the* hymn', as it would seem probable that the reference is to the final Passover hymn which consisted of Psalms cxvi–cxviii.

36. *Gethsemane* means by derivation 'olive-orchard'. The *place* would seem to have been something in the nature of a *hortus inclusus* (cf. Jn. xviii. 1).

37. *To be . . . very heavy* translates *adēmonein* which probably means by derivation 'to be away from home', and so 'not to feel at home', 'to be ill at ease'. Jesus was feeling that 'life was too much for Him'.

38. *Soul* (*psuchē*) here refers, as in John xii. 27, to the seat of human feelings and emotions. It is more accurately rendered in modern English 'heart'.
Even unto death means, as McNeile points out, not 'which makes me wish for death' but 'which is as great as death'. As has been said in the commentary, Jesus' heart was at breaking-point.

40. Both Matthew and Mark state that Jesus expressed His surprise to Peter; but, whereas Matthew has 'could *ye* not', Mark, whose narrative reflects Peter's own reminiscences, has 'couldst not *thou*'. As Chapman notices (p. 49), 'where the words are of blame Peter changes the plural into the singular'.

41. *Peirasmos* in this context should be translated 'trial' rather than *temptation*. (See the commentary, and cf. Jas. i. 2.)

46. *Let us be going* translates *agōmen*. As this verb usually means 'to go forward to meet an advancing enemy', a more vigorous translation is needed here, 'we must go forward' (see the note on Jn. xiv. 31 in the writer's *Tyndale Commentary on St. John's Gospel*).

56. *All this was done.* For the difficulty with which this expression confronts the translator see the note on xxi. 4.

d. The trial before Caiaphas; and the denials of Peter (xxvi. 57–75; cf. Mk. xiv. 53–72 and Lk. xxii. 54–71)

It would seem clear from Matthew's narrative that the Sanhedrin were already in session while Jesus was being arrested. The verb rendered *were assembled (sunēchthēsan)* in verse 57 has a pluperfect sense (so RSV 'had gathered'). It would also seem probable that the Council had been engaged for some time in trying to find evidence on which it could formulate a charge against Jesus that would lead to a death sentence. The verb translated *sought* in verse 59 is in the imperfect tense; and the meaning is not that the Sanhedrin began now for the first time to try to find witnesses (a most unpromising venture on which to embark in the middle of the night), but that it was engaged upon the task of sifting the evidence of those who had already come forward. It was not *false* witnesses that the councillors were especially looking for, though all the Greek MSS make that assertion in verse 59. Mark, however, has 'witness' in place of *false witness*; and it may well be that *false* is due to a slip of a very early copyist. As Torrey points out (p. 296), 'the Greek text which lay before the Old Syriac and Peshitta did not have it. Once in the text, it would not easily have been omitted, anywhere, but it could very easily have been inserted'.

What Caiaphas was most concerned about was not so much the accuracy or inaccuracy of particular allegations, but the discovery of at least two witnesses who were in agreement (so that the Jewish law of evidence would be complied with), and the substance of whose evidence might form the basis for a capital charge. This did not prove to be easy; for although, as verse 60 implies, numerous false witnesses were forthcoming, none was found who produced the kind of evidence that was consistent. Matthew does not state that these two were *false* witnesses, for there is strong ancient MSS authority against the presence of the word *false* at this point in the narrative. Mark, however, makes it clear that their testimony was a misrepresentation of the truth. Jesus had in fact told the Jews, in a challenging statement made in the earlier part of His ministry, that if they destroyed the Temple (meaning the temple of His body), it would be raised again by Him within three days (see Jn. ii. 19). This affirmation had been so distorted in the passage of time that it was now reproduced by these false witnesses in the form *I am able to destroy the temple of God, and to build it in three days.* Nevertheless, true or false, this was the kind of evidence that Caiaphas was wanting—for to speak against the Temple of God directly or indirectly was, in Levertoff's words (p. 91), 'one of the heaviest accusations that could be brought by one Jew against another, cf. Acts vi. 13, 14'. And for Jesus to claim that He possessed the power to work such an architectural miracle as this utterance seemed to imply, was equivalent, in Caiaphas' judgment, to saying that He was Messiah. Consequently when Jesus refused to avail Himself of the opportunity of defending Himself against such an ill-founded accusation, the high priest charged Him in the name of God to tell the Council whether He was in fact *the Christ, the Son of God.* This was a serious and a legitimate question, and Jesus, now put on His oath, did not refrain from answering it. But the form of His reply, as recorded by Matthew, *Thou hast said,* suggested that He and Caiaphas would understand the terms contained in the question very differently. Jesus seems to be saying in effect 'I am not the kind of Messiah that you suppose Me to be, a miracle-worker who merely to demonstrate His supernatural power would destroy a sacred building and then speedily re-erect it without human assistance; but nevertheless I *am* the Messiah. And, although at the moment I appear to be the helpless victim of circumstances, from now onwards (as you will become aware), i.e. from the moment when My apparent defeat in death will result in a triumphant resurrection, I shall be exalted to the right hand of God to reign over His enemies. Thus will the words of the psalmist be fulfilled "The Lord said unto my Lord, Sit thou at my right hand, until I make thine enemies thy footstool" (Ps. cx. 1). Moreover, this exaltation will be the prelude to My coming as the divine Judge in the role depicted by Daniel when he recorded that he had seen in a vision "one like unto a son of man" . . . to whom was given "dominion, and glory, and a kingdom, that all the peoples, nations, and languages should serve him" ' (Dn. vii. 13, 14, RV).

This unreserved application by Jesus to Himself of scriptural prophecies that were generally recognized as messianic relieved Caiaphas from the burden of trying to obtain further evidence. The prisoner, in his judgment, stood self-condemned. And so, after giving visible and symbolic expression to his horror by tearing his robes, he at once called upon the Council to express its verdict. This they did unequivocally. 'He deserves to die.' The Sanhedrin could not, however, itself execute the death sentence; and if it were to call upon the Roman procurator to give the order for Jesus' execution, it was very necessary to present the charge against Him in a form that would be best calculated to rouse Pilate to action. This needed to be carefully thought out. Caiaphas, accordingly, adjourned the meeting till daybreak, when it reassembled, presumably for this specific purpose (see xxvii. 1).

In the meantime, Jesus was subjected to manhandling, though by whom is not certain. It would be possible, grammatically, to suppose that the unexpressed subject of the verbs in verse 67 is 'the members of the Sanhedrin'; but it would seem highly improbable that such an august body would have demeaned themselves by such undignified behaviour. We should probably assume therefore that the perpetrators of the acts of violence were the high priest's servants, the *hupēretai* of Mark xiv. 65 (translated by RSV 'the guards').

While the trial of Jesus before Caiaphas was proceeding, Peter, as all the Gospels relate, was three times disowning Him. He who had so defiantly asserted that he would never be found lacking in loyalty, even if he had to die with Jesus, had followed his Master *afar off* to the high priest's palace—but not because he longed to be near Him, but because he was idly curious, as Matthew alone records, to see how the whole affair would end (58). As he was sitting in the courtyard in front of the palace where the Sanhedrin was meeting, Peter was accosted by a maidservant who pointed out that he was one of Jesus' companions. Perhaps this information had reached her through the gossip that was spreading among the domestic staff in connection with the injury suffered by one of the high priest's servants when Jesus was arrested (51). Peter tells her that her words have no meaning for him. A little later, when another maidservant saw him in the porch and repeated what the first maid had said, he denied emphatically on oath that he had any knowledge of Jesus whatever. Shortly afterwards, what the two maids had said was reaffirmed by some of those standing near, on the ground that Peter's Galilaean accent gave him away. Peter's reaction to this was to break into curses, and to perjure himself once again by repeating contemptuously 'I do not know the fellow'. At that moment a cock crowed, and the prophecy of Jesus, so lightly dismissed by Peter but a few hours before as something that could never happen, surged back to his memory to torture him with what was in truth a self-inflicted pain. He staggered out into the night *and wept bitterly.*

Additional Notes

xxvi. 60. *But found none* and *yet found they none* imply that they found nothing which could be the substance of a capital charge.

64. *Hereafter* is a rather loose translation of *ap' arti*, which does not mean 'at some time in the future' but 'from now onwards'. So RV 'henceforth'. It is therefore probable that the first clause in this saying of Jesus addressed to the Sanhedrin should be regarded as a reference to His entering fully into His kingdom after the resurrection, and that only the second clause should be taken as a reference to the parousia which is not necessarily thought of as imminent (see Stonehouse, pp. 240–243).

Power is a Jewish periphrasis for 'God', the source of all power. As the original has the definite article, the translation should perhaps be 'the Power'.

65. *Clothes* translates *himatia* which is used for outer garments and may refer here to the high priest's robes. Mark has *chitōnas* which would refer to undergarments.

66. *What think ye?* i.e. 'What is your verdict?'

67. *Buffeted* translates *ekolaphisan* which means 'hit him with their fists'.

68. Matthew's and Mark's accounts at this point are supplementary. Each contains details necessary for the full understanding of the other. Mark records that the mockers blindfolded Jesus and then called upon Him to prophesy. Matthew omits the blindfolding, but adds that the mockers addressed Jesus as *Christ*, and called upon Him to exercise His prophetic power by answering the question *Who is he that smote thee?*

69. *Sat* is more accurately rendered 'was sitting', as the verb in the original is in the imperfect (so RSV).

Palace (*aulē*) should be rendered 'courtyard'.

70. *What thou sayest* is better translated 'what you mean' (so RSV).

e. The death of Judas; and the trial before Pilate (xxvii. 1–31; cf. Mk. xv. 1–20 and Lk. xxiii. 1–25)

The members of the Sanhedrin duly reassembled at dawn. The decision had already been made that Jesus must die, but the precise charge best calculated to secure that end had now to be formulated. Matthew does not record the wording that was finally agreed upon, but the reader is led to assume from the subsequent narrative that the key-word in it was 'king', for the opening question in Pilate's examination of Jesus was *Art thou the King of the Jews?* (11). This claim to kingship with all its alleged political implications is underlined in Luke's narrative where the priests inform Pilate that they 'found this fellow perverting the nation, and forbidding to give tribute to Caesar, saying that he himself is Christ a King' (Lk. xxiii. 2).

Matthew does not proceed at once to relate the trial before Pilate. He first turns aside to place on record, alone of the evangelists, the story that was still current in Jerusalem, about the sinister death of Judas. If *Then* (*tote*) in verse 3 is regarded as a connecting link with verse 2, and is not merely a formal introduction to the succeeding narrative, it was apparently the sight of Jesus being led away, a criminal in chains, that filled Judas with remorse, and made him decide as a desperate act of reparation to return to the Sanhedrin his wages for betraying Jesus. The blood of an innocent victim was on his conscience; but it was moral weakness, not repentance, that led him to try to ease his conscience by making this 'satisfaction' for his crime. In reality, his hands could never be clean. The Sanhedrin were unimpressed by his confession of sin; they made it clear that they had no intention to reopen the question of Jesus' influence, and that they were not in the least interested in the state of Judas' conscience. The motive that had actuated his conduct was his business, not theirs; and they expressed no pleasure at his offer to repay the money. But Judas had no further use for it, for he had already made the terrible decision to join the ignoble throng of 'the slayers of themselves'. He therefore threw the money down on the temple floor (the strong verb *rhiptō* used in verse 5 indicating that he did so in angry defiance), *and went and hanged himself*. The priests, who had had no scruples about using money which had presumably been taken from temple funds to secure the arrest of Jesus, now felt unable for conscience' sake to return the same blood money to the temple treasury! And the tradition current in the evangelist's day, to which he alone refers, was that they used the money to purchase a field, originally known as *the potter's field*, but subsequently spoken of as *the field of blood*, for the burial of Gentiles who happened to die in the holy city.

Matthew, familiar perhaps with collections of passages from Scripture, relevant for the understanding of the life of Christ, but drawn from different parts of the Old Testament without any very careful assignment of them to their original authors, finds in the behaviour of Judas and the Sanhedrin a 'fulfilment' of two historically unrelated passages, one from Jeremiah and the other from Zechariah. In verse 9 he is not, it would seem, making a single direct quotation, but combining the substance of Jeremiah xxxii. 7–9 and Zechariah xi. 12, 13, and attributing the whole to *Jeremiah*. In the former passage, Jeremiah is bidden by the Lord to purchase as an inheritance the field of his uncle's son. In the second, Zechariah is instructed by the Lord to reject the price paid to him for his services as a prophet, thirty pieces of silver, and to 'cast it to the potter'. But by a small alteration in the text 'the potter' could be read as 'the treasury'; and both meanings seem to be hinted at in the prophet's statement in verse 13 'I took the thirty pieces of silver, and cast them to the potter in the house of the Lord'. What Zechariah had done on the Lord's instruction, Judas did at the instigation of Satan whose tool he had become. He returned the money to the treasury—as he supposed; but the priests, acting from 'conscientious' motives, used it for doing what Jeremiah had done, viz. purchasing a field as an inheritance for their successors. The words *they took* in verse 9, and *gave* in verse 10, are adaptations of the words *I took* and *cast* in Zechariah xi. 13; but the concluding words of verse 10 show that the evangelist was unable to make his adaptation of these Old Testament passages wholly unambiguous. Judas in returning the money to the Temple did what Zechariah did; but the priests in purchasing a field with the money did what Jeremiah did. This ambiguity has led to the retention of the unrelated word *me* at the end of verse 10. It was very natural therefore, as the textual evidence suggests, that at any early date scribes should have endeavoured to make verse 10 more grammatical by altering *they gave* to 'I gave'.

Attempts have been made to harmonize the account of the death of Judas found in Acts i. 18, 19, where it is added by the author as a parenthesis in Peter's speech, with Matthew's narrative. (See e.g. the *Tyndale Commentary on Acts, ad loc.*) It would seem, however, more probable that the Acts account is based on a somewhat different tradition about the origin of the expression 'the field of blood', more acceptable to those who felt that Judas' death must have been more in the nature of a divine visitation as a punishment for his crime.

The answer given in verse 11 by Jesus to Pilate's pertinent question is made in the same somewhat cryptic language as

His previous answer to Caiaphas. *Thou sayest* means that Pilate is right when he uses the word 'king' about Jesus, but that Jesus would not use the title of Himself in Pilate's presence because Pilate's conception of kingship was very different from His own. Further unspecified, but obviously unfounded, charges were made against Jesus before Pilate by the priests; and Jesus, according to Matthew's narrative, refrained from answering a single one of them, as He had refrained at the trial before the Sanhedrin. Pilate was surprised, and, we may assume, displeased at this, for silence on the part of the accused might well be taken to be a sign of guilt, and Pilate was clearly hoping to be able to dismiss Jesus as 'not guilty', not least that he might be relieved from having to give a decision that would be wholly acceptable to the Jews. He was convinced that their real motive for bringing Jesus before him was that they were jealous that Jesus had won such popularity. He suggested to the crowd, assembled outside his palace, *Jesus* as an alternative to *Barabbas*, the *notable* prisoner whose release Pilate knew they were anxious to secure by the exercise of their Passover privilege. Some little time elapsed, it would seem, before conclusive evidence was given as to whether Jesus or Barabbas was their choice; and Pilate sat on the judgment-seat awaiting their decision.

It was at this juncture, as Matthew alone records, that a message reached Pilate from his wife, urging him, in view of a dream from which she had not long awoken, to meddle no more in the affairs of an innocent man; and this must have still further kindled his desire to let Jesus go free. This incident, assuming its historicity, is evidence, as H. V. Morton has well pointed out, that 'Pilate and his wife had discussed Jesus together, probably on the night before, because the urgency of her message shows a keen appreciation of the danger in which he stood . . . his peril was so much on her mind that she dreamed of him'.[1] What she *suffered* in her dream was the horror of seeing an innocent man being hounded to death, the victim of the world's impassioned hatred. But the intervention of

[1] See H. V. Morton, *The Women of the Bible* (Methuen, 1940), pp. 157–165 for an imaginative study of Pilate's wife.

Pilate's wife came too late. The procurator had exaggerated the degree of the popular support of Jesus; many who had shouted 'Hosanna' when He entered the city a few days before were not prepared now to clamour for His release. Pilate had also underestimated the influence of the Jewish hierarchy over the people of Jerusalem. The priests had, for some time, been moving in and out of the crowd, urging them to secure Jesus' death by raising their voices in favour of Barabbas so loudly that any counter-shouts on behalf of Jesus would be wholly unavailing. It was not surprising therefore that when Pilate, hearing nothing except the word *Barabbas*, ventured to suggest that, even if they insisted upon the release of Barabbas, some more merciful treatment than death might be found for Jesus who had committed no crime at all, their sole reaction was to shout louder and louder, and more and more frequently, *Let him be crucified*. It was clear that a riot was beginning, and that it would rapidly develop if Pilate did not accede to their wishes. And so, conscious of having failed in his efforts, he sought pathetically to exonerate himself from all personal guilt in the matter, by publicly washing his hands, as Matthew alone records, and throwing the responsibility for his decision upon those who had urged him so relentlessly to make it—a responsibility which they were only too ready to accept both for themselves and their descendants (25).

Accordingly, Jesus was flogged and handed over to the Roman soldiers for crucifixion. While the execution squad was making the necessary preparations for carrying out the sentence, the remainder of the soldiers who had been on duty during the trial summoned the rest of the company, and all proceeded to while away the time by mocking their prisoner. They took Him inside the palace, stripped Him of His clothing, dressed Him up in a scarlet tunic, placed a 'crown' upon His head and a 'sceptre' in His hand, and genuflecting before Him saluted Him as 'King of the Jews'! They concluded their 'homage' by spitting in His face, and striking Him on the head with the cane (the *reed* of verse 29) that they had used as a 'sceptre'! Soon the execution squad was ready, and Jesus, reclothed in His own garments, was led away to crucifixion.

Additional Notes

xxvii. 6. *Took*, i.e. took up from the floor where Judas had thrown them.

14. *To never a word* probably does not mean 'did not answer so much as a single word', but 'gave him no answer, not even to a single charge' (so RSV).

16. *They had*, i.e. 'the Romans had in custody'.

Notable translates *episēmon* which may mean either 'notorious' for his crimes, or 'notable', i.e. 'held in high esteem' by the rebellious section of the Jews.

16, 17. There is good textual evidence in favour of the reading 'Jesus' before *Barabbas* in these two verses (see RSV margin); and this is supported by internal evidence, for in verse 17 'Jesus Bar-Abbas' (i.e. 'son of Abbas') seems to be contrasted with *Jesus which is called Christ.* Jesus was a common name, but motives of supposed reverence may well have led later scribes to omit the name of the Saviour before the name of the criminal who was released instead of Him.

22. *All* in this verse is peculiar to Matthew; if interpreted strictly, it indicates a unanimous expression of opinion.

24. *He could prevail nothing.* The Greek could equally well be rendered 'nothing (i.e. 'none of his methods of expediency') was of any use'.

A tumult was made. Better 'a riot was starting'.

For the practice of washing hands as a symbol for the removal of guilt see Deuteronomy xxi. 6 and Psalm lxxiii. 13. Many modern commentators reject this incident as unhistorical, partly on the ground that it was a Jewish and not a Roman custom, and partly because it is assumed that it would have been beneath the dignity of a Roman governor to act in this way. But exceptional men under exceptional circumstances act in exceptional ways. Pilate was a weak vacillating opportunist faced with a wholly unprecedented situation, and his 'dignity' as a Roman governor may well have given way under it.

25. *All the people* indicates, as McNeile points out, 'the Jewish nation' (Greek *laos*), which 'invokes the guilt upon itself'.

His blood, i.e. the guilt for shedding His blood.

27. *The common hall* is literally 'the praetorium' (so RV mg.). It refers to the palace built by Herod the Great, which was now used as the official residence of the procurator when he came up from Caesarea to Jerusalem for special occasions such as the festival of Passover.

28. *A scarlet robe* was a soldier's scarlet cloak. Mark substitutes for it 'purple', the colour of royalty.

29. For *the crown of thorns* see the author's *Tyndale Commentary on St. John's Gospel*, p. 207.

f. The crucifixion and burial of Jesus (xxvii. 32–66; cf. Mk. xv. 21–47 and Lk. xxiii. 26–56)

When the procession moved off from Pilate's quarters, Jesus carried for Himself the cross-bar which would be fixed to the vertical post already in position at the place of execution (see Jn. xix. 17). But after the city-gate had been left (the probable meaning of *as they came out* in verse 32) the soldiers noticed that He was already showing signs of exhaustion. They had no hesitation therefore in pressing into their service, as they were entitled to do, a Cyrenian named Simon, who happened to be coming into the city ('out of the country', as Mark states) at that moment. We know that there was a synagogue of Cyrenians at Jerusalem (Acts vi. 9), and Simon may well have belonged to it. It is usually supposed that he became a Christian as a result of the wholly unexpected experience, resented perhaps at first but regarded in retrospect as a privilege, of carrying the cross after Jesus (see Lk. xxiii. 26). This is an inference from the statement of Mark that Simon was 'the father of Alexander and Rufus', who were presumably mentioned because they were well-known Christians in Rome when Mark was writing. And it is not unreasonable to make the further assumption that they became Christians as a result of hearing the story of the cross unfolded to them by their father. At any rate, it would seem unlikely that Simon went back to the city immediately after he had deposited his burden; and if he stayed to 'see the end', he would have been able to give an eyewitness account of the incidents at the skull-shaped hill of Golgotha, some of which ultimately became enshrined in the Gospels.

The first of these incidents, as related by Matthew, was the offering to Jesus by the soldiers, in accordance with a merciful custom, of drugged wine (Mark's 'wine mingled with myrrh') as an anodyne to afford some relief while the body was being nailed to the cross. According to the best reading in verse 34, Matthew describes the mixture as 'wine mingled with gall'. The later variant *vinegar* is based on the mistaken assumption that it was the soldier's own wine, mentioned in verse 48, into which the anaesthetic was put. The sedative ingredient of the potion was almost certainly called *gall* by Matthew in the light of Psalm lxix. 21 'They gave me also gall for my meat'. The second half of that same verse 'and in my thirst they gave me vinegar to drink' was also fulfilled later, when, as recorded in verse 48, a soldier gave Jesus a drink of his own wine, or *vinegar*. Jesus refused the drug, after tasting it, because it was as a fully-conscious victim that He desired to make His supreme sacrifice. He offered Himself completely and with His faculties unimpaired.

The incident of the fastening of the body to the cross is recorded with impressive restraint in the four words *and they crucified him*. The 'tossing-up' for the different garments of the crucified, which were the perquisites of the soldiers, is stated in verse 35, according to the text of the late MSS followed by AV, to have been in fulfilment of Psalm xxii. 18. It would certainly seem probable that the evangelist had the words of the psalmist in mind when he wrote *they parted his garments, casting lots*, but the remainder of the verse is in fact absent from the most ancient authorities for the text, and is probably a later insertion to harmonize the passage with John xix. 24. Assuming that *they* in verse 36 refers to the soldiers, Matthew alone records that they sat down and kept watch over Jesus, presumably to forestall any attempts that might be made to interfere with Him.

All the evangelists record that a brief statement of the 'crime' for which Jesus was officially paying the penalty, His claim to be *the King of the Jews*, was fastened to the cross; and the words *over his head*, found only in Matthew, are a clear indication that the cross of Jesus was a *crux immissa*, i.e. it was shaped according to the traditional representation of it. All the evangelists also record that two criminals were crucified with Jesus, and that His cross stood between theirs. The men are described as 'bandits' (*lēstai*) by Matthew and Mark, and as 'malefactors' (*kakourgoi*) by Luke. No evangelist, however, draws specific attention to the words of Isaiah which would seem to be patently fulfilled in this incident, 'he was numbered with the transgressors' (Is. liii. 12).

Jesus is abused while He hung on the cross by three groups of people, who might be described respectively as 'ignorant sinners', 'religious sinners' and 'condemned sinners'. First, the careless passers-by arrogantly toss their heads at Jesus, even as the psalmist's persecutors had tossed their heads at him (Ps. xxii. 7). 'You destroyer of the Temple,' they sneer, 'who would build it in three days, save yourself.' And Matthew adds that they also challenged Him to show that He really was *the Son of God* by coming down from the cross. What these self-satisfied people failed entirely to see was that this Son of God *could* not come down from the cross, precisely because He was the divine Saviour 'bearing the sins of many'. The 'religious' sinners were represented by those members of the Sanhedrin who had also come out to mock. Their jeers were not, however, directed at Jesus, but shared among themselves. 'He saved others,' they said, 'he cannot save himself. If he is the king of Israel, he has but to come down from the cross, here and now, and we will believe in him' (Knox's translation of verse 42). And Matthew makes the mocking of the priests parallel to that of the passers-by, by adding, alone of the evangelists, that these priests proceeded to allude to Jesus' claim to be God's Son, and to point out, in words that echo Psalm xxii. 8, that if God still wanted Him as a Son it was up to Him to come and rescue Jesus at once. The same taunts, Matthew adds, were made by the 'condemned' sinners hanging on either side of Jesus. One of them, as Luke records, subsequently became a penitent; but in the narrative of Matthew and Mark it is indeed 'despised and rejected by men', almost it would seem by *all* men, that Jesus dies.

The supernatural darkness, lasting from noon till 3 p.m., intensifies the desolation, which reaches its lowest depth, when Jesus, 'made to be sin' in man's stead, experiences in all its horror the separation from God that sin creates, and cries *My God, my God, why hast thou forsaken me?* These poignant words fall for the most part on unheeding ears. But those who catch an echo of them take them as an indication of the Sufferer's distress, though they misinterpret them as a call to Elijah to come and help Him. One of the soldiers, however, is moved to soak a sponge in sour wine from his own ration and lift it up to the lips of Jesus. According to Mark, it was this man who said 'Let alone; let us see whether Elias will come to take him down,' as though, in the words of McNeile, 'he wished to keep up the strength of the crucified a little longer on the chance that Elijah would come and rescue him before he died'. On the other hand, in Matthew's narrative, according to the translation in AV and RV, it might appear that the soldier's action is resented by the others, for it is they who say *Let be, let us see* (RSV and Knox, 'Wait, let us see') *whether Elias will come to save him*. However, the Greek word translated *Let be (aphes)* may be, and probably is, merely imperatival, so that the meaning is simply 'let us see'. It is clear from John's account that Jesus did drink the wine that was offered Him, and that strengthened by it He uttered the words 'It is finished' (Jn. xix. 30). It is probably this utterance that is alluded to in verse 50, where it is stated that *Jesus, when he had cried again with a loud voice, yielded up the ghost* (RV 'his spirit').

The rending of the veil of the Temple at the moment of Jesus' death is recorded by both Matthew and Mark; and the author of the Epistle to the Hebrews found in it a symbol of the great truth that through Jesus' sacrifice sinners have direct access to God (see Heb. vi. 19, x. 19). Matthew alone mentions the earthquake which caused the veil to be rent; and he further elaborates its effects by stating that rocks were torn asunder, and graves re-opened. This latter phenomenon was also symbolic of a great spiritual truth. By the death and resurrection of Jesus the saints of the old Israel, the prophets who foretold His coming, became united in close fellowship with the believers of the new; and after the resurrection of Jesus, Himself 'the first-fruits of them that slept' (1 Cor. xv. 20), those who were raised at the time of His crucifixion appeared to many in the holy city.

These physical disturbances that occurred during the last moments of Jesus' earthly life transformed the centurion in charge of the crucifixion. He was compelled to admit that Jesus was indeed what he had heard the priests taunt Him for claiming to be, *the Son of God.*

As distinct from the apostles, whose faith for the most part remained dormant till Easter day, the women who had ministered to Jesus during His time in Galilee, and had followed Him up to Jerusalem, remained faithful to the end. Three of them are stated by Matthew and Mark to have been watching at a distance the stupendous event 'which shook the earth and veiled the sun'. The first, Mary of Magdala, once tormented by seven devils, had become an integrated person under Jesus' healing hand (see Mk. xvi. 9); the second, another Mary, was the mother of one of Jesus' apostles, known as 'the little one' (as Mark here notes) to distinguish him from James the son of Zebedee; and the third, named Salome by Mark, is here described by Matthew as *the mother of Zebedee's children*, a description which probably indicates that Zebedee was now dead.

Another disciple of Jesus, Joseph from Arimathaea, introduced by Luke as 'a counsellor, . . . a good man, and a just'; by Mark as 'a respected member of the council' (RSV); and by Matthew as *a rich man*, had been hiding in fear ever since his fellow-councillors had taken decisive steps to get rid of Jesus. But on the evening of the crucifixion before the sabbath began, he plucked up his courage, and boldly approached

267

Pilate with a request that he might be given Jesus' body for burial in what Matthew alone describes as *his own new tomb*. The request was granted; and the body after being wrapped in a clean winding-sheet was laid to rest in a rock-hewn grave in full view of the two Marys, who had watched their Lord's death from afar, but who were now close witnesses of His burial.

Joseph took the usual precautions against possible body-snatchers by rolling a large stone against the aperture of the tomb; but it was destined to be even more securely sealed and guarded. As Matthew alone records, the chief priests and the Pharisees came in a body to Pilate and requested that special care should be taken during the next two days to ensure that the disciples of Jesus did not come and steal the body, and then make out that He was risen from the dead. They had heard Him prophesy, so they alleged, that on the third day after His death He would rise again. This impostor, they pointed out, had deceived the people quite enough by claiming to be Messiah, and it would be the crowning deception if they were to be further tricked into thinking that He was still alive. As events turned out, it was the priests and the Pharisees who proved to be the deceivers of the people, by their persistent assertion after the resurrection that the disciples of Jesus had stolen His body. The Christians' answer to this was that it was at the request of the Jewish ecclesiastics themselves that official action had been taken to make such a theft impossible; for Pilate, though he had had more than enough to do with these turbulent priests already, nevertheless yielded to their request that the tomb should be more strongly secured, and that the extra guard they asked for should be granted.

Additional Notes

xxvii. 32. *Compelled* translates the same verb as is used in v. 41, where see the additional note.

38. As time went on, it was customary to refer by name to the unnamed characters of the Gospels. So here, in a MS representing an Old Latin version, the criminal on Jesus' right is called Zoatham, and the one on His left Camma. Similarly, the name Claudia Procula is assigned to Pilate's wife in the apocryphal Gospel of Nicodemus; and in the apocryphal Gospel of Peter, the centurion at the cross is called Petronius. We have no means of testing the historicity of any of these traditions.

43. The word *now*, which 'heightens the taunt' (McNeile), is added by the priests to the words of Psalm xxii. 8.

45. *All the land* probably means 'all the land of Palestine'.

51. By *the veil* is meant the curtain separating the Holy of holies from the holy place.

54. Although the Greek rendered *the Son of God* can equally well mean 'a son of God' (so RSV), an expression which pagans often used to describe a superhuman person or demigod, it is difficult not to feel that Matthew and Mark intend the reader at this point to understand it in the same sense as in iv. 3, 6 and Mark i. 1, where 'Son' also lacks the definite article. It is claimed that the argument for supposing that the centurion was convinced of Jesus' innocence and of His more than human bearing, but that he was not actually converted, finds support from the fact that Luke, who records the incident of the penitent thief and the two words from the cross in which Jesus specifically spoke to His 'Father', factors which might have led the centurion to acknowledge Jesus as God's 'Son', nevertheless records his 'confession' as 'Certainly this was a righteous man' (Lk. xxiii. 47).

62. *The next day, that followed the day of the preparation* seems a deliberate attempt to avoid the word 'sabbath'. Levertoff suggests that 'the chief priests did not go to Pilate on the actual sabbath, but in the evening after the termination of the sabbath', i.e. after 6 p.m. on Saturday night. But they would by then have lost precious time.

65. *Ye have a watch.* Pilate's frame of mind is better reflected if the verb *echete* is construed as an imperative; 'You can have your guard', Pilate says curtly to the despised Jews. The indicative, represented in all English versions except Tyndale, and in the Vulgate *habetis*, would mean 'You have a guard of your own (the temple guard): don't ask me for additional troops'.

66. *Setting a watch.* The Greek means literally *with the guard*, so RV 'the guard being with them'. RSV rightly returns to the more idiomatic rendering of AV.

XVII. THE RESURRECTION OF JESUS
(xxviii. 1–10; cf. Mk. xvi. 1–8 and Lk. xxiv. 1–12)

The sabbath was over, and dawn was already breaking on what was destined to be the first Christian Sunday when the two Marys, who had so dutifully watched the interment of their Lord, made their way once again to Joseph's tomb. Mark states specifically that they had come to embalm the body, having waited till the sabbath was over before purchasing the necessary spices. Matthew suggests that their object was to gaze once more on the grave. Further embalming, he assumes, would be impossible, for, as he has already recorded, the tomb was by now securely sealed and guarded, and the women would not be able to reopen it themselves. But by the time the women came in view of it, a severe earth-tremor had occurred; the stone had already been shifted; and they found themselves confronted by a theophany. This was an experience so unexpected and bewildering that, when they came later to tell the story of what they had actually seen, their accounts, not unnaturally, varied; and the variations are reflected in the Gospel narratives.

Matthew records the tradition that an angel of the Lord had himself rolled the stone away, and was sitting on it facing the women—a radiant figure, as dazzling as the lightning and with garments white as snow. The apparition so terrified the guards posted at the tomb that they were rendered unconscious; and, according to Mark, the women were also dumbfounded. But the angel at once reassured them that there was no need for *them* to be afraid; for the crucified Jesus, whom he knew to be the object of their search, had in fact been raised in accordance with His prophecy; and if they looked inside the tomb they would see that His body had vanished. They were not, however, to stay any longer, but to hasten with all speed to the disciples and report the good news that the God, who had so often delivered Israel in the past, had now brought about another mighty deliverance by raising His Son from the dead. They were also to inform the disciples that the promise of their Master, made to them as they were on their way from the upper room to Gethsemane (xxvi. 32), was soon to be fulfilled, so that, when in due course they returned to Galilee, they would find Him there already.

It is clear that this reappearance of the risen Jesus in *Galilee* is the climax of Matthew's Gospel. Galilee is to him a district of great significance. It was in heathen Galilee, as he has already noted (iv. 15, 16), that the people who sat in darkness had been illuminated by the mission of the Messiah, whose message, though given first to Israel, was for every nation; and it was to Galilee that the disciples were now to be summoned to receive the commission from that same Messiah, now risen from the dead, to convey that message to all the world. But this underlining by Matthew of the importance of the final appearance in Galilee does not mean that he knew nothing about any appearances of the risen Jesus in Jerusalem, or that his narrative allows no room for them. Readers of the Gospels are not obliged, as many critics insist, to make a historical choice between the tradition of resurrection appearances at Jerusalem and the tradition of resurrection appearances in Galilee. The angel's message in verse 7, *he goeth before you into Galilee* need not mean 'he is now on the way to Galilee', as the verb may well be a prophetic present 'he is going to precede you to Galilee'. Nor do the words of Jesus to the women, when He met them while they were on the way to the disciples to discharge their errand, necessarily imply that He was commanding His brethren to go *at once* to Galilee where they would see Him (10). The very urgency of the message would seem rather to be an indication that the forth-coming reunion in Galilee would be an event of momentous significance. The *brethren*, to whom the order was to be given, would appear to embrace a wider company than the eleven apostles; for, as Stonehouse points out (p. 146) in the light of the use of this expression in xii. 49 and xxv. 40, 'it would most naturally be understood as including all persons attached to His cause who were then in the vicinity of Jerusalem'. It would inevitably take time to convey the message to these brethren, and meanwhile the other appearances of the risen Christ in Jerusalem could have taken place.

Additional Notes

xxviii. 1. The Greek *opse sabbatōn*, rendered somewhat ambiguously *in the end of the sabbath*, could mean 'late on the sabbath' (so RV). It should, however, probably be rendered here 'after the sabbath' (so RSV). The time in fact was 'early on Sunday morning'.

5. *Ye* by its position both in the original and in AV is very emphatic. What should be the reaction of the believing women is set in sharp contrast with what has been the reaction of the pagan guards.

7. The significance of *lo, I have told you* is well brought out in the NEB translation 'This is what I had to tell you'.

9. The words *as they went to tell his disciples* are omitted by the most ancient witnesses to the text, and are not found in RV and RSV. They are a later explanatory addition.

All hail is too fulsome and formal a translation of *chairete*; it obscures the fact that Jesus is addressing the women with the ordinary greeting to which they had long been accustomed. RSV renders 'hail'.

Held him by the feet. By this action the women were showing their submission to the Lord in the manner in which subjects in the East were accustomed to render obeisance to a sovereign prince.

XVIII. POST-RESURRECTION NARRATIVES
(xxviii. 11–20)

a. The bribing of the guard (xxviii. 11–15)

Before the evangelist records the final appearance of Jesus in Galilee, he pauses to strengthen the evidence for the empty tomb by recording a tradition, found only in his Gospel, in which the soldiers on duty at the grave are themselves witnesses that the body was supernaturally removed. According to this tradition, they reported truthfully to the chief priests *all the things that were done*. Their report could not be gainsaid by the hierarchy. But to prevent the truth from spreading, they decided to bribe the soldiers with a considerable sum of money to spread the rumour that the body of Jesus had been stolen by His disciples while the guards were asleep, promising that if the procurator came to hear of their 'crime' of falling asleep on duty, they would *persuade* (Knox 'satisfy') him, and *secure* (Knox 'see that no harm came to') the soldiers. By what means the priests expected to be able to do this is not stated; and the consideration that Pilate would have been unlikely to overlook a breach of discipline on the part of his troops at the request of the hated priests, has been brought forward as a reason for denying the historicity of the entire incident. But, as this particular guard had been placed at the disposal of the Sanhedrin, and was acting under their orders, it may well be that, if the matter had come to the ears of Pilate, he could have been persuaded to do nothing about it. The soldiers accepted the bribe, and circulated the concocted story so widely that it was still being propagated among the Jews at the time the evangelist was writing.

b. The final commission (xxviii. 16–20)

This Gospel began with a statement that Jesus was of the royal lineage of David, and recorded that while still an infant He was acknowledged 'King of the Jews' by astrologers from the East. Now after being crucified as 'King of the Jews' He has been raised from the dead; and in His glorified state as the risen Christ He claims unreservedly to possess complete authority *in heaven and in earth*. On this note the Gospel ends. As Swete well pointed out:[1] 'The field of Jesus' authority seems to grow as His ministry advances; at the outset He has authority to forgive sins on earth; as the days pass on, we read of authority to act as the final judge of all human lives, to determine the bounds of His own life, laying it down and taking it up at pleasure; on the eve of the passion He speaks of authority given to Him over all flesh, i.e. all mankind. But none of these great claims reaches the boundless magnificence of the words "All authority is given to me in heaven and on earth".' Jesus could have had authority over 'all the kingdoms of the world' before His earthly ministry began without having to spend Himself in the service of His fellow-men and to endure the agony of the passion, had He allowed Himself to listen to the words of the tempter in the wilderness (iv. 9); but precisely because He rejected Satan's offer, and, remaining loyal to the Father who had sent Him into the world, had not shrunk in obedience to His will from treading the way of the cross, He now possesses in all its fullness Lordship over the entire universe. As Knox has put it, 'He was given heaven and earth to do what He liked with them.'

What He did choose to do, as the word *therefore* in verse 19 indicates, was to send forth His apostles not, as He had done earlier in His ministry, on a restricted mission 'to the lost sheep of the house of Israel' (x. 5), but to *all nations*. From these various nations His universal Church was to be formed—a company of learners to be brought by baptism into union with the Father the Creator, the Son the Redeemer and the Holy Spirit the Sanctifier, and enabled in the strength of this divine fellowship to live obediently to the precepts that Jesus had taught His original disciples, that they might transmit them to others.

The historicity of these final instructions of the risen Christ has been doubted on two main grounds. First, it is said that if the apostles had received an explicit charge to embark on

[1] H. B. Swete, *The Appearances of our Lord after the Passion* (Macmillan, 1912), p. 70.

world-wide evangelization, they would not have been so hesitant, as it would seem from the narrative of Acts that they were, about receiving Gentiles freely into the Church. But it was surely not to be expected that they would be able to grasp all at once the full implication of their commission, or that a 'catholic' Church would immediately emerge from what was originally a movement within Judaism. Many difficulties had to be overcome, and many adjustments had to be made, before it was fully understood that 'in Christ Jesus there is neither Jew nor Gentile'.

Secondly, it is often affirmed, that the words *in the name of the Father, and of the Son, and of the Holy Ghost* are not the *ipsissima verba* of Jesus, but either the evangelist's words put into His mouth, or a later liturgical addition. It is argued that on the lips of Jesus they are an anachronism; that the early Church did not in fact use them as a baptismal formula till the second century; and that Eusebius of Caesarea in quoting this passage often omits or varies these words. On the other hand, the words are found in all extant MSS; and it is difficult to see why the evangelist should have inserted them if at the time when he was writing they formed no part of the Church's liturgy. It is also difficult to suppose that, if Eusebius had really known of MSS which omitted these words, some trace of the influence of these MSS would not have survived in the textual tradition. Furthermore, it may well be that the true explanation why the early Church did not at once administer baptism in the threefold name, is that the words of xxviii. 19 were not originally meant by our Lord as a baptismal formula. He was not giving instructions about the actual words to be used in the service of baptism, but, as has already been suggested, was indicating that the baptized person would by baptism pass into the possession of the Father, the Son, and the Holy Ghost. There is good evidence that the Greek idiom *eis to onoma* ('into the name' not 'in the name') could convey this meaning. Moreover, it would seem that the baptism which the risen Christ is here instructing His disciples to practise was not just a revival of John's baptism of repentance, nor even a continuation of the baptism practised by Himself and His disciples earlier in His ministry. It was essentially a *new* sacrament, by which men and women were to come under the influence of the Triune God, to be used in His service. The words *in the name of the Father, and of the Son, and of the Holy Ghost* are therefore both emphatic and essential to the text. Without them, the reference to baptism would be indeterminate and conventional.

Nor is the fact that it is somewhat startling to find the three Persons of the Trinity mentioned together by Jesus an insuperable argument against the historicity of the words. He had already constantly spoken of 'the Father'; in xi. 27 and xxiv. 36, and frequently in the Fourth Gospel. He is represented as speaking of Himself as 'the Son'; and He had frequently made reference to 'the Spirit' who would be 'the other Comforter' when His own earthly ministry was finished. How natural then that in this final commission to His disciples He should have given, in Swete's words,[1] 'a magnificent summary of all His scattered teaching about the Father, the Spirit, and His own relations to both . . . not delivering it as a dogma to be preached, but communicating a life of fellowship, of consecration, of divine fulness and strength'. And how closely is this 'communication' bound up with the comforting words with which the Gospel ends. The risen Christ assures His followers, in what Levertoff calls 'the greatest conclusion that any book could have', that whatever the future may hold in store for them, He will be with them in the Spirit whom He will send to them from the Father, *alway, even unto the end of the world*, i.e. as the Greek *heōs tēs sunteleias tou aiōnos* means, 'until the consummation of the present age', when the new age will begin, inaugurated by the Lord's return in glory.

Additional Notes

xxviii. 16. The translation *where Jesus had appointed them* indicates that the 'mountain' in question was where Jesus had originally commissioned the Twelve and given them the instructions contained in chapter x. The probable meaning

[1] *Op. cit.*, pp. 77, 78.

of the Greek, however, is conveyed in Knox's translation 'where Jesus had bidden them to meet him'; cf. RSV 'to which Jesus had directed them'.

17. If *the eleven* alone were present on this occasion, then *some doubted* must mean 'some at first doubted', presumably because they were not able to identify Jesus all at once in the distance. But it is probable that others were also present, the *brethren* mentioned in verse 10, and some of them may have doubted in a more serious sense. It is also probable that this appearance of the risen Christ should be identified with that mentioned by Paul, when he says that the Lord appeared to 'above five hundred brethren at once' (1 Cor. xv. 6).

18. The word *exousia*, here rendered *power*, should be translated 'authority' as in RV and RSV.

19. *Teach* translates a different word from the word similarly translated in verse 20. The word used in this verse is *mathēteuō*, from which *mathētēs*, 'a disciple', is derived. It is found also in xiii. 52 and xxvii. 57, and means here 'make disciples, or learners, of'. A disciple is not one who has already learned, but one who is always learning. The 'school-days' of a Christian are never over.

APPENDIX

THE commentaries in this series are based on the Authorized Version; but all the commentators have found it necessary to point out that the more recent English versions are not only based on more reliable witnesses to the Greek text, but in many places convey the meaning more intelligibly to English readers today. As many readers of the present commentary will have already become acquainted with *The New English Bible* by the time this present volume is published, it seems appropriate by examples taken from the Gospel of Matthew to draw attention to some of its more salient features. These may be classified as follows:

1. *The nature of the underlying Greek text.* As is the case with all English versions later than the AV, the Greek text translated in the NEB is shorter, being based on MSS earlier in date than those used by King James' men, but in some cases comparatively recent discoveries. As time went on, the tendency was to expand the text. This was particularly the case with the Gospel of Matthew, which, as we have seen, was the most 'popular' Gospel in the early Church. Sometimes, the expansion took the form of a liturgical addition such as the doxology at the end of the Lord's prayer (vi. 13b). In other cases, passages were inserted from other Gospels, often in places where they were little suited to their new context. Examples of this are: 'But the Pharisees said, He casteth out devils through the prince of the devils' (ix. 34); 'howbeit this kind goeth not out but by prayer and fasting' (xvii. 21); 'For the Son of man is come to save that which was lost' (xviii. 11); 'for many be called, but few chosen' (xx. 16); 'And whosoever shall fall on this stone shall be broken: but on whomsoever it shall fall, it will grind him to powder' (xxi. 44). There are also instances

where words came to be added to the text to make its meaning clearer, as in the addition of the words 'without a cause' in v. 22.

In all these cases the NEB, in the library edition, indicates in footnotes that these passages are additions found in 'some witnesses to the text'; and their absence from the text itself signifies that in the view of the translators they were originally not part of the Gospel of Matthew. On the other hand, it is interesting to note that for the first time in any 'official' English version the *longer* reading '*Jesus Bar-Abbas*' (xxvii. 16, 17) has been placed in the text of the NEB. This reading, discussed in the present commentary, was noted in the margin of the RSV.

2. *The recording of alternative possible translations.* This is not of course a new feature; but several interesting instances of it a re to be found in the NEB. The translation in the text in each case represents the interpretation of the Greek advocated by the members of the translation panel, or a majority of them. Examples are: (a) ii. 2, where *pou estin ho techtheis basileus tōn Ioudaiōn* is rendered 'where is the child who is born to be king of the Jews', in the text, and 'where is the king of the Jews who has just been born' in the margin. (b) viii. 7, where *egō elthōn therapeusō auton* is taken as a statement in the text, 'I will come and cure him', and as a question in the margin, 'Am I to come and cure him?' (c) xxiii. 32, where the difficult words of Jesus to the Pharisees *kai humeis plērōsate to metron tōn paterōn humōn* are translated, in the text, 'Go on then, finish off what your fathers began!', and, in the margin, 'You too must come up to your fathers' standard'. (d) xxvi. 15, where the statement *hoi de estēsan autō triakonta arguria* is, in the text, given the sense 'They weighed him out thirty silver pieces', and, in the margin, 'They agreed to pay him . . .'. (e) xxvi. 50, where the puzzling words of Jesus to Judas at His arrest, *hetaire eph' ho parei*, are translated 'Friend, do what you are here to do' in the text, and 'Friend, what are you here for?' in the margin. Reasons for the necessity of providing alternative renderings for some of these passages have been given in the present commentary.

3. *The translation of the same Greek word by different English*

words. It is a great defect of both the AV and RV that their makers, by rendering *one* Greek word nearly always by *one* English word, on the false supposition that this was the best way of preserving the closest contact of the reader with the original, violated what is recognized today as a cardinal principle of all true translation, that the particular sense of any given word is necessarily conditioned by the context in which it is found. How vastly more meaningful translation becomes when a variety of English words is drawn upon to translate the same Greek word in different contexts. This truth can be illustrated by the following comparison of the renderings by the AV and the NEB of certain words which play an important part in the Gospel of Matthew.

a. *dikaiosunē*. (i) iii. 15. 'Suffer it to be so now: for thus it becometh us to fulfil *all righteousness*' (AV); 'Let it be so for the present; we do well to conform in this way with *all that God requires*' (NEB). (ii) v. 6. 'Blessed are they which do hunger and thirst *after righteousness*' (AV); 'How blest are those who hunger and thirst *to see right prevail*' (NEB; marginal alternative '*to do what is right*'). (iii) v. 10. 'Blessed are they which are persecuted *for righteousness' sake*' (AV); 'How blest are those who have suffered persecution *for the cause of right*' (NEB). (iv) v. 20. 'except *your righteousness shall exceed the righteousness* of the scribes and Pharisees' (AV); 'unless you *show yourselves far better men* than the Pharisees' (NEB). (v) vi. 33. 'seek ye first the kingdom of God, and his *righteousness*' (AV); 'Set your mind on God's kingdom and his *justice* before everything else' (NEB).[1]

b. *skandalizō*. (i) v. 29, 30. 'if thy right eye *offend thee* . . . if thy right hand *offend thee*' (AV); 'if your right eye *leads you*

---

[1] R. A. Knox, in drawing attention to the variety of meanings covered by the word *dikaiosuné*, remarked, 'Only a meaningless token-word, like 'righteousness', can pretend to cover all these meanings. To use such a token-word is to abrogate your duty as a translator. Your duty as a translator is to think up the right expression, though it may have to be a paraphrase, which will give the reader the exact shade of meaning *here* and *here* and *here*.' (*On Englishing the Bible*, pp. 11, 12.) It should be added that the NEB uses 'righteousness' to translate the peculiarly Pauline sense of *dikaiosuné* as the new status of the Christian before God into which he is brought by faith. There is of course no English word really adequate to denote this, for it is something unique.

astray . . . if your right hand *is your undoing*' (NEB). (ii) xiii. 57. 'they were *offended in him*' (AV); 'So they *fell foul of him*' (NEB). (iii) xvi. 23. 'Get thee behind me, Satan: thou art *an offence unto me*' (AV); 'Away with you, Satan; you are a *stumbling-block* to me' (NEB). (iv) xviii. 6. 'whoso *shall offend* one of these little ones' (AV); 'If a man is *a cause of stumbling* to one of these little ones' (NEB). (v) xxvi. 31. 'All *ye shall be offended* because of me this night' (AV); 'Tonight *you will all fall from your faith* on my account' (NEB).

c. *ekklēsia*. By translating this word 'church' at both xvi. 18 and xviii. 17, AV fails to bring out the distinction between the local congregation and the Church universal. Contrast NEB, 'on this rock I will build my church' and 'report the matter to the congregation'.

d. *kurios*. In the vocative, this word is often a polite and respectful form of address, corresponding to our 'Sir'. Care is taken in the NEB to translate it 'Lord' only in passages where Jesus is being addressed by those who are His disciples. Thus the leper (viii. 2), the centurion (viii. 6), the woman of Canaan (xv. 27), the father of the epileptic (xvii. 15), all address Jesus as 'Sir' in the NEB. In *all* these cases the AV has 'Lord'.

e. *ponēros*. (i) vi. 23 'if thine eye be *evil*' (AV); 'if the eyes are *bad*' (NEB). (ii) vii. 11. 'if ye then, being *evil*, know how to give good gifts to your children' (AV); 'if you then, *bad* as you are, know how to give your children what is good for them' (NEB). (iii) vii. 17. 'a corrupt tree bringeth forth *evil* fruit' (AV); 'a poor tree (always yields) *bad* fruit' (NEB). (iv) xx. 15. 'Is thine *eye evil*, because I am good?' (AV); 'Why be *jealous* because I am kind?' (NEB). (v) xxv. 26. '*Thou wicked and slothful servant*' (AV); '*You lazy rascal*' (NEB). (vi) xviii. 32. '*O thou wicked servant*' (AV); '*You scoundrel*' (NEB).

4. *Occasional use of paraphrase, i.e. adding something to the text to elucidate what is in the text.* This is usually done either to indicate to the reader, what he would not otherwise suspect, that there is a play upon words in the original; or else to establish the force of conjunctions and connecting particles. Illustrations of this are (i) 'you shall give him the name Jesus (*Saviour*), for he will save his people from their sins' (i. 21). (ii) 'And you, *like*

the lamp, must shed light among your fellows' (v. 16). (iii) 'You need only say the word and the boy will be cured. *I know*, for I am myself under orders' (viii. 9). (iv) 'And if it is by Beelzebub that I cast out devils, by whom do your own people drive them out? *If this is your argument*, they themselves will refute you' (xii. 27). (v) 'You are Peter, *the Rock*; and on this rock I will build my church' (xvi. 18). (vi) 'Never despise one of these little ones; I tell you, they have their *guardian* angels in heaven' (xviii. 10).

5. *The interpretation rather than the transliteration of obscure words*, e.g., 'astrologers' for Magi; 'Money' for 'Mammon'; 'Prince Herod' for 'Herod the tetrarch'; 'Mary of Magdala' for 'Mary Magdalene'. 'Phylacteries' is retained, but a footnote reference is given to passages in the Old Testament where it is explained. The word *grammateus*, misleadingly rendered 'scribe' in the AV, is variously rendered 'lawyer', 'doctor of the law', 'teacher of the law', 'teachers'. And for the meaningless 'whosoever shall say to his brother, Raca, shall be in danger of the council' (v. 22, AV) the NEB has 'If he abuses his brother he must answer for it to the court'.

6. *The substitution of English idioms for Hebraic idioms*. The frequent use of *behold*, the Semitic way of introducing a statement, is retained in the translation only where it is really significant, and not just a conventional manner of speech; and the constantly recurring 'he answered and said', always retained in that form in the AV, is variously interpreted in the NEB in the light of the context. Very often it indicates not a reply given to a specific question, but the reaction of a speaker to a particular situation. Peter's interventions on the mount of transfiguration (xvii. 4), after Jesus' words about the difficulty of a rich man entering the kingdom (xix. 27), and after hearing the parable about the blind leading the blind (xv. 15), are illustrations of this. The designation of a person as 'a son' or 'a child' of something, when he exhibits or will exhibit a characteristic of it, is Hebraic but not English idiom. So instead of the literal renderings 'the children of the kingdom', 'the children of the bridechamber', 'the child of hell', in the NEB we read about 'those who were born to the kingdom' (viii. 12), 'the

bridegroom's friends' (ix. 15); and 'fit for hell' (xxiii. 15). Similarly, 'binding and loosing' when used with reference to interpreting the law becomes 'forbidding and allowing' (xvi. 19, xviii. 18).

Furthermore, when a literal translation, though making good sense in English, fails to bring out an underlying Old Testament reference, the rendering in the NEB is conditioned by that reference. Thus, in the message heard from heaven at the baptism and transfiguration of Jesus, the words *en hō eudokēsa* reflect the thought of Isaiah xlii. 1, 'mine *elect*, in whom my soul delighted'. Hence, where AV translates 'in whom I am well pleased' (iii. 17, xvii. 5), the NEB rendering is 'on whom my favour rests'. For the same reason *nai ho patēr hoti houtōs eudokia egeneto emprosthen sou* (xi. 26) 'Even so, Father: for so it seemed good in thy sight' (AV) appears in the NEB as 'Yes, Father, such was thy *choice*'. The thirty or more occurrences of the Hebrew *amēn*, used to give solemn emphasis to what is being said, and always rendered 'Verily' in the AV, are usually rendered in the NEB 'I tell you this'.

7. *The style of English is varied to suit the literary genre of the passage translated.* The NEB has been criticized by some for being too modern, and by others for not being modern enough. The former and larger class of critics find the style too 'light-weight' for Holy Scripture, and tend to feel that what is ancient and venerable is *ipso facto* more 'holy'! They are apt to forget that within the New Testament there is a great variety of literary styles, and that much of it is written in the colloquial Greek of the day—a fact which is almost totally obscured by the even semi-poetical prose style which is maintained throughout the AV. It is therefore somewhat unintelligent to draw up lists of 'light-weight' expressions from the NEB, *regardless of the nature of the context in which they are used*. Expressions wholly unsuitable in one passage may well be suitable in another. For example, it is surely of vital importance to remember that the man who '*makes off with*' the strong man's goods happens to be a burglar (xii. 29)! And surely we ought not to be surprised to hear that the malicious 'enemy' in the parable who ruined his neighbour's crop by sowing 'darnel

among the wheat' '*made off*' after he had done his dirty work (xiii. 25); or that the workmen in the parable of the labourers in the vineyard should have expressed their grumbles by saying 'These latecomers have done only one hour's work, yet you have put them on a level with us, who have sweated the whole day long in the blazing sun!' (xx. 12). No workers in similar circumstances today would use the 'exalted' AV expression 'borne the burden and heat of the day'; and it is very doubtful whether they would have talked like that in the days of King James! Similarly, is it not equally natural that the people in Jesus' home town, jealous of His 'success', '*fell foul of him*' (xiii. 57); and that the panic-stricken men in charge of the pigs '*took to their heels, and made for the town*' (viii. 33) after witnessing the destruction of the whole herd for which they were responsible?

On the other hand, where the nature of the narrative calls for it, the NEB is as solemn as the AV, and in the opinion of the present writer, always more meaningful. A comparison between the story of Peter's 'denials' in the two versions confirms this, particularly if we can imagine that we are reading both for the first time.

'Now Peter sat without in the palace: and a damsel came unto him, saying, Thou also wast with Jesus of Galilee. But he denied before them all, saying, I know not what thou sayest. And when he was gone out into the porch, another maid saw him, and said unto them that were there, This fellow was also with Jesus of Nazareth. And again he denied with an oath, I do not know the man. And after a while came unto him they that stood by, and said to Peter, Surely thou also art one of them; for thy speech bewrayeth thee. Then began he to curse and to swear, saying, I know not the man. And immediately the cock crew. And Peter remembered the word of Jesus, which said unto him, Before the crock crow, thou shalt deny me thrice. And he went out, and wept bitterly' (xxvi. 69–75, AV).

'Meanwhile Peter was sitting outside in the courtyard when a serving-maid accosted him and said, "You were there too with Jesus the Galilean." Peter denied it in face of them all.

"I do not know what you mean", he said. He then went out to the gateway, where another girl, seeing him, said to the people there, "This fellow was with Jesus of Nazareth." Once again he denied it, saying with an oath, "I do not know the man." Shortly afterwards the bystanders came up and said to Peter, "Surely you are another of them; your accent gives you away!" At this he broke into curses and declared with an oath: "I do not know the man." At that moment the cock crew. And Peter remembered how Jesus had said, "Before the cock crows you will disown me three times." He went outside, and wept bitterly' (xxvi. 69–75, NEB).

It is of course true that the *perfect* translation never has been and never will be made. It is also true that no translation, however good, can ever render the work of the commentator redundant. Nevertheless, there is no doubt whatever that the labours of the commentator are considerably lessened if he has at his disposal a good translation into contemporary speech, particularly if it is the work not of a single scholar, which must of necessity bear to some extent the impress of his idiosyncrasies, if not his prejudices, but of a group of Christian scholars working as a team, who have had at their disposal the findings of a much larger number of research workers in the fields of linguistic and textual studies. It is the humble opinion of the present writer that in *The New English Bible*, imperfect though it inevitably is, the English-speaking world of our day has been given a translation of this nature, which will prove itself to be an instrument of the greatest value for the understanding not only of the Gospel of Matthew, but of the entire New Testament. It has always been an axiom of evangelical Christians that the Scriptures should be available for the people *in a language they can understand*. There is no merit in obscurity; and in spite of the beauty of much, though by no means of all, of the Authorized Version, a great deal of it is obscure to the point of being unintelligible to men and women of the mid-twentieth century.